Spy Swap

Spy Swap

The Humiliation of Putin's Intelligence Services

Nigel West

FRONTLINE
BOOKS

An imprint of
Pen & Sword Books Ltd

FRONTLINE
BOOKS

First published in Great Britain in 2020 by

Frontline Books
An imprint of
Pen & Sword Books Ltd
Yorkshire – Philadelphia

ISBN 978 1 52679 213 6

Typeset in Chennai, India
by Lapiz Digital Services.

Printed and bound by CPI Group (UK) Ltd, Croydon, CR0 4YY

Pen & Sword Books Ltd incorporates the Imprints of Aviation, Atlas, Family History, Fiction, Maritime, Military, Discovery, Politics, History, Archaeology, Select, Wharncliffe Local History, Wharncliffe True Crime, Military Classics, Wharncliffe Transport, Leo Cooper, The Praetorian Press, Remember When, Seaforth Publishing and Frontline Publishing.

For a complete list of Pen & Sword titles please contact

PEN & SWORD BOOKS LTD
47 Church Street, Barnsley, South Yorkshire, S70 2AS, England
E-mail: enquiries@pen-and-sword.co.uk
Website: www.pen-and-sword.co.uk

Or

PEN AND SWORD BOOKS
1950 Lawrence Rd, Havertown, PA 19083, USA
E-mail: Uspen-and-sword@casematepublishers.com
Website: www.penandswordbooks.com

Contents

Acknowledgments . . . . *vi*

Abbreviations . . . . *vii*

Dramatis Personae . . . . *ix*

Introduction *1*

    Chapter I: Recruitment. 3

    Chapter II: KARAT 26

    Chapter III: *Konspiratsia*: The Soviet Legacy 48

    Chapter IV: GHOST STORIES 80

    Chapter V: Take Down 112

    Chapter VI: Negotiations 123

    Chapter VII: Aftermath 133

    Chapter VIII: Salisbury. 140

    Chapter IX: Directorate S 147

    Chapter X: Consequences 168

Appendix 1: Organization Chart. 170

Appendix 2: Chronology. 171

Appendix 3: Timeline of Events 172

Appendix 4: Kalaris and McCoy Monograph. 178

Notes 186

Index 190

Acknowledgements

The author owes a debt of gratitude to those who have assisted his research, among them Jack Platt, Vladimir Kuzichkin, Brian Kelley, Oleg Gordievsky, Vladimir Rezun, Dan Mulvenna, Oleg Sutyagin, Alan Kohler, Arthur Martin, Charles Elwell, Bill Hood, Keith Melton, Pete Bagley. Jack Barsky, Joe Reilly, Marti Peterson, Stan Levchenko, Elena Vavilova, Art Lindberg, John Guilsher, Stanislav Lunev, Tom Hayden, Ron Olive and Oleg Kalugin.

In Memoriam
Brian Kelley (1943–2011)
Jack Platt (1936–2017)

Abbreviations

ABW	Polish Security Service
AH	Hungarian Security Service
AIVD	Dutch Security Service
BfV	German Federal Security Service
BIS	Czech intelligence service
BMD	Federal German intelligence service
CESID	Centro Superior de Información de la Defensa
CI	Counter-Intelligence
CIA	Central Intelligence Agency
CNI	Centro Nacional de Inteligencia
CPGB	Communist Party of Great Britain
CSIS	Canadian Security Intelligence Service
DDO	Deputy Director of Operations
DLB	Dead-letter drop
ETA	Basque separatist organization
FBI	Federal Bureau of Investigation
FCD	First Chief Directorate
FISA	Foreign Intelligence Surveillance Act
FSB	Russian Federation Security Service
GDR	German Democratic Republic
HVA	East German foreign intelligence service
ILO	International Labour Organization
KaPo	Estonian Security Service
KGB	Soviet foreign intelligence service
KR	Counter-intelligence
Line KR	Counter-intelligence
Line PR	Political intelligence collection
Line X	Scientific and technical intelligence
MI5	British Security Service

MI6	British Secret Intelligence Service
MIVD	Dutch defence intelligence service
NIS	US Naval Investigative Service
NOC	Non-Official Cover
NSA	National Security Agency
NYFO	FBI New York Field Office
OKW	German High Command
OPCW	Organisation for the Prohibition of Chemical Weapons
OSS	Office of Strategic Services
RCMP	Royal Canadian Mounted Police
SB	Soviet Bloc Division, CIA
SBU	Ukrainian security service
SCD	Second Chief Directorate
SD	Sicherheitsdienst
SE	Soviet/Eastern Europe Division
SIS	British Secret Intelligence Service
Stasi	Ministry of State Security
SVR	Russian Foreign Intelligence Service

Dramatis Personae

Ames, Aldrich	CIA officer
Anschlag, Andreas	SVR illegal in Germany
Anschlag, Heidrun	SVR illegal in Germany
Baré, Charles	KGB mole inside ASIO
Barsky, Jack	KGB illegal in New York
Bezrikov, Andrey	Russian illegal in Cambridge, Mass.
Bloch, Felix	State Department diplomat and KGB spy
Boone, David	NSA analyst and KGB spy
Boshirov, Rusian	Dr Alexander Mishkin
Brodie, Ian	SVR illegal in Canada
Brodie, Laurie	SVR illegal in Canada
Brunet, Gilles	KGB spy in the RCMP Security Service
Buryakov, Evgeni	SVR officer in New York
Cassidy, Joe	US Army double agent
Chapman, Anna	SVR spy in New York
Cherepanov, Sergei	SVR illegal in Madrid, alias Henry Firth
Cherkashin, Viktor	KGB officer at the Washington *rezidentura*
Chernyaev, Rudolf	KGB officer imprisoned in the US
Cohen, Helen	KGB illegal code-named Mrs KILLJOY by MI5
Cohen, Peter	KGB illegal code-named KILLJOY by MI5
Danilin, Mikhail	KGB officer
Delisle, Jeffrey	Canadian spy for the GRU
DesLauriers, Richard	FBI Supervisory Special Agent
Droulimsky, Dmitri	FBI Special Agent
Elliott, John	ASIO mole suspect
Elwell, Charles	MI5 officer
Enger, Valdek	KGB officer imprisoned in the US
Flores, Roberto	Spanish CNI intelligence officer
Foley, Tracey	Alias of **Elena Vavilova**
Fradkov, Mikhail	Director of the SVR

Frith, Henry	Alias of **Sergei Cherepanov**
Gee, Ethel	KGB spy code-named TRELLIS by MI5
Geiger, Donna	NIS double agent
Gordievsky, Oleg	KGB spy code-named NOCTON
Gundarev, Viktor	KGB defector in Athens
Guryev, Lydia	Russian illegal, in Montclair, New Jersey
Guryev, Vladimir	Russian illegal, in Montclair, New Jersey
Hampel, Paul	Russian illegal based in Montreal
Hanssen, Robert	FBI officer, code-named KARAT, RAMON and GRAY DAY
Heathfield, Donald	Alias of **Andrey Bezrikov**
Hoffman, Daniel	CIA Station Chief in Moscow
Houghton, Harry	KGB spy code-named REVERBERATE by MI5
Howard, Edward Lee	Ex-CIA officer
Juchniewicz, Tadeusz	GRU illegal in Poland
Kalugin, Oleg	KGB general exiled in the US
Kappes, Steve	CIA officer
Kapustin, Pavel	Russian illegal
Karetnikov, Alexei	Russian illegal in Redmond, Seattle
Kelley, Brian	CIA expert on Soviet illegals
Kohler, Alan	FBI Special Agent
Kroger, Helen	Alias of **Lona Cohen**
Kroger, Peter	Alias of **Morris Cohen**
Kruminsch, Karl	KGB illegal in Zurich code-named KONRAD
Kruminsch, Katerina	KGB illegal in Zurich code-named EVA
Kushchenko, Vasili	Anna Chapman's father, an SVR officer
Kutzik, Mikhail	Russian illegal in Arlington, Virginia
Kuzichkin, Vladimir	KGB Line N defector in Tehran
Lazaro, Juan	Alias of **Mikhail Vasenkov**
Lipka, Robert	KGB spy in the NSA betrayed by **Mitrokhin**
Lonsdale, Gordon	Alias of **Konon Molody**
Metsos, Christopher	Alias of **Pavel Kapustin**
Miller, Pedro	British MI6 officer
Mills, Patricia	Alias of **Natalia Pereverzeva**
Mitrokhin, Vasili	KGB defector

Molody, Konon	KGB illegal *rezident* in London code-named LAST ACT by MI5
Murphy, Cynthia	Alias of **Lydia Guryev**
Murphy, Richard	Alias of **Vladimir Guryev**
Ojamae, Valeri	SVR spy for MI6
Page, Carter	FBI informant
Panetta, Leon	CIA Director
Pelaez, Vicky	Russian illegal in Yonkers, New York
Pelton, Ronald	NSA analyst and Soviet spy
Pereverzeva, Nayalia	Russian illegal in Arlington, Virginia
Petrov, Alexandr	Anatoli Chepiga
Pettit, Valerie	MI6 case officer for Gordievsky
Pitts, Earl	FBI officer and Soviet spy
Podobny, Viktor	SVR officer in New York
Poeteray, Raymond	Dutch diplomat and SVR spy
Polikarpov, Boris	Soviet naval attaché in Washington
Polyakov, Dmitri	GRU officer recruited in New York by the FBI
Poteyev, Alexander	KGB officer recruited in New York code-named DUMB LUCK
Ratkai, Stephen	KGB spy in Canada
Rivas, Gilberto	KGB illegal in Mexico
Rochford, Mike	FBI officer
Samoshkin, Aleksandr	Line N SVR officer in Madrid
Semenko, Mikhail	Russian illegal in Arlington, Virginia
Shcherbakov, Aleksandr	SVR retiree paid $7 million to betray Bob Hanssen
Simbirsky, Anton	Line N officer in Madrid
Skripal, Sergei	GRU colonel code-named FORTHWITH
Smith, Geoffrey	ASIO mole suspect
Sporyshev, Igor	SVR officer in New York
Sulick, Mike	Head of the CIA's Clandestine Service
Sutyagin, Igor	Russian arms control analyst
Sypachev, Alexander	SVR officer imprisoned in Russia in 2002
Szady, David	FBI officer
Tretyakov, Sergei	SVR defector
Trofimoff, George	KGB spy betrayed by **Mitrokhin**
Vasenkov, Mikhail	Russian illegal in Yonkers, New York

Vasilenko, Gennadi | Former KGB major. Code-named MONOLIGHT and DOVKA by the FBI; GLAZING by the CIA
Vavilova, Elena | Russian illegal in Cambridge, Mass.
Vertefeuille, Jeanne | CIA officer
Yurchenko, Vitali | KGB defector
Zaporozhsky, Aleksandr | SVR retiree, code-named AVENGER
Zharko, Vyecheslav | Russian tax inspector and MI6 spy
Zimyakin, Vladimir | KGB officer expelled from New York
Zottoli, Michael | Alias of **Mikhail Kutzik**

Introduction

For much of the Cold War, and until the dismissal of the CIA's counter-intelligence chief James Angleton in December 1974, Soviet defectors were regarded with considerable suspicion as possible provocations, perhaps deliberately dispatched to the west with false information. This policy, advocated by Angleton, had been inspired by a KGB defector, Anatoli Golitsyn, who had warned of a novel concept, the 'fake defector', had instilled doubts about the integrity of a subsequent KGB turncoat, Yuri Nosenko, and was largely responsible for a climate of suspicion that would be described by critics as 'the monster plot'. During that era some CIA careers were wrecked by mole hunts, defectors were regarded as hostile, and Soviet operations conducted by the CIA's Clandestine Service came close to paralysis.

At the end of 1974 the DCI Bill Colby fired Angleton in an effort to appease Congress after the *New York Times* had published reports alleging that the Agency had undertaken illegal domestic operations against American citizens. In the wake of the Watergate scandal Colby justified his Augean stables approach by claiming that the very survival of the Agency was in the balance.

Angleton was followed into retirement by his senior staff, among them his loyal subordinates Bill Hood, Scotty Miler and Ray Rocca. Their departure from Langley heralded the introduction of a new doctrine intended to encourage the recruitment of sources inside the KGB and the GRU. The programme, designated COURTSHIP, was the brainchild of Angleton's successor, George Kalaris, and his FBI counterpart, James Nolan. This was indeed a clean sweep, as Kalaris had no experience in counter-intelligence, nor of Soviet Bloc (SB) operations, and his deputy, Leonard McCoy, had been a reports officer who had distinguished himself by defending the KGB defector, Yuri Nosenko, whom his initial handler Pete Bagley, as well as Angleton, believed had been a plant.

Previously, Kalaris had served in Athens, Jakarta, Manila and Rio de Janeiro, but was best known for having acquired an SA-2 anti-aircraft missile manual from a contact in the Indonesian military, an item that had proved very useful during the Vietnam War when more than a thousand of the weapons had been fired at Blackbird high-altitude reconnaissance aircraft without a single loss. Born in Billings, Montana, his mother took him to Greece at the age of eleven, where he remained during the Nazi occupation. After the war he returned to the United States and spent two years in the army. He then obtained a law degree from the University of Montana and worked for the National Labor Relations Board before joining the CIA in 1952, aged thirty. Kalaris, who set out his counter-intelligence doctrine in a co-authored internal monograph in December 1989 (see Appendix 4), declared that Soviet penetration had severely damaged American interests, and that only a robust counter-intelligence strategy could prevent further betrayals. The irony is that much of the paper could have been written by Angleton himself, who had died two years earlier, in May 1987. Significantly, during Angleton's tenure there was not a single example of high-level hostile penetration, nor of a senior officer selling out to the adversary. There may have been an isolated case or two of low-echelon personnel working for the Soviets, and Angleton thought he had detected a potential KGB source in Igor Kopazky, supposedly a mole code-named SASHA, and a former Berlin Base staffer. As so often happens, there was no neat, satisfactory resolution to the investigation, but the professional spy known as Igor Orlov was able to retire quietly to his picture-framing business in Alexandria, Virginia.

In the years since Angleton's removal from his post, he was vilified as a near-paranoid eccentric who succumbed to the labyrinthine theories of a Russian defector that inflicted great damage on western interests, peddled bizarre theories about Kremlin conspiracies and undermined orthodox, objective analysis of Soviet intentions. However, Angleton's sometimes ruthless approach to counter-intelligence, undoubtedly adversely influenced to some extent by his close proximity to Kim Philby over the twenty months between 1949 and 1951 they worked together, made him few friends, and his achievements have been somewhat underestimated.[1] In retrospect, it can be seen that he laid the foundations for a remarkable period of operational activity that resulted in unprecedented success, and brought the once mighty Soviet (and then Russian) intelligence monolith to the point of total collapse.

Chapter I

Recruitment

The COURTSHIP programme, based on the rather risky tactic of making an approach to almost any identified KGB or GRU officer, in almost any environment, a technique known as a 'cold pitch', soon yielded good results. Within five years this joint venture had netted about twenty assets, most of whom admittedly were that most prized commodity, the self-recruited walk-in.

The situation regarding the treatment of potential defectors had become so serious under the previous regime that one prospect, Yuri Loginov, a Directorate S illegals support officer, had been thrown to the wolves. He had tried to defect while on a training mission to Finland but had been persuaded by the CIA's Richard Kovich to remain in post so as to increase his value, but when he reappeared subsequently, on an assignment to South Africa in 1967, the ever-suspicious Angleton had arranged for his arrest and interrogation by the local security apparatus, the Bureau of State Security. Fluent in Czech and English, he was taken into custody as a Canadian of Lithuanian extraction named Edmund Trinka.

Prior to his arrest in Johannesburg, Loginov had attended a rendezvous in Nairobi where he had provided the CIA with an account of his Directorate S activities and detailed the local *rezidentura*, headed by Gennadi Bekhterov. Critically, in one of his debriefing sessions Loginov, code-named AE/GUSTO, had asserted that Nosenko's defection had been entirely genuine and had caused consternation in Moscow. This unwelcome item served to undermine Loginov's credibility and when Angleton concluded that he was actually part of an elaborate deception scheme, he authorised the release of his debriefing record, which was presented as his confession to the South African police.

Loginov's information was sufficiently detailed to persuade his KGB controllers that he had volunteered a very incriminating statement containing details that only he could have known. In it he revealed that his wife Nira was also a KGB officer who had bungled a mission to Cuba. He disclosed that he had travelled to West Germany on the Kiel Canal hidden in the captain's cabin aboard a Soviet vessel, the *Kamenski*. He named his KGB handlers as Yuri Modin (alias Yuri Lyudin), Vitali Pavlov (alias Nikolai Kedrov), and Konstantin Frolov. These specifics were intended to embarrass the KGB and demonstrate that Loginov had co-operated with his captors, but stop short of revealing his history of contact with the CIA.

Much to his dismay, after two years in gaol, Loginov was returned to the Soviet Union through a spy swap in Germany where he was exchanged in July 1969 for eleven Bundesnachrichtendienst assets freed by the Stasi. Astonishingly, Loginov survived his cool reception in Moscow and was exiled, but not actually imprisoned.[1]

Under the new administration the CIA offered a warmer welcome to KGB and GRU personnel, and had encouraged 'walk-ins' to earn their defection by remaining in their post where they could provide valuable data from inside their organization. These individuals were promised that if they felt endangered, they would be exfiltrated and then resettled in Florida with a house, swimming pool and pension. Among those who took advantage of such an attractive deal was MOTORBOAT, a Bulgarian military intelligence (RUMNO) officer who would prove exceptionally valuable when he passed on details of RUMNO's participation in May 1981 in the attempt on the life of Pope John Paul II.

The Washington end of COURTSHIP, based in anonymous offices in the Hayes Building at Buzzard Point, overlooking the Potomac, was the FBI's CI-4 Squad, targeted against KGB Line KR counter-intelligence specialists at the embassy *rezidentura*, headed by Dmitri Yakushkin, who had succeeded Mikhail Polonik in 1975. The FBI relied on three sources to identify which Soviet employees were genuine Ministry of Foreign Affairs (MFA) and those that were intelligence professionals: physical surveillance, conducted by the FBI's specialist unit, known as 'the Gs' who kept a watch on the Russian staff and their offices; technical surveillance on the Russian premises; and a very secret source, Colonel Boris Piguzov. Code-named JOGGER, he had been a walk-in at the US embassy in Jakarta and had proved his worth in 1979 by betraying a former CIA officer, David Barnett, who had retired from the Agency in 1970 to set up his own business in Indonesia. In desperate need of funds, Barnett had started to sell information to the KGB but had been arrested by the FBI upon his return to the United

States. Meanwhile, JOGGER had been appointed to a teaching post at the KGB's training school, the Andropov Institute, where, as secretary of the local Party branch, he had access to all the personnel files of the graduates. This fortuitous promotion for JOGGER meant the CI-4 Squad enjoyed a valuable method of spotting the new arrivals working for Yakushkin. As for the *rezident* himself, he was extremely cautious, except in his private life. He had two mistresses, a young teacher working at the embassy school, and an American girlfriend supplied by the FBI. Professionally, he was always on the look-out for provocations, having experienced some embarrassment early in his tenure when three of his subordinates were duped in April 1978 by a double agent, Lieutenant-Commander Arthur Lindberg, in New York offering details of the US Navy's submarine detection apparatus, and exposed. The operation, code-named LEMONADE by the Naval Investigative Service, caught three KGB officers serving Lindberg's dead drop on the Jersey Turnpike and resulted in fifty-year prison terms for Valdik Enger and Rudolf Chernyaev who, as employees of the UN Secretariat, were not entitled to diplomatic immunity, although their companion, Vladimir Zinyakin, was released without charge as an accredited member of the Soviet UN mission with the rank of third secretary.[2]

Thereafter, Yakushkin had shown great reluctance to engage in anything that smelled of entrapment, a handicap that led him to ignore three approaches from a genuine CIA source, Edwin G. Moore, who was a disgruntled retiree formerly employed until three years earlier as a junior clerk in the Office of Research and Reports.[3]

Yakushkin's *rezidentura*, having been targeted by CI-4, would be thoroughly penetrated, for two other members became sources. First, there was Major Sergei Motorin, a Line PR political intelligence expert, whom the FBI's David Morton would cultivate for two years before he finally succumbed, having been caught bartering embassy duty-free vodka. He was followed by the Novosti press agency correspondent, Colonel Valeri Martynov, a Line X scientific and technical intelligence specialist run by the FBI's Jim Holt and the CIA's Rod Carlson. Code-named MEGAS and PIMENTA respectively, neither KGB officer knew that the other was actually a CI-4 asset, and the trio of Motorin, Martynov and Gennadi Vasilenko all acting independently of each other would give CI-4 a unique insight into the KGB's local activities. All came from different branches with, perhaps most importantly, Vasilenko having a background in Directorate K.

One of those targeted for recruitment in Washington, DC in late 1977 was a suspected KGB officer, a new arrival at the *rezidentura* who had been flagged by JOGGER as a Line KR counter-intelligence officer. Surveillance showed his talent for volleyball, and Platt, five years older, working under alias and posing as a Pentagon contractor, began the time-honoured process of pre-recruitment cultivation based on a shared passion for the sport and a love of the outdoors. Both, by their natures, were unconventional, rule-breakers and heavy drinkers.

At that time Platt, aged forty-one, was an experienced CIA case officer and ex-Marine Corps officer who had served in Vienna, Vientiane and Paris, but had been withdrawn from his last posting after he had been identified as a CIA officer by a renegade, Philip Agee. Together with some two thousand other officers and agents, Platt's details had been published by Agee in his exposé, *Inside the Company: A CIA Diary*, and in a series of magazine articles.[4] Disaffected by a broken marriage, Agee had left the CIA in Mexico in 1968 and sold out to the Cuban DGI, having been rebuffed when he first approached the KGB. The Cubans embraced Agee, who became a long-term asset, destroying the careers of hundreds of Operations officers. In Platt's case the damage was significant because, despite his unorthodox appearance and behaviour, he had a real grasp of the counter-intelligence business. Shortly before his posting to France he had been selected to accompany Yuri Nosenko on a 'dog-and-pony' worldwide tour of CIA stations and Allied intelligence agencies during which the defector had delivered lectures, and answered questions, on his eleven years in the KGB's Second Chief Directorate.

The Agee carnage had been unprecedented, and had forced Platt to adopt the alias of 'Chris Llorenz', but while he was reporting progress on his cultivation of Vasilenko, his quarry had identified 'Llorenz' as Platt, and obtained permission from his Line KR chief at the *rezidentura*, the wily Viktor Cherkashin, to continue the contact in the hope of making a recruitment. Although Platt routinely worked under alias, the Texan was easily recognizable to the KGB because of his penchant for cowboy clothes and a physical peculiarity: he had lost half of the middle finger of his left hand while in the military.

Cherkashin, who had previously served in Bonn, Vienna, Delhi and Beirut, had come to realise that there was mounting evidence suggesting his own *rezidentura* had been penetrated. As he later recalled, the FBI seemed to know exactly when and where a KGB operation was planned, and who would be participating. None of the usual KGB tradecraft, of employing regular diplomats co-opted to act as decoys, seemed to distract the FBI surveillance, which manifested an uncanny ability to concentrate its limited resources on the intelligence professionals.[5] In particular, the FBI's distinctive local radio traffic, intercepted by a special signals unit attached to the *rezidentura*, invariably detected an FBI presence in locations intended for some type of operational activity. Whatever countermeasures he took, inevitably there would be the unmistakable telltale indications of sophisticated frequency-hopping mobile transmissions, communications of the kind associated with the FBI.

While Cherkashin was pondering the challenge of hostile penetration, his subordinate Vasilenko was transferred to Moscow in June 1981, and then in 1984 was posted to Georgetown, Guyana. This meant that during the period of maximum penetration in Washington, Vasilenko was not a candidate for suspicion.

The era of FBI prescience would terminate dramatically on 15 May 1985 when a senior CIA officer, Aldrich Ames, walked into the Soviet embassy and offered Cherkashin the solution to the *rezidentura*'s poor performance. In return for a cash payment of $50,000 Ames agreed to a further meeting, the so-called 'big dump', on 13 June, at which he provided a list of current cases, but in an exercise in blatant self-preservation he probably named MEGAS and PIMENTA as moles currently operational inside Cherkashin's *rezidentura*. Both men would be recalled to Moscow on pretexts, and simply disappear, leaving the FBI to ponder their fate. The KGB took very deliberate steps to conceal the fact that Motorin and Martynov had been arrested, charged with treason and executed. These measures worked, and effectively prevented the CIA from learning about the deaths of some for a year, and others even until 1992.

What made some of the arrests in Moscow so odd was the lengths the KGB went to in order to conceal the exact date on which they had occurred. In the example of Motorin, he had been taped by the FBI as he had telephoned his girlfriend in Washington, DC, assuring her he was alright, months *after* he had been detained in Moscow. The pattern that emerged was of sources being recalled to Moscow or disappearing while on home leave, and for reasons that intrigued the CIA mole hunters, the KGB evidently had attempted to conceal the undeniable fact that between May and September 1985 the majority of the Soviet/Eastern European Division's spies had been caught.

Indeed, the KGB used numerous ruses to distract the CIA investigation into its own losses, which was anyway handicapped by the certainty that Edward Howard had betrayed a wealth of secrets. According to Oleg Kalugin, one such was

> our man in West Germany who was in charge of cultivating 'ille-gals' – Soviets who spoke German and were to be infiltrated into the West German government, army or intelligence agencies. The turncoat KGB officer was forcibly abducted from West Germany, returned to the USSR, tried, and put to death.[6]

Another known source of leaks was the Marine guard detachment in the US embassy in Moscow, which had allowed KGB personnel access to sensitive areas in the building. In December 1986 Sergeant Clayton Lonetree confessed to having been honeytrapped into helping the KGB, and Corporal Arnold Bracey admitted to a similar affair, so there was a possibility that listening devices had been installed in the embassy's comms equipment. The big question was whether the CIA's 1985 losses were evidence of a dangerous, currently active mole, or could be rationalised by other more mundane explanations. The DDO, John Stein, concluded in a ten-page report that there was no proof of a mole and opined that poor tradecraft had been at the root of each loss, a view that was rejected by the Agency's counter-intelligence experts. However, it was equally true that not everything could be blamed on Howard's treachery. After all, Sergei Vorontsov's recruitment had occurred *after* he had left the Agency, so he could never have been in a position to compromise him to the KGB.

The CIA mole hunters were to take nearly nine years to identify Aldrich Ames as the source of the SE leaks, in part because the Soviets laid several false trails, including the initially plausible assertion, made in March 1986 through an anonymous source in Germany who turned out to be a KGB-controlled double agent, that the security of the CIA's communications had been compromised by the successful penetration of its principal radio facility at Warrenton, Virginia. The information, hand-delivered by letter to a CIA officer in Bonn, contained some genuine information about Gennady Varenik, code-named GT/FITNESS, and correctly named his CIA case officer as Charles Leven. An inevitably lengthy investigation had concluded finally that no such breach had occurred, and that the entire tale had been a skilfully constructed ploy. Similarly, another KGB source, Aleksandr Zhomov, code-named GT/PROLOGUE, sold his CIA handlers dozens of supposedly authentic internal SCD documents that seemed to disclose how the KGB's ubiquitous surveillance on US embassy staff had been responsible for identifying the CIA agents lost in 1985. Once again, Zhomov was finally exposed as an elaborate hoax, presumably intended to divert the CIA from the existence of a well-placed mole within the SE Division.

Lack of confidence at headquarters in Moscow station operations had a long history. In August 1977, when the organization was struggling to survive in the post-Watergate era with a Director, Admiral Stansfield Turner, who had banned all activity in the Soviet Union and would decimate morale by firing two hundred Clandestine Service officers in the notorious Halloween Massacre, the Moscow embassy suffered an extensive fire. The classified spaces in the three top-floors were affected after the conflagration had been detonated by a power-surge in an antiquated junction box. The KGB routinely used this tactic to harass the embassy building, and on this occasion attempted to use the inferno as a pretext to enter the sensitive floors. Famously, the station chief, Gus Hathaway, a decorated Second World War veteran, blocked the entrance to his suite of offices and prevented the KGB personnel dressed as firefighters from gaining access to them.

Management of covert operations in the Soviet capital was very high risk and numerous CIA case officers had been caught trying to communicate with assets, among them Marti Peterson, who was the first woman CIA officer deployed to Moscow. She was arrested in June 1977 while attempting to service a dead drop for the diplomat Aleksandr Ogorodnik. Similarly, in later years, Peter Bogadyr, Richard Mueller and Erik Sites were all apprehended by undertaking such assignments. In June 1980 an engineer, Alexei Nilov, was imprisoned on a charge of having spied for the CIA after he had been recruited in Algeria.

* * *

In his eventual confession, traded for a five-year prison sentence for his wife, Ames admitted having betrayed for cash amounting to $2 million more than two dozen CIA spies, among them a pair close to him who were never arrested. Sergei Fedorenko, code-named GT/PHYRRIC, and a scientist code-named BYPLAY originally recruited by the FBI in San Francisco, had been handled by Ames personally in New York. Fedorenko had been run until his return to Moscow in 1977, and both later reported that they had come under sustained KGB surveillance. Fedorenko, who had worked as a subordinate to Arkadi Shevchenko in the UN Secretariat, had suspended contact with the CIA following the arrest in June 1977 of a colleague, Aleksandr Ogorodnik, who had worked in the same department of the Foreign Ministry. He had taken even more precautions, including the destruction of his secret communications equipment, when his colleague at the USA and Canada Studies Institute, Vladimir Potashov, was caught. Despite having been named by Ames, the KGB apparently had been unable to arrest so senior a political figure as Fedorenko, who was to be promoted to one of Mikhail Gorbachev's advisers. Like GT/BYPLAY, Fedorenko survived despite Ames's treachery, and subsequently went to live in the United States, while the scientist chose to stay in Moscow. Ten others suffered confiscation of their assets and the KGB's traditional execution of a bullet fired at point-blank range in the back of the neck, an unmarked grave and a perfunctory form letter mailed to the next of kin. While the CIA remained anxious to channel financial support to the families of his victims, it was not always possible to do so without jeopardising further innocent lives so, in the case of Adolf Tolkachev's son Oleg, he was effectively orphaned and forced to carry the KGB's punishment into the next generation.

Although the KGB attempted to exploit Ames's list of traitors with a degree of subtlety, it became obvious to the CIA that there was a major security breach when two sources in Moscow fell silent. One was Piguzov, based at the Andropov Institute, and the other was AE/SPHERE, an aeronautical engineer named Adolf Tolkachev who was self-recruited and eventually had made successful contact with the Moscow station in March 1978 after several failed attempts. He had been handled with consummate skill by the CIA's John Guilsher, but nothing had been heard from him since he had failed to turn up at a rendezvous scheduled for January 1985, and there were other indications that something had gone badly wrong in Soviet/Eastern Europe Division. Two technical operations, involving a telephone cable tap under a Moscow street, code-named TAW, and another collection apparatus concealed in a railway freight container, designated ABSORB had been compromised.

Losing assets, especially in such a hostile environment as the Soviet Union, was considered an occupational hazard, but the pattern set in 1985 suggested a serious leak, and the obvious candidate was Ed Howard, a former CIA officer who had been dismissed in May 1983 when his routine polygraph had extracted an admission of drug-taking and theft. Unfortunately, his sacking had occurred *after* he had received a detailed briefing on various cases he was expected to handle in his imminent posting to Moscow. Crucially, Howard was a common denominator in some of the cases that had been compromised, and the record showed that he had been indoctrinated into SPHERE, ABSORB and TAW, so he was a strong suspect for those betrayals, but there were others to which he could not have had access. Howard was questioned and placed under FBI surveillance, but in August 1985 he slipped away from his home in Santa Fe and wound up in Moscow, an option that was interpreted as an eloquent admission of his guilt.

Howard's shrewd use of tradecraft had been taught to him by Jack Platt, who introduced and managed the PIPELINER project from a CIA office in Rosslyn. Candidates for the programme, the Internal Operations Course (IOC), were known as ZEPHYRS and they were imbued with the skills required to 'go black' and evade hostile surveillance in territory hitherto considered too dangerous to operate orthodox case officers. Almost all Agency personnel destined for a tour of duty on the espionage front line participated in the counter-surveillance exercise to graduate from the IOC and were suitably impressed with Platt, who acquired a very wide circle of acquaintances, admirers and useful contacts.

Howard and his wife Mary had both attended the PIPELINER course and this advantage had enabled him to evade the FBI team watching his home, but details of his betrayal were provided by Vitali Yurchenko, who unexpectedly defected to the CIA in Rome at the beginning of August 1985. Previously based at the Washington *rezidentura*, Yurchenko had been sent from Moscow on a mission to Italy to assess a US Navy chief petty officer, Thomas E. Hayden, a decorated Vietnam veteran who was in fact a relatively low-level Naval Investigative Service (NIS) double agent participating in an operation code-named SACKETT LAND, which had commenced soon after he had been posted to Naples and recruited by a KGB officer, Aleksandr M. Chepil. The classic 'dangle', handled by NIS Special Agents Ron Olive and Joe Riccio, had been initiated in January 1983 by an approach to the Intourist office in Rome. Having held a rendezvous with Hayden, Yurchenko had seized the opportunity to defect.

Yurchenko's debriefing in the United Sates, in which Aldrich Ames participated, proved very helpful and exposed Ron Pelton as a Soviet source inside the NSA. The former Washington *rezidentura* security chief, apparently unaware that the MI6 asset Oleg Gordievksy had been exfiltrated to Finland ten days earlier, also mentioned that he was under investigation in Moscow, news that was related to his bemused London handlers.

Yurchenko also disclosed details of a mole inside the Australian Security Intelligence Organisation (ASIO). Neither he, nor anyone else in the KGB, apparently knew the mole's true identity as the spy had taken elaborate pre-cautions to protect himself, and his wife who was also an ASIO employee, in a clerical post. When this tip belatedly was passed to Canberra, ASIO launched a mole hunt, code-named JABAROO, and headed by a former seminary student, Gerard P. Walsh, to ferret out the culprit, a lengthy inves-tigation that examined some forty potential suspects. As ASIO then only employed about 850 staff, this exercise amounted to scrutiny of 5 per cent of the entire organisation. Eventually the shortlist was narrowed down to three candidates, John C. Elliott, Charles F. Baré and Geoffrey R. Smith.

Elliott was a German-speaking officer born in Norway who ran ASIO's operations in Canberra and had been posted to Luneburg Heath with the British Army to supervise a post-war de-Nazification programme. He would later be seen to visit Eastern Europe, and in particular Finland. MI6's assistance was used to keep Elliott, codenamed BOOKBINDER, under surveillance when he toured Europe, but he skilfully eluded his watchers in Finland, and then re-emerged, leaving MI6 to speculate that he had been slipped across the frontier for meetings with his controller. When he retired, before the enquiry had been completed, Elliott ran a recruitment agency that became a conduit for entry into the organization, thus allowing him close contact with his former colleagues. The second suspect, Baré, was of Hungarian Jewish origin but his wife was a librarian, and had worked for ASIO's counter-subversion branch, mainly in the policy field, rising to be staff officer to the Deputy D-G.

While Yurchenko's contentious comments were being pursued by the mole hunters, confirmation of the Australian mole was found in 1992 among the documents donated to MI6 by another FCD defector, Vasili Mitrokhin, and two years later further collateral was provided unexpectedly by General Oleg Kalugin. Although not a defector in the conventional sense, Kalugin was too senior and specific to ignore. He had been forced into exile in the United States in 1993, having been pushed out of the KGB in 1990 where he had enjoyed a meteoric career in the FCD's 1st Department. Sophisticated and cosmopolitan, he had studied in New York as a Fulbright exchange scholar at

Columbia University, and then operated in New York under Radio Moscow journalistic cover. Fortuitously for him, in August 1959 he was approached in New York by Anatole Kotloby, a chemical engineer of Russian origin employed on a classified project designing solid-fuel rockets, who had been persuaded by his Chinese wife to adopt Communism. Until he was interviewed by the FBI in October 1964, when he fled to Moscow, Kotloby had been one of the KGB's star agents, and his success had reflected well on Kalugin.

In late 1969, after nearly five years at Boris Solomatin's *rezidentura* in Washington, Kalugin had been appointed deputy chief of Directorate K at the Centre and, at the age of forty, promoted the KGB's youngest ever general. However, his unparalleled career had nosedived after he had been elected to the Duma as a reformist, and had become a vocal critic of Russia's supposedly new, post-Soviet intelligence structure. Although exiled, Kalugin remained fiercely critical of 'traitors' such as Stanislas Levchenko, whom he had called 'scum' to his face, and Oleg Gordievsky, both defectors who had traded KGB assets for their resettlement.

With his professional experience and the knowledge he had accumulated over three decades of KGB espionage, it might be imagined that Kalugin would be regarded as an exceptionally valuable defector, but the CIA narrative remains that there was no need to resettle Kalugin under alias as he was such a senior figure, and anyway he had made clear that he was only prepared to discuss cases that were already known to allied authorities.

Despite this self-imposed discipline, Kalugin's 1994 memoirs contained an astonishing disclosure relating to his consultation with Kim Philby, at a time when the former MI6 officer was languishing unemployed in Moscow, and this caught the attention of the Australian mole hunters:

> I also called on Philby for advice on operational matters and sought his opinion on whether some 'volunteers' who had come to us were genuine or not. In one case, an Australian sent a letter to our embassy in Canberra, enclosing top-secret documents and requesting that payment be made to a post office box in the capital. The anonymous volunteer promised to supply us with more information if we sent the money. Fearing a set-up by Australian security services, we debated whether to send the cash to the donor. Finally, we decided there was no harm in transferring the funds anonymously to a post office box. Thus began a fruitful relationship in which

the anonymous Australian – apparently someone in their intelligence agency – supplied us with extremely useful information about the Australian Secret Intelligence Organisation *(sic)* and its American and British partners. At some point, I showed Philby the Australian's letters and the classified material he had supplied us. I had blacked out any references to the country, so as not to compromise the security of the operation, but Philby quickly surmised that the 'volunteer' was from Australia and that he was genuine. Eventually, our Australian began passing on so much material that we set up a series of dead drops similar to those used by Walker, although I lost touch with the information after 1980. I don't think the Australian was ever caught.[7]

In this passage Kalugin, who was already residing and teaching in Washington, DC, confirmed the existence in about 1975 to 1977 of an ASIO mole who supposedly emulated the tradecraft of John Walker, the US Navy spy who had started selling secrets to the KGB in 1968, but took measures to protect his true identity. This was a precaution against betrayal by a defector and the use of a Post Office box as a cut-out was a familiar expedient intended to insulate the source. Alarmingly, in a second reference to KGB activities in Australia, Kalugin used the plural, with the implication there was more than one mole:

The KGB also had excellent sources in Australia and Canada, including a valuable mole in Royal Canadian Mounted Police Counterintelligence. We had productive moles in Australian intelligence who passed us documents from the CIA and British intelligence as well as providing us with information on subjects as varied as the peace movement and the Australian military.[8]

Kalugin had been demonstrably right about the RCMP spy, Gilles Brunet, who had headed the RCMP Security Service's Russian section in Montreal. A high-level, long-term mole since he approached the KGB in January 1968, Brunet had died in April 1984, having been dismissed over disciplinary issues in 1973. Yurchenko's debriefing on this subject cleared up what had become an unresolved historical conundrum for the RCMP as Brunet had never been interrogated about his espionage. Once again, Kalugin's version had matched and enhanced an assertion already made by Yurchenko.

More confirmation would come from Oleg Gordievsky, who reported to his MI6 handlers that the (unusually long-serving) KGB *rezident* in Canberra had been heard boasting to his Third Chief Directorate colleagues that he had been decorated with the coveted Order of the Red Banner as a reward for his recruitment of the Australian mole. This news had brought an ASIO counter-intelligence analyst to London to question Gordievsky further.

The unsolicited accounts given separately and independently by Kalugin and Gordievsky, which seemed to confirm a self-recruited anonymous ganisation of ASIO with grave implications for British and American allied services, would invigorate the investigation that came to focus on Geoffrey Smith, who seemed to fit the Mitrokhin profile in every respect, and was traced and confronted. He had been paid huge sums for his deliveries of secrets, many of them from MI6 and the CIA, but he was by then a retiree and declined to co-operate with his interrogators. Smith, who had been posted to London as deputy to ASIO's liaison officer, T. Hardy Palethorpe, and then had headed the organization's Soviet Operations Group until 1979, had not come under suspicion during his career, and died after his retirement of stomach cancer. Smith had enjoyed access to vast amounts of British classified material, and had undergone a training course at MI6's facility at Fort Monckton. Palethorpe, who had previously served in Washington, DC, had never suspected Smith, but later colleagues recalled that, somewhat unusually, he had kept a photocopier in his office. As an experienced intelligence officer who had already shielded himself from any KGB attempts to learn his identity, Smith knew only too well the limitations that would handicap ASIO's efforts to entrap a pensioner.

An independent report into the JABAROO enquiry, written by the diplomat Michael Cook in 1994, suggested that the mole had been active between 1977 and 1985, and had been handled by the then KGB *rezidents,* Geronty Lazovik and his successors Gennadi Nayanov (formerly his deputy *rezident* and then acting *rezident*), and then Lev Koshliakov. However, even Cook did not know the mole's name, which was eventually traced in 1992 through a clue to the date of his retirement from ASIO, found in Mitrokhin's papers.[9] By this time Smith had refused to cooperate, so no further action could be taken. Indeed, the original, inconclusive JABAROO investigation was so inept that some ASIO staff even came to suspect that Walsh himself might have been a candidate for the elusive mole, claiming that there had been several security breaches on his watch, including the discovery of an air-conditioning engineer with access to ASIO's headquarters who had been recruited by Koshlyakov but had never been granted a security clearance.

The identification of Koshlyakov as *rezident,* later confirmed by Gordievsky, was significant because ASIO's original candidate had been his colleague, Gennadi P. Nayanov, another Line KR officer. Koshlyakov would remain in Canberra for seven years, until March 1984 when he was succeeded by Nayanov. The unusual fact that counter-intelligence specialists, instead of Line PR political reporters, were being selected for the *rezidentura*'s top job was interpreted as reflecting the local priority.

The issue of hostile penetration of ASIO had been raised originally during the lengthy review conducted by the Royal Commission led by an appeals court judge, Robert Hope, which concluded its work after three years in 1977. Hope had been briefed by MI6 and the CIA and, in coded civil service language, suggested that ASIO's antiquated management systems left the organization vulnerable to the kind of episodes experienced by almost all other allied intelligence agencies. However, Hope explained that it was beyond his remit to investigate penetration, but instead of taking up the gauntlet, ASIO downsized the D5 counter-intelligence section and then absorbed it into a new, under-staffed Security Review Branch that was also responsible for vetting new personnel. With an average of just five officers to pursue these enquiries, ASIO seemed reluctant to face up to the possibility that it had harboured at least one long-term mole. Furthermore, other ASIO investigations left the organization open to external criticism and internal dissent.

The controversy centred on two major enquiries, the first of which was an apparently routine security clearance required for the appointment of an English-born academic, Paul Dibb, as director of the National Assessments Staff. This investigation should have been straightforward, but as ASIO delved into Dibb's background, his links to a GRU *rezident* and confirmed KGB personnel based at the embassy raised suspicion. When interviewed, Dibb retorted that he had received Soviet help for his doctoral thesis, later published in 1988 as *The Soviet Union: The Incomplete SuperPower,* a plausible motive that explained his meetings and telephone contacts. ASIO was unconvinced, noting that some of the author's statistics were contradicted by American estimates, but Dibb, who was married to a Russian, received his clearance anyway, and was even promoted deputy director of the Joint Intelligence Organisation in 1978.

Dibb would complain vociferously about his security review and claim that he had actually worked for ASIO against the Soviets for over twenty years, a view that was not entirely shared by some ASIO staff, which became a matter of lasting internal contention and was exacerbated by the plethora of JABAROO candidates.

In June 1993, during the course of JABAROO, another potential security breach inside ASIO was discovered when a Russian analyst and linguist with twenty-five years' experience, George Sadil, was caught taking classified papers home. Aged fifty-seven, Sadil had been filmed removing files from his office, concealing them in a jacket tailored with a specially enlarged pocket, and had also been seen in the company of an SVR officer, Vycheslav Tatarivnov, based at the Canberra *rezidentura*, when they had both attended the same Russian Orthodox church.

The investigation of Sadil revealed that his brother ran a real estate business with a partner in Sydney with Soviet connections, and led ASIO to study Sadil's sister, Jenny, who was employed as a Russian interpreter in Canberra.

However, espionage charges against Sadil were dropped in March 1994 and he was sentenced in December 1994 to three months' imprisonment after he had pleaded guilty to illegal possession of classified material. As a lead to the loss of CIA secrets, the Sadil investigation, code-named LIVER, went nowhere as he clearly did not fit Yurchenko's profile, his wife had never worked for ASIO, and no evidence had been found of any illicitly acquired wealth. The enquiry, involving nearly two hundred federal police officers, and some very sophisticated surveillance techniques, would be inconclusive.

* * *

According to Yurchenko, Edward Howard had visited the KGB in Vienna late the previous year and had volunteered a mass of information so as to establish his credentials. However, as the losses mounted it was reluctantly acknowledged that not all of them could be blamed on Howard since he had been fired in June 1983, and that most likely the CIA harboured a currently active mole.

One example of the losses was a GRU general, Dmitri Polyakov, who had self-recruited while serving at the United Nations in New York in 1961, and had been active until June 1980 when he had been withdrawn without explanation from his military attaché post in Delhi. The CIA had been confident of his good health because of 'proof-of-life' articles he had contributed to a hunting magazine, *Okhota*, but they ceased in 1986, just as his son, a regular MFA diplomat, was recalled to Moscow.

A further example was GT/WEIGH, a KGB Line PR officer named Leonid Poleschuk who had been recruited in Nepal during his first overseas assignment, following a disagreement with his *resident*. He had re-established contact with the CIA in Lagos in early 1985 but failed to return from a scheduled vacation in September. After missing two meetings, the CIA realised that he had been detained in Moscow.

And there were others too. Boris Yuzhin, code-named GT/TWINE who had been recruited in 1979 while at the *rezidentura* in San Francisco under TASS cover, disappeared off the radar in 1986, having been sentenced to fifteen years' imprisonment. Gennadi Varenik, a Line N illegals support officer at the Bonn *rezidentua*, code-named GT/FITNESS, in March 1985 volunteered very specific information about KGB plans to exploit the then prevalent urban terrorism in West Germany by detonating bombs in venues frequented by NATO forces so as to create disaffection within the United States. However, in November 1985 he was lured to East Berlin and arrested. Another victim was GT/COWL, a KGB Second Chief Directorate officer who in early 1984 approached the CIA station in Moscow through a State Department intermediary but refused to reveal his true name. At a second meeting later in the year he passed his contact Mike Sellers a packet of the 'spy-dust' used by KGB surveillance teams, but when Sellers attended a third rendezvous in March 1986 he was ambushed and arrested. The CIA only learned GT/COWL's name, Sergei Vorontsov, when his trial and execution was announced. Yet another casualty was Vladimir Potashov, code-named GT/MEDIAN, a Soviet arms control expert who had volunteered to collaborate with the CIA in 1981. He had routinely returned to Moscow, where he had not been contacted by the station, but had been arrested in July 1986.

In late May 1985 Colonel Sergei Bokhan, the GRU deputy *resident* in Athens, sought an emergency meeting with the CIA to disclose his recall to Moscow, and to request his immediate exfiltration. Code-named GT/ BLIZZARD, Bokhan had been recruited in 1976 on his first tour to Greece by his occasional tennis partner, and was certain his new orders represented a trap. Abandoning his wife and daughter, Bokhan was smuggled out of Athens and resettled in the United States.

Another GRU source, Colonel Vladimir Vasilyev, code-named GT/ ACCORD, was not so lucky. Having been recruited in Budapest in 1982, Vasilyev had rotated back to Moscow in 1984, where he was in contact with the CIA station through a dead drop in December. He was arrested in early June 1986.

A third GRU asset was Gennadi Smetanin, code-named GT/MILLION, who was recruited in Lisbon in late 1983 by his tennis partner with the active support of his wife Svetlana, who worked in the embassy as a consular official. A routine meeting had been scheduled for 4 October after the couple had returned from their home leave, but they failed to attend the rendezvous, having been arrested in Moscow as they prepared to depart to Portugal by train.

One of the final pieces of the betrayal jigsaw, which would be unknown to the CIA for some months, was the role played by Oleg Gordievsky, a KGB Line PR officer recruited by the British MI6 in Copenhagen in October 1974. At the end of June 1982 he had been posted to London, and had been appointed *rezident*-designate three years later, receiving an invitation on 16 May to fly to Moscow for urgent consultations with the KGB Chairman and Vladimir Kryuchkov, head of the First Chief Directorate. Code-named NOCTON by MI6, Gordievsky immediately discussed the wisdom of complying with the recall message at a meeting with his MI6 case officer, Valerie Pettit, but in the absence of any adverse information, it was agreed that Gordievsky would travel as bidden two days later, on 28 May.

Although not arrested upon arrival, Gordievsky discovered that his flat had been searched, and when he visited Yasenevo he was subjected to a detailed interrogation and placed under very obvious surveillance. Concerned for his future, Gordievsky would request an emergency exfiltration from the MI6 station in Moscow, and this was undertaken, code-named PIMLICO, on 20 July, with total success. Once across the Soviet frontier, Gordievsky was reunited with Pettit, driven to Norway and then flown to England for a lengthy debriefing and resettlement.

Gordievsky's true identity had never been disclosed by MI6 to the CIA, but as a counter-intelligence specialist who had seen much of the MI6 reporting over the past decade, Ames had completed his own analysis of the KGB material originating first in Denmark and then in England, and narrowed the likely field down to a single individual who was code-named AE/TICKLE.

* * *

Among all the losses, the most distressing for Jack Platt was the disappearance of Vasilenko, who had vanished from Guyana in 1988, and it would be six years of fearing the worst before he learned what had happened.

In January 1988 Vasilenko had received instructions to report to Havana for a routine consultation, but as soon as he had arrived in the Cuban capital he had been driven not to the *rezidentura*, but to a villa where he had been violently assaulted and then interrogated about his contacts with the CIA. His interrogators were obviously convinced that he had sold out to the 'main adversary' (*'Glaviny Vrag'*) and when he refused to confess he was bundled aboard a Soviet freighter for a long voyage to Odessa, enduring maltreatment every day. Once back in the Soviet Union, he had been taken to Lefortovo prison, where the questioning and beatings continued for a further six months.

During this painful period Vasilenko came to suspect, from the repetition of certain questions relating to visits to Guyana made by Platt and his FBI partner James Nolan, that the KGB possessed a detailed knowledge of some parts of their relationship, to the point where it occurred to him that Platt might have betrayed him or maybe exaggerated his role as a fully-fledged CIA asset. However, he had an insurance policy that he repeatedly conveyed to his captors that, he asserted, proved his innocence of their charges: in January 1980, while at the Soviet embassy in Washington, DC, he had been responsible for the handling of an unexpected NSA walk-in, Ron Pelton. A retired linguist, Pelton had been declared bankrupt the previous year and he had offered to sell information about a highly classified project code-named IVY BELLS that had accessed Soviet and Libyan underwater telephone cables. Terms were agreed, and the embassy security officer, Vitali Yurchenko, had directed Vasilenko to shave off Pelton's beard and smuggle him out of the building's rear exit in a staff minivan, so as to avoid the FBI surveillance that, they calculated, must had spotted his arrival. Pelton was dropped off at a bus-stop on Old Courthouse Road in Virginia, and went undetected for a further five years, during which he travelled to Vienna to sell more NSA secrets to the KGB.

Pelton would be arrested in October 1985, having been compromised by Yurchenko, and it was Vasilenko's argument that gained traction in Lefortovo that quite obviously he had not been responsible for the betrayal. If he had been recruited by CIA, he alleged, Pelton would not have remained at liberty until 1985. Indeed, the KGB knew this to be partly true because upon his return to Moscow in November 1985, Yurchenko had acknowledged having told the Americans about Pelton during a drug-induced interrogation.

Only partly persuaded by this strategy, and in the absence of a confession, Vasilenko was released from Lefortovo, and in October 1988 was demoted and dismissed from the KGB. Years later, the CIA would learn that Vasilenko had been betrayed as a source by Robert Hanssen, but Ames had provided contradictory information, suggesting that MONOLIGHT was a target that had not yet been recruited. This discrepancy probably saved his life.

The evidence of Hanssen's complicity turned up on a computer disc that would be purchased almost exactly thirteen years later by the FBI in November 2000. The data contained three items that had been provided to the KGB by RAMON on Monday, 23 November 1987: a summary of Vitali Yurchenko's debriefing in 1985; a technical description of the US intelligence community's internal intranet inter-agency communications system known as COINS-II; and a cable report of Platt's meeting in Georgetown in October 1987 with a 'valuable source' referred to by the KGB as 'M', which was instantly recognized as Vasilenko's code name MONOLIGHT.[11] This was eloquent proof that Vasilenko had been betrayed by the spy who called himself RAMON.

Taking advantage of his new freedom, and the changing business and political climate in Moscow, Vasilenko found a job as a security adviser to a new company exploiting the nationwide shortage of photocopiers. One of the partners was Viktor Cherkashin's wife, Elena, and Vasilenko settled into his new existence, careful to avoid any contact with the west. On the one occasion he attempted to travel, by train on business to Warsaw, he was turned back, so he fully understood that even if the political atmosphere was being liberalised by Mikhail Gorbachev, the KGB was unforgiving,

A few months later he was telephoned by Platt and in 1992 acquired a passport and a visa to travel to the United States. This was the first opportunity for the two men to compare notes, and begin to understand what had happened in Guyana, and since. From Vasilenko's account of his interrogation, which had concentrated on certain narrow subjects, it was clear to Platt that one of his reports had been leaked to the KGB. As a matter of routine, Platt had filed a detailed account of his visit to AE/MONOLIGHT in Georgetown, but one of them evidently had been passed to his interrogators. Who was the culprit? This was another 'serial' for the Langley mole hunters but at least Vasilenko came to realise that he had not been betrayed by his old friend. Nevertheless, Platt felt a burden of responsibility for having placed Vasilenko in harm's way, albeit unintentionally.

* * *

In the light of the continuing losses and growing evidence of penetration, a joint CIA–FBI task force, designated AM/LACE, convened in the autumn of 1986 to review the situation. There would be many distractions along the way, some of them undoubtedly orchestrated by the KGB. Some of the red herrings were ingenious, involving on one occasion a potential KGB FCD defector, Aleksandr Zhomov, code-named GT/PROLOGUE, who in June 1988 offered entirely misleading information about the source of the losses. However, Sergei Papushin, from the Second Chief Directorate (SCD), supplied contradictory evidence. A thirty-four-year-old alcoholic, Papushin had been arrested in New Jersey in November 1989 while drunk and had opted to defect, despite his father being the KGB *rezident* in Sofia, who had been flown to the United States to persuade him to change his mind, but he refused to re-defect.

Papushin, who had resigned from the KGB to join an oil business shortly before his trip to New York, told the FBI that his SCD role in Moscow was to identify and monitor the local MI6 station personnel. He also said that during the course of his duties he had learned that the CIA station had been penetrated. Code-named DECANTER by the CIA, Papushin would be found dead of alcohol poisoning in his Maryland apartment in February 1991.

Against this background noise of deliberate deception, the Moscow station had to endure a penetration scandal implicating the US Marines employed to guard the CIA and NSA premises on the embassy's top floors.

The KGB's SCD had spent years, devoting considerable resources, to targeting the embassy, and in April 1984 yet more bugs were discovered inside a consignment of IBM Selectric III typewriters used in the classified spaces. Out of the 250 'golf-ball' machines used throughout the Moscow embassy and Leningrad consulate, sixteen were found to have been delayed at customs at Sheremetyevo and modified with miniature, low-power transmitters that relayed individual key strokes to an ingenious apparatus constructed in a disused chimney space. This was a familiar technique, code-named GUNMAN, and had happened before, but knowledge of how they had been planted did not emerge until December 1986 when a US Marine, Sergeant Clayton J. Lonetree, approached Jim Olson, the CIA station chief in Vienna, and confessed to having allowed KGB personnel into the classified areas of the embassy in Moscow at night. Lonetree had been the victim of a honeytrap conducted by a KGB agent, Violette Seina, while he had been posted to Moscow between September 1984 and March 1986. Seina previously had worked at the embassy as a locally employed telephonist and translator, but her genial 'Uncle Sasha' was actually a skilled KGB officer, Aleksei G. Yefimov, who manipulated the young Native American and persuaded him to compromise classified information.

Lonetree's confession resulted in the detention of six other Marines, including Corporal Arnold Bracey, who was suspected of having had several affairs with various Soviet women. In the end, the charges against all except Lonetree were dropped, and he was convicted in August 1987 in a military court on 12 counts of espionage and collaborating with the Soviets to supply floor plans of the embassies in Moscow and Vienna, and identifying US intelligence personnel. Lonetree was sentenced to thirty years' imprisonment but, following a further, detailed inquiry by the Naval Investigative Service, it was concluded that the KGB never did gain access to the embassy, and his sentence was cut in May 1988 to twenty-five years, in 1992 to twenty years, and then to fifteen years. Finally, he was released in February 1996, in part an acknowledgment that the KGB had been attempting to misdirect the mole hunters in Washington.

A year later, in July 1997, former Director of Central Intelligence James Schlesinger completed a review of security procedures at the embassy in Moscow and recommended that the top three floors of the new embassy be rebuilt and that a new, six-floor annex be constructed to accommodate a high-security unit, but the new site would not be completed until May 2000.

One of the curiosities of the Langley mole hunt was the behaviour of the Soviets as they methodically closed down the CIA's assets across the globe. Although the KGB could be seen to have adopted various ruses to conceal the disappearance of so many agents, the lack of subtlety was uncharacteristic. As the toll rose, and evidence of hostile penetration grew, the existence of the mole became a certainty, so why had the KGB not exercised more discretion and simply sidelined their suspects into non-sensitive posts, of which the organization had literally thousands. The answer would only emerge years later when Vladimir Kryuchkov's ambitions became clear. He had coveted the role of KGB chairman and had intended to replace Viktor Chebrikov, as indeed he would in October 1988, but he was anxious not to steer a course between an overnight purge, which would alert the Americans, or be accused of complacency and inaction in the face of large-scale treason. In these circumstances, Kryuchkov had opted to deal with the traitors ruthlessly, but to minimise the perceived impact.

The AM/LACE investigation would rumble on for years, partly driven by the mole hunter Jeanne Vertefeuille's determination to find out what had really happened to General Polyakov, an asset she had never met, but whose reporting she had handled at headquarters for many years. According to her version of events, *Circle of Treason*, authored with her task force colleague Sandy Grimes and published with the CIA's approval, it had been dogged determination that had whittled down a long list of suspects to just Rick Ames.[12] Although not popular in SE Division, where he supervised the counter-intelligence branch, Ames was fluent in Mandarin, spoke some Russian and Italian, and had married into a prominent and wealthy Colombian family, which was an explanation for the couple's conspicuous consumption. Vertefeuille and Grimes claim their suspicions were aroused by the fact that the records demonstrated Ames had read most, but not all, of the contaminated case files, and that his bank account showed large unexplained deposits that coincided with his foreign travel.

In reality the two CIA women had written their book, which was largely true, in an attempt to shield the real source of the information that had led to Ames being placed under intensive surveillance during the two months before his arrest in February 1994. Discretion was required because the clinching clue to the identity of the mole had been provided inadvertently by a recent walk-in, Aleksandr Zaporozhsky, who had joined the KGB in 1975 and had approached the CIA station in Addis Ababa fourteen years later, in 1989, to make an unusual deal. He wanted to pass occasional information to the CIA on his own terms, whenever he deemed it convenient, so as to earn a quiet retirement in the United States. He would decide when to initiate contact, and he would control the flow of information. Assured by Vasilenko that Zaporozhsky was a genuine former colleague from Directorate K, coincidentally having been his volleyball partner, the CIA accepted his proposal, and in due course was rewarded, when the source was transferred to the 1st (North American) Department, with details of David Boone, a retired NSA cryptologic traffic analyst who had been a walk-in at the Soviet embassy in Washington in October 1988. In the meantime, when asked in May 1993 about his knowledge of any indications of a mole deep inside the CIA,

Zaporozhsky, now code-named AVENGER, had claimed ignorance, but had mentioned that he had heard from a friend in Yasenevo that an important spy had been run by an acquaintance, Vitali Karetkin, who had flown to Lima to meet him. He also said that the mole was somehow connected to the State Department spy Felix Bloch.

When the AM/LACE analysts compared Zaporozhsky's story to the dates of Ames's declared visits to Colombia, there was a match. Further research revealed that at that time there were no direct flights from Moscow to Bogota, and that a change of plane was required in Lima. This was the ostensibly innocuous item, supplied inadvertently by Zaporozhsky, that would seal Ames' fate. However, as Zaporozhsky was still at liberty, climbing through the ranks of the KGB and heading for a quiet retirement, it was important for the AM/LACE team to put up a smokescreen regarding the precise information that closed the case:

> Luckily, in 1993 additional information became available. This new information, while it did not identify Ames, pointed in his direction. It added to the comfort level of those who had not been convinced by the results of our analytic efforts and forced the FBI to open a full-scale investigation of Ames.[13]

Once Ames was subjected to the physical and technical surveillance applied to his office, home and car, his arrest, and that of his wife, it was only a matter of time and convenience before the investigation, code-named NIGHTMOVER, had him taken into custody. However, no sooner had he been detained than further evidence emerged of another mole active inside the Agency.

Chapter II

KARAT

The 'loose ends' from NIGHTMOVER amounted to a list of incidents that suggested hostile penetration of the CIA that could not be attributed to Ames who, between July 1986 and December 1989 had been based at the CIA station in Rome and therefore could not have been involved. This analysis was especially true in the case of Felix Bloch, formerly the deputy chief of mission at the US embassy in Vienna and currently director of regional economic and political affairs in the European Bureau, who received an early morning telephone call on 22 June 1989 at his apartment in Washington, DC, from 'Ferdinand Paul' who warned him that 'Pierre' was 'ill' and that 'a contagious disease is suspected'. Thereafter Reino Gikman, a suspected Soviet illegal masquerading as a Finnish businessman supposedly employed by IBM who had come under the CIA's surveillance and called himself 'Pierre', disappeared from Austria, and the FBI concluded that their investigation into a high-level leak from the State Department had been compromised. Gikman's relationship with Bloch had been under the FBI's scrutiny since 28 April 1989, following a tip from the CIA.

Soon afterwards, in May, Gikman was identified in Paris by the French Direction de la Surveillance du Territoire as the person to whom Bloch had twice handed over a briefcase while dining at the Hotel Meurice. When Bloch returned to his home in Washington, his calls were monitored, and he had received the somewhat transparent warning from the Soviet embassy within five weeks of the FBI initiating its enquiries.

Under interrogation by the FBI the same day that he received the warning call, Bloch explained his visits to Paris and Brussels as opportunities to buy stamps for his collection and to spend time with his girlfriend, Tina Jirousek, a woman he had met through the escort section of the Vienna telephone directory's yellow pages. When the blonde was interviewed, she revealed a bizarre relationship with Bloch over seven years in which he had paid her an estimated $70,000 to participate in sado-masochism and bondage sessions on

Saturday mornings when he had told his wife he was working at his office. Bloch subsequently was interrogated at length but made no further admissions, and in December 1990, after thirty years in the Foreign Service, he was fired and denied a pension.

The case was to have wide ramifications, not least because it convinced the FBI and the CIA that there had been a high-level leak that had compromised the investigation at a very early stage. Ironically, the senior CIA counter-intelligence officer, Brian Kelley, who had initiated and supervised the CIA's surveillance of Gikman, himself became the subject of a secret mole hunt code-named GRAY SUIT for a spy allegedly code-named KARAT by the KGB. The FBI rationale was that only someone indoctrinated into the Bloch investigation could have compromised the case, and the best candidate was Kelley himself, a former Air Force colonel now code-named GRAY DECEIVER, who had headed the Counterintelligence Center's (CIC) illegals branch for seven years, and the double agents section for two. That Kelley had been selected as the FBI's prime suspect for the GRAY SUIT mole hunt had considerable ramifications, for not only was Kelley well liked and greatly admired by his colleagues for his professionalism, his daughter was also a CIA officer attached to Director Tenet's personal security staff.[1] Furthermore, Kelley had recently received a decoration from Tenet for his work on Gikman.

To identify Gikman as a Soviet illegal, Kelley had undertaken a lengthy analysis of Line N travel patterns and had devised a scheme to flag up possible suspects. Kelley's project was ingenious and promised to become an invaluable counter-intelligence technique that might expose other Soviet spies. Study of Gikman's movements across Europe, using the passport of a dead Finn, showed that he was based in the Viennese suburb of Hietzing, living with his girlfriend Helga Hobart, but flew irregularly to and from Austria through Budapest and Belgrade, unnecessarily transiting through third countries, but characteristic of the behaviour of Soviet illegals. However, according to some of the FBI 'true believers', including the squad leader David Szady, Kelley's methodology, based on a study of the two routes chosen by illegals to travel to Moscow, was just too clever by half and maybe indicated an attempt by the KGB to enhance the status of one of its own assets. According to Kelley's analysis, the average illegal routinely returned to Moscow every other year, usually to undergo an operational briefing and enjoy some family leave, and took one of two distinct itineraries. One was northern, through a Scandinavian airport, the other was southern, probably through Rome or Zurich. Kelley reasoned that, if the flight data could be retrieved, this pattern might suggest some suspicious passengers worthy of further study.

As the FBI looked further for the mole, a review code-named PENNYWISE was conducted by the senior FBI analyst for Soviet operations, described as the 'senior penetration analyst'. He was given the task of looking at all fifty FBI-sponsored operations against the Soviet HUMINT and technical targets that had occurred over a ten-year period from the late 1980s through the late 1990s, and had all failed. His conclusions, based on a matrix linking suspects to serials, were that there was no discernible pattern, and that the mole must be inside the CIA.

It later emerged that this analyst, who had been the FBI's primary mole hunt analyst since 1986, beginning with his participation in AM/LACE, had been supervised since the late 1980s, mentored and at various times had shared a cubicle at his office in the FBI Headquarters with a senior officer, Bob Hanssen. Apparently Hanssen had influenced the analyst's thinking as to who the mole might be, and had posed two questions that greatly impacted the decision that the mole 'had to be at CIA'. Hanssen had told the analyst to pay close attention to the breadth of the losses that the FBI had suffered in its Soviet counter-intelligence programme, meaning the HUMINT and technical dimensions, and reportedly had asked, 'Who in the FBI would have that kind of broad-based access? The question was significant as CIA personnel would be expected to have far more extensive knowledge than anybody in the FBI.' Further, 'The person who is the spy we are chasing has to be a genius. Who in the FBI do you know who is that smart? It has to be somebody at CIA.'[2]

The new FBI squad gathered at the WFO amounted to some fifteen agents and analysts assembled by Robert Bryant, sifted through between fifty-eight and sixty-two items thought to be relevant, and then studied the 245 case officers and others associated with them. The challenge was immense and would boil down to thirty-four names, and then just seventeen, all Agency case officers, there being an institutional acceptance that the culprit was most likely a member of the Counterintelligence Center, but definitely a CIA officer.

After Hanssen's arrest plenty of his colleagues recalled odd, suspicious incidents that had gone unreported. For example, in 1985 Eddie Worthington had challenged Hanssen in a Xerox room on the fourth floor of headquarters making copies of the reports on Vitali Yurchenko's debriefing. On another occasion he had been caught by Bob King hacking into a Soviet espionage analytical group database to read a file compiled by Ray Matlock and Jimmy Holt relating to the Ames investigation. Personnel assigned to the Washington Field Office found themselves being targeted by Hanssen for an uncomfortable cultivation intended to elicit information about the progress of the mole hunt. In hindsight, these episodes gained significance, but at the time Hanssen had a strange reputation, dating back to his first assignment in New York in 1979 where he had shown a talent for developing databases and digitising the NYFO's paper counter-intelligence records, at a time when such skills were rare and valued.

Although disliked by most of his FBI field agent colleagues, who avoided him as an oddball, Hanssen did ingratiate himself with junior staff during the two periods he headed the counter-intelligence analytical groups at head-quarters, and once purchased a special program to help a subordinate who was struggling to tackle a particular data-processing problem. She had been impressed that her superior had bought the program with his own money.

According to one of Kelley's interrogators, the FBI had acquired some information about KARAT from an unknown Soviet source, now known to be Zaporozhsky, earning his meal ticket before his planned retirement. Allegedly KARAT had provided 'tightly held' insider's information about Felix Bloch, was paid in part in diamonds and had participated in opera-tional activity at Nottoway Park, in Virginia, as well as other parks in Fairfax County that had been used as dead drops and signal sites. The source, code-named AVENGER, also disclosed that an advertisement had been placed in the *Washington Times* as part of the covert communications process, and at some point New York City had been used as a venue for operations. As the GRAY SUIT investigators noted, some of these clues might fit Kelley, who as a divorcee conducted a very energetic love life and lived close to Nottoway Park, where he jogged regularly. The FBI became convinced Kelley was the mole when they recovered his jogging map drawn on a scrap of paper that included three of KARAT's known drop sites.

In addition, KARAT had possessed knowledge of highly compartmented FBI recruitments of three KGB officers, Motorin, Martynov and Yuzhin, and had sold this information to the KGB. The source also revealed that KARAT was connected with strip clubs, and had a stripper girlfriend. According to the source, KARAT's home had a sealed off room where, presumably, he was able to indulge in some of his espionage. He also claimed that KARAT's true name had never appeared on the matrix used by the AN/LACE mole hunters during their long search for Ames.

Various techniques were deployed by the FBI to entrap Kelley or extract an incriminating admission, but he passed his polygraph examinations and protested that he had been in Panama on an Agency counter-intelligence assignment during the year that some of the acts he was accused of had taken place.

Doggedly convinced that Kelley was KARAT, the FBI took a different approach to the challenge by asking Zaporozhsky to draw up a list of the very senior KGB officers who would be expected to have been indoctrinated into KARAT. On one of his visits to the United States to visit Platt, Vasilenko was given the same task, so the results could be compared and cross-referenced. This tiny circle, an *ad hoc* cadre of five specialists who had run Ames successfully for nine years, would develop into the Co-ordination Unit, and then become GROUP NORTH, the very existence of which was a closely guarded secret. Chaired by the ambitious FCD chief Vladimir Kryuchkov's subordinate Vadim Kirpichenko, GROUP NORTH was totally compartmentalised within Directorate K to prevent rumours about its activities or its sources. Its management consisted of the chiefs of the KGB's various directorates (or occasionally their deputies), its personnel communicated with headquarters on a separate, dedicated channel, and it had access to unvouchered funds so major recruitments could be managed with the minimum risk of a leak. Ad hoc operational teams would be assembled when circumstances required, and this had happened with the handling of Ames and Hanssen. The group's operational doctrine was to talent spot and pitch American officers posted away from the United States, just as the CIA had concentrated on targets when they were physically outside the Soviet bloc.

Once the GROUP NORTH membership list had been delivered, the FBI's Mike Rochford gathered a small team of special agents and analysts, designated the MC-43 Squad, to track down and pitch some twenty-seven targets, some of them GROUP NORTH members.

The creation of GROUP NORTH extended beyond the FCD's Directorate K, which anyway underwent a considerable reorganization and its role looked, to some the FBI analysts, as a mirror image of the CIA's Counterintelligence Center, Later the mole hunters would hear that the concept had been adopted by the KGB based on advice from the elusive spy, and served to convince the Bureau that the unidentified quarry, known as the UNSUB, was almost certainly to be found in the Agency.

The son of a Chicago policeman, Rochford had joined the FBI as a clerk in 1975 but attended a Russian language course at Monterey and gained a degree in accounting. He left agent training at Quantico in November 1979 and was posted to CI-4 in Washington, DC to participate in the then current investigation of a CIA officer, David Barnett. For the following ten years he worked at the Washington Field Office and was then assigned in 1989 to Nashville, Tennessee, for three years. In 1992 he returned to the WFO to work on the Ames investigation, designated Major Case 43, having met Ames in 1985 while debriefing Vitali Yurchenko with the CIA's Colin Thompson. During this period Rochford was seconded to the CIA's Central European Division and spent two years travelling each month to England to debrief Mitrokhin.

Top of Rochford's list was, of course, Viktor Cherkashin, whose daughter Alyona lived in California, but he politely declined the invitation to co-operate. He also turned down a further offer of $1 million.

Cherkashin's reaction to the bribe reflected an FCD *esprit de corps* and a discipline that had largely evaporated from Russian life in the post-Communist era when thousands of former KGB officers were left unemployed, and criminal gangs were operating with impunity, looting state assets and engaging in protection rackets and similar activities. The KGB itself had been dissolved, with Kryuchkov's FCD transformed into the SVR in December 1991, followed by the SCD becoming the Federal Security Service (FSB) in 1995. The changes in names were largely cosmetic as the personnel stayed much the same, working in the same premises and fulfilling an almost identical mission. What certainly changed dramatically were the social and economic realities that encouraged some disaffected officers to capitalise on their accumulated knowledge. One such defector was Vasili Mitrokhin who, in March 1992 aged sixty-nine, walked into the British embassy in Riga and asked to see a member of MI6. He had arrived on the overnight train from Moscow, spoke no English, but explained that he had joined the KGB in 1948, and that from late 1956 until his retirement in 1984 he had been in charge of the FCD's archives at Yasenevo. For the previous twenty-five years, since the premature conclusion of his only overseas assignment, to Israel, he had supervised the tens of thousands of FCD files and during his retirement he had reconstructed his own version of what he regarded as the most significant dossiers.

In 1972, when he was made responsible for checking the FCD files being transferred from the old headquarters in the Lubyanka to the KGB's modern building on the outskirts of Moscow, he embarked on an illicit history of the Soviet Union's most secret operations. Mitrokhin asserted that he had simply copied the original files and walked out of the heavily guarded KGB compound with his handwritten notes stuffed into his socks. He had then redrafted a detailed account of the files from his scraps of paper into exercise books and other convenient binders that he had hidden in a milk churn concealed under his country dacha. In return for political asylum for himself and his family he offered his entire collection, amounting to a full six cases of documents. He returned to Riga on 9 April with more samples of his handiwork and was met by MI6 officers, who examined some 2,000 sheets of his archive and scrutinised his Party membership card and his KGB retirement certificate. Acknowledging the authenticity of what he had shown them, a further appointment was made two months' hence to meet the man now code-named GUNNER by MI6, and on 11 June he returned to Riga carrying a rucksack containing yet more material.

Mitrokhin subsequently made a third journey to Riga on the anniversary of the Bolshevik revolution, accompanied by his wife and son, and an MI6 officer later visited his empty dacha outside Moscow and recovered his secret hoard of papers amounting to 23,000 documents, and carried them undetected to the British embassy. Now code-named JESSANT, no official announcement was made of Mitrokhin's defection, and in the chaos of 1992 his disappearance from the Russian capital probably went unnoticed, but in the months that followed, numerous counter-intelligence operations were mounted across the globe.

Mitrokhin revealed that before turning to MI6 he had initially approached the CIA station in Riga, but had been rebuffed, the SE Division supposedly overrun with similar offers, so the CIA and FBI agreed to pay equal shares with MI6 for access to his material. He was largely motivated by his desire to help his sick son, who could not get proper medical attention in Russia, but resented having been rejected by the Americans, who had been his first choice. For more than two years the American participation in his debriefing consisted of two FBI officers attached to the CIA, Mike Rochford and Bob Way.

Mitrokhin always resented his original rejection by the CIA, but the decision not to pursue him had not been entirely arbitrary, for 1992 was truly 'the year of the defector'. In March a GRU officer, Colonel Stanislav Lunev, had been granted political asylum in the United States, and later the same month Vladimir Konoplev had left the KGB *rezidentura* in Brussels. In July, the KGB's Viktor Oshchenko, based in Paris, defected to the British. Mitrokhin had chosen a busy time to offer himself, and as a retiree he was probably a less attractive prospect than someone currently serving. Certainly the Kryuchkov coup the previous year had created a political climate in which many supporters of the former regime felt able to capitalise on their accumulated knowledge.

Buried in Mitrokhin's notes was sufficient information to identify two American traitors, a retired US Army officer, Colonel George Trofimoff, and a former NSA cryptographer, Robert Lipka.[3] Both spies would be entrapped by the FBI and imprisoned, but cover stories were constructed so as to protect the integrity of the many other investigations then under way, inspired by the same source. In Trofimoff's case, Oleg Kalugin was made to appear as a prosecution witness during his trial in Florida in June 2000, and in Lipka's it was suggested that Kalugin's indiscreet 1994 memoirs had been the cause of his compromise. In his book he had described 'a soldier in the mid-1960s' working at the NSA who had been a walk-in at the Washington embassy but he had not provided enough detail for the FBI to trace Lipka, who indeed had begun to sell NSA secrets to the KGB in September 1965.[4] He was entrapped by the FBI in May 1993 but was not arrested at his home in Millersville, Pennsylvania, until February 1996 and in May the following year was sentenced to eighteen years' imprisonment as part of a plea bargain.

In reality General Kalugin, who had been forced to retire from the KGB in February 1990, moved to the United States and was convicted *in absentia* of treason in 2002. The following year he acquired American citizenship.

Another of the KGB sources compromised by Mitrokhin was Albrecht Dittrich, alias Jack Barsky, who was placed under surveillance by the FBI in Mount Bethel, Pennsylvania, in the summer of 1993. The defector's papers referred to a spy operating in the US north-east with the surname Barsky, and when the FBI checked the thirty or so relevant individuals, only one had acquired a social security number after the age of thirty. Once identified, the FBI launched an operation code-named FARBSTIFT to watch and listen to Dittrich in the hope of spotting any co-conspirators. Initially the Department of Justice was reluctant to apply for a FISA warrant but when eventually one was granted the FBI recorded a kitchen argument between Dittrich and his wife Penny, who was an illegal immigrant from Jamaica. Her sister had acquired citizenship by marrying an American, and she thought she had done the same until Dittrich reluctantly explained that his position in the United States was far from secure, as he was in danger from both the KGB and the FBI. This taped admission would prove enough for his FBI investigator, Special Agent Joe Reilly, who was based at the Philadelphia Field Office's satellite at Allentown, as he later recalled:

> Our investigation during the many months that followed revealed that Barsky was an energetic, focused, and intelligent man who would do well in almost any undertaking, except perhaps diplomacy. He was advancing quickly at his job and was well liked and respected. An ideal spy! But what was he actually doing for the Russians, or what had he been doing for them? We were well aware that the KGB's internal operations were in disarray after the collapse of the Soviet Union, but how did this affect Barsky? Was he still receiving instructions, or had he been put in sleeper mode? Months turned into years of investigation and surveillance. At one point, we even purchased the house next door to Barsky's to better observe him.

The FBI surveillance on Dittrich's isolated, rural home was run from a neighbouring property, the only one in eyesight of his house. During a family visit to Canada, the FBI took the opportunity to conduct a search and install an eavesdropping device. The search only turned up seven $100 bills hidden in the basement. The FBI guessed this was his escape funds, but in reality it was Dittrich's savings for the purchase of a diamond ring for his wife.

Dittrich had been concerned about the reliability of his US citizenship because he had never received the passport that he had applied for in Barsky's name. In fact, as the FBI discovered, a passport *had* been issued to him but had either been lost or stolen in the mail. Although concerned about the absence of his expected passport, Dittrich had not complained when it had not been delivered.

Reilly was an experienced counter-intelligence officer, having served ten years in Boston and another six in Honolulu, although he had plenty of disagreements with his supervisor at headquarters, Susan Gregory, who had wanted to extend the surveillance. Instead, Dittrich was detained by Reilly while driving home from work in New Jersey in what appeared to be a routine traffic stop in May 1997. He then underwent six weeks of intermittent interrogation at a local motel, the Pocono Inn at Delaware Water Gap, where he made a detailed confession in which he described his childhood in East Germany and his entry into a KGB training programme in February 1973. He also recalled the cover names of his handlers and recalled how he had been taught English in Moscow by a disappointed woman married to a Soviet military intelligence agent who had operated undercover in the west. He was also given lessons on how to behave in the United States by Morris Cohen, the illegal arrested in London in January 1961 who had been released in a spy swap in July 1969.

On his first overseas mission, to Chicago in 1978, Dittrich had travelled via Mexico City on a Canadian passport in the name of William Dyson, and then established himself in New York as Jakob Barsky, a child who had died in 1955, and enrolled in a four-year business degree course, majoring in computer technology at Baruch College. In 1984 he found a job with the Metropolitan Life Insurance Company but continued to maintain contact with the KGB, occasionally undertaking missions on instructions, one of which had taken him to Canada. There he had surveyed several dead drops in Montreal and Windsor, but never actually used them himself.

Although principally deployed as a talent spotter, directed to gather information on members of influential policy think tanks, Dittrich was also sent to California to trace a KGB defector, Nikolai Khokhlov, then working as an academic in San Bernardino. Although evidently the KGB had been keen to find Khokhlov, who had defected in Germany in 1954, and had survived an attempt on his life in Frankfurt three years later, no further action was taken and he died of a heart attack in September 2007.

On another occasion Dittrich was tasked to find a site in Keene, New Hampshire, suitable for a dead drop that could conceal a large object the size of a suitcase. The FBI later speculated that the drop might have been connected to some emergency exfiltration plan for an unknown asset, perhaps Aldrich Ames.

Dittrich, who returned to Moscow four times during his assignment, eventually received an emergency recall at a signal site in 1988 and was ordered home during a rendezvous with a contact in a New York subway station. No explanation was ever offered about the nature of the emergency, nor the reason for the order. However, by then Dittrich was married with a son, and ignored his instructions and responded with a message that he had been diagnosed with AIDS. As he later joked, 'Russians fear only two things: Jews and AIDS.' Dittrich calculated that his ruse would pander to the SVR's prejudices, and deter future contact.

During his FBI debriefing, which ended with a polygraph test, Dittrich asserted that he had not engaged in espionage since 1988 and, having co-operated with the FBI, acquired American citizenship in 2014.[5]

Mitrokhin's archive, which would take years to translate and manually enter into a computer database before it could be exploited, revealed the KGB's strategic plan to develop up to six illegal networks across the United States, supported by more in South America.[6] The ambitious project was intended to create an organization that could survive the withdrawal of the legal *rezidenturas* in time of political crisis, and enjoy the freedom to penetrate US government agencies and associated institutions. The core purpose for the illegals' operational doctrine was to take over the management of existing assets when the conventional lines of communication were broken. Such a commitment required extraordinary resources, and a discipline that the decadent west could never hope to match. In a sense, the Russian dedication to the covert life actually defined the true Chekist, the willingness to risk everything for the *rodina*.

Dittrich had been given the task of insinuating himself into the Hudson Institute, and a similar goal had been entrusted to GORT and LUIZA, then based in Queen's, New York.[7] Also East Germans, the couple worked in Astoria as a computer engineer and a tax adviser respectively, and had ignored a recall signal in 1988 as they had a small baby. After the Soviet collapse they reported to Moscow and then returned to their home in Germany, where they were interviewed by the BND. By the time Mitrokhin identified them as GORT and LUIZA they had long abandoned their illegal activities, and no action was taken against them.

* * *

The GRAY SUIT investigators travelled to London several times in the hope that the Mitrokhin treasure trove might contain a lead relevant to their enquiries, but they drew a blank. It was not until 1999 that Vasilenko revealed his knowledge of Aleksandr Shcherbakov, another member of GROUP NORTH who, he said, had served in the Washington *residentura* in Line KR, worked in Moscow under his mentor, Colonel Vladimir Adrianov, the deputy chief of Directorate S, and in that capacity had been declared to the CIA station so he could act as a liaison link with the Moscow station chief. Later, and quite unexpectedly, Shcherbakov had been promoted to Directorate S's security branch, in charge of maintaining the integrity of the KGB's worldwide network of illegals. Most significantly, Shcherbakov was now out of a job, and had been squatting in the office of Vasilenko's new enterprise, Securitar, where he had been making a nuisance of himself, running up phone bills to find work. Furthermore, he was in desperate financial straits after a caviar export scheme had failed, leaving him heavily in debt to the Irkutsk mafia and in fear of his life. Although Shcherbakov had been pitched during the PENNYWISE trawl of potential sources, an approach that he may, or may not, have reported to the SVR, he now made himself available for recruitment, and used Vasilenko to pass a message to Platt indicating that he was now ready to trade.

Rochford's intention was to lure Shcherbakov to New York with a spurious business proposal and then pitch him for his knowledge of KARAT. What the FBI officer did not realise was that, like a few other KGB officers, Shcherbakov had acquired his own personal pension plan. At the height of the August 1991 coup, when Vladimir Kryuchkov had plotted to remove Mikhail Gorbachev and laid siege to the Russian duma, the KGB FCD had panicked, fearing the Yasenevo headquarters would be invaded and occupied by an angry mob, just like the Stasi building in Berlin's Normanienstrasse in December 1989. Accordingly, Shcherbakov had been one of a small trusted team of senior officers who relocated the GROUP NORTH records to a more secure site at Smolensk, some 200 miles west of Moscow. During this frenzied episode Shcherbakov had seized the opportunity to hide an armful of files in a convenient cupboard, and then remove them from the compound altogether, to be hidden in his mother's garage. Eight years later, this cache would hold the key to KARAT's identity, although the SVR had only known him as RAMON. In his communications to his Russian handlers, the mole had gone to elaborate lengths to protect his own identity, and had signed off his messages simply as RAMON.[8]

In July 2000 Shcherbakov arrived in Manhattan, supposedly unaware that his flights had been paid for by the FBI, and that his invitation to discuss the sale of Russian art objects to the Frick Collection was a sham. Jack Platt met him and escorted him to the Frick, but absented himself when Rochford introduced himself at Shcherbakov's hotel, where he was booked in for the week. Although Rochford would later pretend that this was his first encounter with Shcherbakov, and that he had made more than two dozen similar pitches to other potential sources, both men had met previously, but on the earlier occasion Shcherbakov had not been ready to open negotiations.[9]

During his stay in New York Shcherbakov was constantly in Rochford's company, and urged to reveal what he knew of GROUP NORTH's secrets. He was invited to a lobster dinner to break the ice, but the shrewd KGB retiree appeared quite aggressive and resentful of the pitch and made a similar recruitment offer to Rochford, inviting him to Moscow. The G-man countered with a promise to make a deal that he said had already been authorised by the DCI George Tenet and FBI Director Louis Freeh.

The Russian, conscious that there would not be a business coup with Frick, and worried about how he was going to pay off the Irkutsk gangsters, embarked on discussions for the sale of another precious commodity, which he referred opaquely to as 'volume 1' of the KARAT file. By the time Shcherbakov returned to the airport to catch his flight home he had agreed a price of $7 million (to include resettlement and associated costs), with a down payment of $750,000 paid by the CIA, a schedule of meetings to be held within the month at which the final exchange would take place, and a five-page handwritten contract duly signed by Mike Sulick on behalf of his Director, George Tenet.

In the event Shcherbakov was too frightened of the Irkutsk gangsters to emerge from his Moscow apartment to attend the first rendezvous, but he did eventually turn up on 4 November and hand over a package, which was then placed in the Bureau's custody. FBI officers flew from Washington to open a 'green sheet' to certify the chain of custody, and it was delivered via the US embassy bag by the CIA on 11 November to the FBI laboratory for forensic examination. On 18 November 2000, after Shcherbakov had travelled to the United States, a sealed envelope within the parcel was opened unceremoniously in the MC-4 office at headquarters. It was found to contain some computer discs, various documents in Russian, and a tape cassette. When the audio tape was played it proved to be of immense significance because it was the only recording, made surreptitiously, of two telephone calls initiated by RAMON in July and August 1986 following a series of miscommunications during that summer.

The deliberate hiatus had been prompted by RAMON's concern about the defection in the middle of February of Viktor Gundarev, a Line KR officer from the KGB *rezidentura* in Athens, as he explained in a letter he mailed to the home address in Alexandria of Viktor Degtyar, a Line PR officer officially listed as the embassy's press attaché:

> I apologise for the delay since our break in communications. I wanted to determine if there was any cause for concern over security. I have only seen one item which has given me pause. When the FBI was first given access to Viktor Petrovich Gundarev, they asked ... if Gundarev knew Viktor Cherkashin. I thought this unusual. I had seen no report indicating that Cherkashin was handling an important agent and heretofore he was looked at with the usual lethargy awarded Little Chiefs. The question came to mind, are they somehow able to monitor funds ie to know that Viktor Cherkashin received a large sum of money for an agent? I am unaware of any such ability, but I might not know that type of source reporting.

Subsequent investigation showed that the FBI had received a report dated 4 March 1986 concerning Colonel Gundarev's debriefing that had included a reference to the defector confirming from Cherkashin's photo that he too was a Line KR counter-intelligence specialist. Although RAMON included a tempting morsel of intelligence relating to an NSA breakthrough involving the interception of Soviet satellite communications, doubtless included as an incentive for the KGB to resume the relationship, his main purpose, inspired by his instinct for self-preservation, had been to check if Gundarev, as a senior Line KR officer, posed any threat to him. RAMON's letter had concluded:

> If you wish to continue our discussions, please have someone run an advertisement in the *Washington Times* during the week of 1/12/87 or 1/19/87, for sale, 'Dodge Diplomat, 1971, needs engine work, $1,000'. Give a phone number and time-of-day in

the advertisement where I can call. I will call and leave a phone number where a recorded message can be left for me in one hour. I will say 'Hello, my name is Ramon, I am calling about the car you offered for sale in the Times.' You will respond 'I'm sorry but the man with the car is not here, but can I get your number.' The number will be in Area Code 212. I will not specify that Area Code on the line.[10]

Thus RAMON had signalled his intention to revive his espionage activities after deliberately missing a set of dead drop exchanges several months earlier. Having broken off contact, RAMON had acquired some important information for the KGB and he needed their assent to renew the relationship, so in a clever use of operational tradecraft, RAMON had written the letter, which the KGB received in July 1986, setting out the procedure for re-establishing a secure line of communications. Even this message contained an in-built security precaution, as it had been agreed years earlier that any times and dates referred to should be subtracted by six. Accordingly, RAMON was requesting a newspaper advertisement on 6 July or 13 July at 0700 and the KGB responded with:

DODGE '71 DIPLOMAT, NEEDS ENGINE WORK $1000
Phone (703) 451-9780 (CALL NEXT Mon. Wed. or Fri. 1pm)[11]

This number was a payphone at the Keene Shopping Centre in Fairfax, Virginia, and was answered by a member of the *rezidentura*, Aleksandr K. Fefelov, who was told by RAMON to call 628-8047, which he did, an hour later, adding the New York 212 prefix as instructed. RAMON answered, and was informed that a drop had been made at a prearranged site, designated PARK, which was actually under a wooden footbridge in Nottoway Park.

This ingenious procedure ensured that if the FBI or NSA monitored the conversation, it would not reveal the full contact telephone number to be dialed as only the recipient of the letter would know that the area code to be used was for New York, and not Washington D.C. Perhaps even more remarkably, the number in New York chosen by RAMON was actually registered to an operational cut-out for the FBI's New York Field Office, and had been used previously in an operation that the spy had known about.

He also knew that, although still active, this particular line was no longer used operationally. This extraordinary arrangement was intended to prevent detection, and the initial call was made in late July 1986 to arrange the drop, but RAMON could not find the package and two weeks later sent a second letter to Degtyar requesting another attempt. Thus, on Monday 18 August, RAMON held another conversation with Fefelov, which he recorded:

RAMON: Tomorrow morning?

FEFELOV: Yeah, and the car is still available for you and as we have agreed last time, I prepared all the papers and I left them on the same table. You didn't find them because I put them in another corner of the table.

RAMON: I see.

FEFELOV: You shouldn't worry, everything is okay. The papers are with me now.

RAMON: Good.

FEFELOV: I believe under these circumstances it's not necessary to make any changes concerning the place and the time. Our company is reliable, and we are ready to give you a substantial discount which will be enclosed in the papers. Now, about the date of our meeting. I suggest that our meeting will be, will take place without delay on February thirteenth. One three, one pm. Okay? February 13th.

RAMON: February second?

FEFELOV: Thirteenth, one three.

RAMON: One three.

FEFELOV: Yes. Thirteenth. One p.m.

RAMON: Let me see if I can do that. Hold on.

FEFELOV: Okay. Yeah.

RAMON: Six ... Six ... That should be fine.

FEFELOV: Okay. We will confirm you. The papers are waiting for you with the same horizontal tape in the same place as we did it at the first time.

RAMON: Very good.

FEFELOV: You see, after you receive the papers, you will send the letter confirming it and signing it as usual. Okay?

RAMON: Excellent.

FEFELOV: I hope you remember the address. Is … if everything is okay?

RAMON: I believe it should be fine and thank you very much.

FEFELOV: [Laughs] Not at all. Not at all. Nice job. For both of us. Have a nice evening Sir.

RAMON: Dozvidanye.

DEGYTAR: Bye-bye.[12]

The audio recording revealed the stilted language used by Fefelov and RAMON to discuss the mistake, and it sounded quite comical. The KGB officer told RAMON that the package had been left inadvertently on 'the wrong side of table' and that was why he had not found it. The spy then took several moments to figure out what the substitute words actually meant, and then he acknowledged that he had understood.

Those present listening to the tape, among them analysts Jim Milburn and Robert King, suddenly realised, despite the brevity of the conversation, that the voice was not Brian Kelley's, as they had expected, but someone else known to them all: Robert Hanssen, whose office was only a few yards away, on the same corridor. Once the voice had been recognized, the tape was taken the next morning to Rochford, then at his DD-1C office at the CIA, and then to Sheila Moran at FBI Headquarters. Finally, it was played to Tim Caruso at the WFO, who was so angry he had thrown his headphones across the room, and then to FBI Director, Louis Freeh, and his deputy, Tom Pickard. When all were satisfied that Hanssen had been unmasked, Rochford went over to the Department of Justice to brief the attorney-general John Ashcroft and, in his absence in Chicago, found himself addressing his acting deputy, Robert Mueller.

Hitherto considered above suspicion, Hanssen, now code-named GRAY DAY, became the subject of an intense surveillance operation, but the FBI was especially circumspect because they knew that their adversary was familiar with every technique likely to be deployed by the mole hunters. Indeed, on one occasion Hanssen's car radio experienced unusual interference, and he later claimed that he had suspected the noise as indicating the concealment of some device, perhaps a tracker, inside the vehicle.

A new GRAY DAY team of specially indoctrinated investigators was assembled at the WFO to watch Hanssen, who in January was transferred from his current assignment as liaison with the State Department to a cyber-crime research role, and three subordinates were briefed to monitor his daily activities. One was his personal assistant, Eric O'Neill, actually from the SSG; another was the analyst Bob King, who reassured his friend that the mole hunt was still focused on the CIA, and the third was Richard Garcia, his immediate Cyber Division supervisor. After two months of watching Hanssen, O'Neill's covert access to his private PalmPilot III enabled the FBI to anticipate and plan for an ambush at a dead drop scheduled for 18 February in Foxstone Park, Virginia.

Hanssen was arrested by the heads of the two squads involved, Special Agents Doug Gregory and Stephan Pluta, during the evening, their guns drawn, just as he had loaded the dead drop with three classified documents. His home was only a short distance away in Whitecedar Court, the same street in which Kelley had lived between 1981 and 1985. In his confession, Hanssen admitted having alerted the SVR that the FBI was closing in on Felix Bloch, thereby confirming the validity of Zaporozhsky's tip.

In preparation for Hanssen's arrest on capital charges the Bureau prepared an astonishing 103-page affidavit based on Shcherbakov's forensic evidence, the audio cassette and the content of several KGB computer discs that were read by NSA cryptographers at Fort Meade and found to contain a comprehensive account of Hanssen's espionage. The overall effect was intended to completely overwhelm any legal defence Hanssen might contemplate. The retrieved data showed that between 1985 and 1989 the spy had passed the KGB some 6,000 classified documents and, apart from prodigious quantities of cash, had been given three diamonds (two of which he had later returned for the money). The encrypted files also showed that the same Nottoway Park drop site had been used seventeen times in addition to Foxstone Park where he was detained. Perhaps most remarkable of all was Shcherbakov's declared willingness to appear as a prosecution witness if the trial judge agreed to protect his anonymity at a death sentence hearing after his conviction by a jury. Shcherbakov agreed to testify that Hanssen, and Hanssen alone, had been directly responsible for the death of the FBI's asset Valeri Martynov. This threat would prove a knock-out blow for the defence lawyers, who settled a plea bargain in July 2001.

The fact that Hanssen's name had never appeared on any shortlist of potential moles was profoundly troubling, for two reasons in particular. Firstly, his own brother-in-law, Special Agent Mark Wauck, had reported his suspicions in 1990 after two odd incidents. One was an offhand remark Hanssen had made to another family member about retiring to Poland. This was considered a strange thing to say, the more so considering that Wauck was then a counter-intelligence officer working Polish and eastern European cases at the Chicago Field Office. Secondly, Hanssen's wife Bonnie had confided in a family member, who then had told Wauck's wife, about her discovery of an envelope containing $5,000. How could a GS-14 with six children accumulate such cash? Although Wauck was adamant he had filed an official report about his concerns, FBI denied any record of it at headquarters.[13]

Secondly, there was the inference of a post-mortem damage assessment drawn up by Special Agents Tom Kimmel and Pete O'Donnell, who had researched the espionage of another FBI special agent, Earl Pitts, who had been imprisoned for twenty-seven years in June 1997, having been arrested the previous year on charges of spying for the KGB for a period of five years, from 1987 to 1992.

In December 1996 Pitts, a forty-three-year-old special agent with thirteen years of experience, was arrested in the Behavioural Sciences Unit at the Quantico training academy. He had served with Special Forces as an army officer during five years of military service,, but while assigned to the New York Field Office (NYFO) had approached a KGB officer attached to the Soviet mission to the United Nations in the New York Public Library with an offer to sell him information, including a document entitled *Counterintelligence: Identifying Foreign Agents*. The KGB accepted the offer and paid Pitts $129,000, with another $100,000 allegedly placed in a foreign bank account,

Pitts broke off contact with the KGB in 1992, but when he was compromised by Zaporozhsky in 1996, the FBI attempted to recruit one of Pitts' handlers, Aleksandr V. Karpov, whom Pitts had met at least nine times between 1987 and 1988. Simultaneously, a sting operation was mounted to entrap Pitts into further acts of espionage, a scheme that was complicated at the outset when Pitts' wife Mary, an ex-FBI support employee, reported her suspicions about her husband within two days of the operation being initiated.

The FBI ran the operation for fifteen months from August 1995, during which Pitts was watched making twenty-two drops of classified information in exchange for $65,000. He also held nine telephone conversations and attended two rendezvous with 'false-flag' FBI officers posing as his SVR contacts. In February 1997, after the FBI had seized his personal computer at Quantico, which contained a highly incriminating letter addressed to his supposed SVR case officer, Pitts pleaded guilty to two counts of espionage, thus obviating the need to adduce evidence that might have endangered Zaporozhsky.

In conversation with Kimmel, as part of his co-operation with the Bureau post-conviction, Pitts asserted that he had deduced from the attitude of his KGB handlers, and a particularly indiscreet question that Karpov had posed, that there must have been another, more senior penetration of the FBI, probably in the New York Field Office. When asked who he thought the other mole might have been, Pitts had replied, 'Robert Hanssen'.[14]

During thirty-three interrogation sessions conducted by the WFO, having reached a plea agreement in which his wife would receive his FBI pension, Hanssen admitted having engaged in three distinct periods of espionage, all apparently motivated by his need for money. The first was between 1978 and 1981, when he had been working GRU surveillance at the NYFO, and the second was in Washington for the KGB, commencing in October 1985 until 1991, when he learned of the Ames investigation, and a third, also for the SVR, from 1996, terminating with his arrest.

Hanssen acknowledged having warned the SVR that Bloch was under investigation, and knew that Brian Kelley was the subject of a mole hunt, news that might have prompted another phase of intense espionage. The FBI had been puzzled that Hanssen had risked renewed contact with the SVR just two years before his scheduled retirement in the autumn of 2001, but speculated that he had been encouraged by the knowledge that the FBI's mole hunt had focused on the wrong person, in the wrong agency.

It had taken the FBI ten years to track down the UNSUB described by Zaporozhsky, and when the investigators realised their mistake in having chased six innocent CIA officers, they were unable to tell Kelley for fear that the news might filter back to Hanssen and alert him to his imminent arrest. Understandably, Kelley had been infuriated by the extension of his torment of suspension from duty by an additional two and a half months. Professionally, Kelley was especially offended that the FBI's refusal to look at any suspects within the FBI had given Hanssen the freedom to inflict yet more damage. Indeed, one of the largest dumps made by Hanssen had taken place coincidentally on 11 November 2000, the very day Shcherbakov sold the RAMON file in Moscow. On that occasion Hanssen had handed over a bundle of papers two inches thick, and in that material were references that compromised dozens of CIA assets across the globe, among them Alexander Zaporozhsky and Gennadi Vasilenko.

* * *

After the arrest of Aldrich Ames in February 1994 he had pleaded guilty and submitted to lengthy interviews in a bargain for a reduced sentence for his wife Rosario, and the avoidance of the death penalty. In Hanssen's case, his deal with the prosecution included retention of his pension for his wife Bonnie, and co-operation with the authorities. Thus, in neither case was there any need to disclose the roles of Zaporozhsky or, more recently, Shcherbakov. In 1997, within a month of having retired from his post as deputy head of the FCD's 1st Department, Zaporozhsky moved with his wife Galina and sons Pavel and Maxim to the affluent suburb of Cockeysville, Maryland, where he had his own business, the Water Shipping Company. Fatally, ten months after the arrest of Bob Hanssen, Zaporozhsky accepted an invitation to bid for a lucrative contract in Moscow, which would require his presence, and he flew back, ignoring the pleas of Rochford, Steve Kappes and several senior CIA officers who begged him not to take the risk. Although it was strongly suspected that Zaporozhsky had been compromised by Hanssen's 'big-dump' the previous November, the CIA did not have absolute proof, so the arrogant Russian ignored the pleas, pointing out that he had previously returned for a reunion attended by many of his former colleagues, and the visit had gone uninterrupted. There was, he insisted, no danger and no leak. Before his departure, Zaporozhsky visited the Russian consulate to renew his passport, thus alerting Moscow to his imminent arrival. As soon as his plane landed at Sheremetyevo he was arrested, and in June 2003 was sentenced to eighteen years' imprisonment.

The Russian reaction to Hanssen's arrest was delayed until August 2005, when Vasilenko was detained on a charge of terrorism, based on the discovery by the FSB of an unregistered hunting rifle and a quantity of ammunition at his dacha outside Moscow. His trial followed in May 2006 and he was sentenced to three years' imprisonment, but as his release date approached he was rearrested and in December 2007 made to face new vague charges 'of resisting the authorities'. Mounting a defence, or even consulting with lawyers, was made almost impossible by the FSB's procedure of moving Vasilenko around Russia's extensive penal system, thereby requiring con- stant 'quarantine' treatment in isolation, which meant he was hard to trace for anyone interested in his welfare. At one stage in this undisguised campaign of harassment he was transferred to a prison at Smolenskaya, where he encountered his old friend Aleksandr Zaporozhsky in the exercise yard. Vasilenko concluded that the FSB intended to consign them both to oblivion. What he could not know was that the SVR's attitude to him had changed after Hanssen had compounded the suspicions originally raised by Ames.

When his son Ilya finally tracked his father down to IK-11, a penal colony near Bor in the Nizhny Novgorod region, 220 miles east of Moscow, he learned that he was suffering a daily beating at the hands of the FSB and, at the age of sixty-six, was unlikely to survive much longer. Jack Platt had already mobilised many of his Agency connections, including his former student Mike Sulick, the CIA's Deputy Director of Operations who had signed off on the Shcherbakov down payment, and the Counterintelligence Chief, Cindy Webb. Platt's self-appointed mission was to rescue Vasilenko, but what had the United States to offer in return for his freedom?

Chapter III

Konspiratsia: The Soviet Legacy

The history of Soviet illegals dates back to the Soviet Revolution and the tradition adopted by the Bolsheviks, including Lenin and Stalin, of avoiding the attention of the Czar's ubiquitous Okhrana. In the absence of recognition of the Communist regime, the Kremlin came to rely on unofficial representatives overseas, and on a network of committed adherents to the cause who travelled abroad, usually under alias, to develop illegal *rezidenturas* from which to manage mainly ideologically motivated volunteers who could not be contaminated by contact with the local Communist Party apparatus or a diplomatic mission. Although Arnold Deutsch worked in London under his own name, his colleagues Theodore Maly and Dmitri Bystrolyotov operated under alias. Almost nothing was known in the west about this bifurcated structure until Walter Krivitsky, the GRU illegal *rezident* in The Hague, who had operated under art dealer cover, defected and revealed the existence of a GRU and an NKVD illegal organization.

Born Samuel Ginsberg in Galicia, Krivitsky had operated as the Soviet military intelligence service's illegal *rezident* in Holland. When, in late 1937 he had learned that he was to be liquidated he had defected, staying in Paris under the ineffective protection of the French Sureté until he took his valuable knowledge to America and then to Canada. However, for two months after his arrival in New York the authorities were reluctant to take him seriously, and one of his most significant revelations, regarding the existence of a Soviet spy in London, did not reach the British government until early September 1939 when Isaac Don Levine, a Russian-born journalist collaborating on a series of articles with Krivitsky, sought an interview with Lord Lothian, the British ambassador in Washington, DC. Levine disclosed enough of Krivitsky's information for MI5 to identify Captain John King, an important Soviet source working in the Communications Department of the Foreign Office, and arrest him in September. King was convicted in October

1939, but no public announcement was made regarding his subsequent trial until after the war. Under interrogation he identified his recruiter as Ernest Oldham, a disaffected former Foreign Office colleague who had resigned his post in September 1932 and had been found dead, gassed in his London home, a year later.

Installed in London's Langham Hotel in January 1940 for an extensive debriefing conducted by MI5's Jane Sissmore, Krivitsky described an extensive network of illegals across Europe. His remarks about the dependency of the GRU (referred to as the Fourth Department of the Red Army's general staff) on illegals would form the basis of Sissmore's comprehensive, forty-five-page report in which she described the illegal *rezidenturas*:

Illegal *Rezidents*

The third section of the Fourth Department employ three types of regular illegal agents for work abroad. Head agents in control of organization are always staff officers of the same type as Krivitsky himself. Then there are *rezident* agents holding responsible permanent posts, or acting as principal assistants to the senior agent or *rezident*. These men have almost invariably been staff officers of the Fourth Department but, having failed to procure promotion, have worked abroad so long and out of personal contact with Moscow that they have lost standing there. Sometimes they have even lost their membership in the Russian Communist Party, for this to remain valid has to be periodically renewed from within the Soviet Union.

The third class of agent is called the 'speculant' class. These 'speculants' – mainly Austrian, Czechs, Hungarians or Roumanians – are usually people who have become outlaws from their own countries on account of their communist activities. They have nothing to lose by employment in the Fourth Department and hope to gain a good deal. Krivitsky while acknowledging the necessity of employing this type both as regular and casual agents, regards them as a danger in that if bribed by a promise of permanent domicile in a foreign country and the means to live they might in many cases be prepared to betray their service. Krivitsky emphasised the horror which this class of agent and sometimes also the second class view the possibility of a recall to Moscow and the necessity of living in the Soviet Union.

The question of agents for the United Kingdom was always a difficult one. In the early years after the Bolshevik revolution there were a number of *rezident* Russians here, refugees from the Tsarist regime. These men made excellent agents, a number of them had a sound political background and a special knowledge of the United Kingdom. Theodore Rothstein, father of Andrew Rothstein of the TASS Agency, belonged to this class and was a successful agent of the Fourth Department for many years.

Later it became very difficult for the Fourth Department to place head agents here. The *rezident* head agent had to be a staff officer of the Fourth Department and there were few who knew the language sufficiently well and enough about this country to make it possible for them to work.

One man who was earmarked to act as head agent here was Krivitsky's assistant Max Unschlicht. The proposal to use him in this capacity was cancelled in November 1927 after the arrest and imprisonment in the United Kingdom of the young German Communist Georg Hansen. Hansen was employed by the Fourth Department. His association with Macartney, with whom he was arrested, was only incidental to his visit. His main purpose was to ascertain the best means of establishing Unschlicht in the United Kingdom, and if possible, to prepare the ground for his residence here. Krivitsky stated as a definite fact that from 1935 until 1937 the Fourth Department had no *rezident* senior staff officer of the first grade in the United Kingdom, but as long visits as possible were paid by Fourth Department agents from the Continent, with instructions to 'stay as long as you can and photograph all you can'. This was partly due to the difficulty of getting Army staff men with a knowledge of English who could get permission for permanent residence, and partly to the fact that after 1935 the OGPU, on Stalin's orders, began to work on military information and build up a military espionage organization in this country. The chief objective of Stalin's espionage during these years was details regarding the mechanisation of the Army.

Passports for illegal *rezident* or visiting agents

Although the Fourth Department in Moscow were able to produce perfectly forged passports of any country it was much preferred that espionage agents should travel on genuine passports procured, if necessary, by means of forged documents of identity.

Up to 1928 or 1929 Soviet agents usually travelled on Austrian, German or Danish passports. At one time genuine Austrian passports were easily obtainable in Austria. To obtain the issue of a legal Austrian passport a certificate of domicile was more important than a birth certificate. At one time the Fourth Department had as their agent the head of the local council of a small town in Austria. This man issued false certificates of domicile whenever required. A confederate in a nearby town issued false birth certificates if these were necessary. Sometime before 1934 both these men were arrested and the Department was obliged to use Moscow-made Austrian passports for the time being.

A foreign passport obtained by a Soviet agent never bears any indication that he has been in Russia. If for instance the agent is to come to the United Kingdom posing as an Austrian with an Austrian passport he will travel from Russia to Vienna on his Soviet passport and pick up his new passport in Vienna. He will then leave his Soviet passport at the Soviet embassy or legation for use on a return journey to Russia at a future date, or else give instructions that it shall be returned to Moscow until he indicates where he wishes it to be sent for his return journey.

About 1928–1929 it was discovered how easily American and Canadian passports could be obtained, and they came into very frequent use both for Foreign Department and OGPU agents. Krivitsky explained that anyone could pass as a citizen of the USA who could speak little English, and the same applied to French Canadian passports so long as the agent in question could speak French.

Krivitsky states most emphatically that he had never known a Soviet agent to travel on a passport of the United Kingdom, nor did the Fourth Department ever ask for a United Kingdom passport to be forged in Moscow. None of the officers of the Fourth

Department knew English sufficiently, or enough about this
country to use an English passport without incurring enquiries or
suspicion.

Cover for Illegal Resident Agents

It sometimes happened that a senior staff officer or an officer of the
second class of agent might be an expert in some matters outside
his military capacity, or have, such as Krivitsky at The Hague, an
opportunity to pose as such. In these cases permission for residence in the United Kingdom could be obtained on these grounds.

Most frequently some form of business cover would have to be
arranged. Sometimes a firm was actually created for a particular
purpose and sometimes it was possible to arrange through an intermediary that the intended agent should come to this country as the
representative of some genuine and important Continental firm. In
these latter cases the firm would probably be quite unaware of the
true character of their representative.

A highly important firm called Wostwag or the Eastern Trading
Co. was created by the Fourth Department in Berlin in 1922. It
provided a genuine business cover for a large number of Fourth
Department agents. The principal business of the firm was the
sale of Russian produce in Germany. The business was passed to
them through the Soviet Trade Delegation in Berlin. In one year
the firm made over a million roubles profit. As Krivitsky points out
this profit was merely the putting of money from one Soviet pocket
into another. Nevertheless the proceeds of Wostwag trading were
retained by the Fourth Department to augment their espionage
and internal disruption grants.

Two junior staff officers of the Fourth Department, the brothers Abraham and Aaron Ehrenlieb, were put in charge of the
organization and espionage side of the firm. They were of Polish
origin naturalised Austrians. The business side of Wostwag, and
later its various branches, was in the hands of an old Bolshevik – a
Latvian – a personal friend of General Berzin. He travelled a good
deal with a speculant agent – Leo Katz – a Romanian. Leo Katz
visited this country at some time in connection with the affairs of

the firm. (He must not be confused with a Hungarian, an OGPU agent, of the same name.)

About 1925 or 1926 the Fourth Department suspected that the activities of the firm had become known to the German police. They decided to withdraw the Ehrenlieb brothers and other members of the Russian General Staff and let the firm continue purely commercial activities under a speculant agent called Zloczower. A man called Stuchka also worked in connection with Wostwag and its affiliated companies.

After their recall from Berlin the brothers Ehrenlieb worked for a time in the Fourth Department. Both men were first class accountants and managed the accounts of the Fourth Department in the second section. After a time Abraham Ehrenlieb was sent to Tientsin where he founded and built up a very important firm – the Far Eastern Trading Co. The profits were retained for their work in China by the Fourth Department, and were a useful source of foreign currency. Incidentally Abraham managed to inspire sufficient confidence in Tietsin to be appointed president of the Austrian Chamber of Commerce there. Later Adam Purpis, a Lett, who travelled on a Honduras passport became head of the Tientsin firm. He passed through London in 1937 or 1938, but probably only in transit to Russia from some other Western European country. Soviet ships sailed regularly to Leningrad from Hay Wharf, London, and the Fourth Department frequently used this means of returning agents to Moscow.

The other brother Aaron was sent to Urga, the Soviet colony in Outer Mongolia. In 1935 he was recalled to Moscow with the idea that he should go to the American branch of Wostwag. The firm in the USA became very active and a lot of material can be obtained from the American authorities. This plan fell through owing to the difficulty of obtaining an American visa. It was decided, in 1936, to send him to London where an affiliated company of Wostwag, known as the Far Eastern Fur Trading Co. was formed in February 1936.

The Far Eastern Fur Trading Co. is properly registered in the United Kingdom and is staffed by commercial men carrying on legitimate business. Certain members of the staff however devote a proportion of their time to Fourth Department work. Zloczower was in London working for a time with Ehrenlieb and during the Spanish war Krivitsky sent a man called Samuel Hockstedt or Hochstedt to meet Ehrenlieb in London and the two worked together in the export of arms from Sweden to Spain. Stutchka, at that time in Paris, was also involved in these deals. Samuel Hochstedt is now in the USA.

Incidentally Krivitsky is of the opinion that both Zloczower and Katz could be bullied or cajoled into acting as double-cross agents for the British. He always considered Katz more trustworthy than Zloczower but neither of these men have any strong political beliefs and money counts for a great deal with them. A threat to make it impossible for them to live in any Western European country and thus force them to return to the Soviet Union would, he thinks, make either of them disclose all he knew.

Krivitsky does not know Rubin Clucksmann, the present chief of the Far Eastern Fur Trading Co. in London, but is certain he is a Fourth Department man. He believes that he is not an Austrian and that his passport is Moscow made. Krivitsky regards it as highly important that a thorough investigation should be made into the whole personnel of the Far Eastern Fur Trading Co., although it is possible that Clucksmann himself is actually still under training and held in reserve for more active work at a later stage. This is the usual procedure for newly appointed heads of companies established by the Fourth Department.

In regard to the creation of the firm, Krivitsky feels sure that the solicitor – Herbert Oppenheimer – would not have been used accidentally for the legal formalities. Something must already have been known about him in the Fourth Department. Krivitsky believes that he actually met him in Paris in connection with arms deals for Spain.

A firm established by the Fourth Department in Paris was a firm for the Importation of 'Legumes Secs' in the rue de Neuilly. The firm was founded by a Fourth Department man called Eisenberg who in 1928 was working in a private firm in Danzig. A most important senior staff officer of the Fourth Department who had a false American passport in the name of Kleges or Klages subsequently became head of the firm. His real name can probably be ascertained as he was acting as Second Consul in the Soviet Legation in Prague in 1927/28. The firm is still operating although the entire staff was changed in 1938.

Methods of Work

When a legal or illegal *rezident* agent merely goes to a country to take over from a predecessor his task is comparatively easy, but when he has to create an organization, the position becomes much more complicated. In such cases when the agent has been chosen and a suitable cover or place at the embassy arranged, it is still necessary that he should become personally known or receive a special introduction to a senior official of the Communist Party of the country in which he is to work.

During Krivitsky's service this was usually arranged personally between General Berzin, head of the Fourth Department, and Piatnitsky, head of the OMS (*Otdyel Mezhdunarodnoi Svyazi*), the Foreign Liaison Department of the Comintern. As regards the United Kingdom an opportunity was usually taken to introduce prospective agents to senior members of the Executive Committee of the Communist Party of Great Britain who might be visiting the Soviet Union. Pollitt and Gallacher were frequently used in this way. It would always be arranged that each chief Fourth Department agent should have a specially tried and trusted member of the Communist Party put at his disposal. The *rezident* Embassy agent has probably only a man earmarked whom he can use when necessary, but he has his own special man, and not a Party member already working for the OGPU legal *rezident*. The OGPU embassy agent is always a thorn in the side of the Fourth Department legal *rezident*. There is sharp friction between the two. Material and visitors to the Embassy are frequently withheld from the Fourth Department agent in favour of the OGPU *rezident*. The position has become still more difficult since the GUGB began to control the Razvedupr in 1935.

When a chief illegal agent of the third section of the Fourth Department starts work in the United Kingdom, a picked member of the Communist Party is put entirely at his disposal. He is usually not a manual labourer, but a man of the clerical type. It sometimes happens that the best man that can be obtained is already an important Communist Party organiser, but any objections to his release are always overruled on the grounds that intelligence work takes precedence over purely Party matters. The selected Communist Party member drops all his political work and is gradually trained by the Fourth Department agent. The period of training lasts six months or more, during which time the man is instructed to make contacts wherever possible but on no account to attempt to obtain any secret information. In order to keep him fully occupied during his period of training he is sent to public libraries to obtain information on industrial and economic questions. He looks up trade directories and visits industrial districts to gain information as to the numbers of factories turning out military material and if possible full details about them.

The Fourth Department illegal *rezident* invariably employs a woman through whom he maintains contact with his colleague in the Embassy. This woman is often a German or Austrian here in the guise of a student and it is her sole work to act as intermediary between him and the woman 'runner' for the Fourth Department agent in the embassy.

After about six months when the illegal *rezident* has thoroughly established himself in this country and trained his assistants, he begins to work. He meets people useful for his purpose in different walks of life and gains their confidence. For instance, as the Soviet Government are always particularly interested to receive confidential maps, the illegal *rezident* tries to cultivate a man in a map making establishment. He finds out his private circumstances, gives him presents and subsequently money, and eventually recruits him as a sub-agent. Russian-made maps are very bad and always have been. The best maps in the possession of the Mobilisation Department of the Soviet Army are British. Krivitsky could not remember the name of the department, but he said that about 1930 the Fourth Department had an agent in a department or institute which made military maps, and from this source the Soviet obtained a large number of maps made from aerial photographs.

Through his Communist Party assistant the Fourth Department agent gradually recruits as agents, workmen and technicians in important factories. Details regarding these workmen and technicians are checked up by the Communist Party. Later plans are brought out of the works and photographed. Plans are never stolen; the originals are always replaced. The Fourth Department would have a photographic studio installed either at the back of a small shop or in a house. Material from a distance is brought up over a weekend, or if this is not possible, a Leica camera is used on the spot.

The Fourth Department agent is himself always an expert photographer. Someone carefully trained by him would be sent to a distant town with a small suitcase containing everything he could want for photographing documents. This portable suitcase was frequently used and after several failures had been experienced with small makes, always a Leica camera.

Although as a general rule the Fourth Department agent arranged for his own photography, there were occasions when the plan or document was taken to the Soviet embassy to be photographed. Krivitsky recalls an instance when he was at The Hague and managed to obtain for a very short time a large and highly important plan of a French submarine. He could only retain the plan for a short time, not long enough to make trial photographs on his own apparatus. He therefore took it to the Soviet Legation who had a much larger and permanently erected apparatus and where moreover there could be no risk of molestation.[1]

Krivitsky was silenced by a mysterious shooting in a Washington hotel in February 1941, and nothing more became known of illegals in the west until some two years after the German surrender when MI5 gained an unexpected opportunity to study Soviet illegal methodology in July 1947 with the defection of Allan Foote in Germany. Upon identifying himself to the Control Commission's Intelligence Division in Berlin as a Soviet spy on a mission to the United States, Foote was flown from Hanover to RAF Northolt and installed at an MI5 safe house at 19 Rugby Mansions in West Kensington, where he was code-named SNEAK and interviewed by two MI5 officers, Michael Serpell and Bob Hemblys-Scales. The self-confessed spy was a former RAF fitter who had deserted from his unit in Gosport in December 1936 after just fifteen months' service to join a Communist Party of Great Britain (CPGB) group of volunteers intending to join the 15th International Brigade and fight in the Spanish Civil War.

Under interrogation, Foote gave a lengthy account of his soldiering in Spain, his recruitment as a Soviet agent and his espionage for the GRU in Switzerland until his arrest by the Bundespolizei's Inspector Paasche at his flat in Lausanne in November 1943 following pressure from the Germans. He identified the other members of the spy ring, known as ROTE DREI (or EDELSWEISS by the Sicherheitsdienst) which had been led by a Hungarian cartographer, Sandor Rado, code-named DORA, and had consisted of three wireless links to Moscow. Both well-known Communists, Rado and his wife Lena had lived in Berlin and Paris, and she had worked for the Soviet embassy in Berlin.

Foote, code-named JIM by the GRU, had been trained by Ursula Kuczynsky, code-named SONIA, who had moved to England in December 1940, and he handled Rado's wireless traffic from March 1941. Another transmitter was operated by Edmund and Olga Hamel, who owned a shop selling radios in Geneva, and Rado's principal source was Rudolf Rössler, code-named LUCY, who was run through a cut-out, Rachel Dúbendorfer. The information they transmitted appeared to consist of high-grade OKW and Luftwaffe messages, designated WERTHER and OLGA. A third radio was operated by Rado's mistress Marguerite Bolli, but she too would be arrested in October 1943, at the same time as the Hamels.

A contemporary German assessment of the ROTE DREI wireless traffic made by Wilhelm Flicke described it as 'enough to take many a person's breath away'.

> During the entire eastern campaign, during the first German offensive in 1941, during the preliminary stages of the campaign of 1942, during the critical period of the battles around Stalingrad and the Caucasus, and later in 1942 when the eastern front was being pushed back and one hoped to make a stand, possibly on the Dnieper, and check the on-rushing tide of the Russian armies, precisely during those days, weeks and months, the most secret information regarding the German military situation in the east – troop units, tanks, assembly areas, intentions – was being passed

currently through Switzerland to Moscow. This was information which must have come from the highest level of the German military command. The sender always signed DORA; the sources were designated as WERTHER, SISSY, TEDDY, FERNAND, TAYLOR, LUCIE, PAKBO, MAUD, EDUARD, ALFRED, JIM, WALTER, etc. The man who directed the work from Moscow signed DIREKTOR.[2]

The chief German cryptographer monitoring the traffic, Flicke, never discovered the true identity of Rado's well-informed sources, and concluded 'it was and remains the most fateful secret of World War II'. Another senior SD officer, Horst Kopkow, then a prisoner of the British in occupied Germany, had been questioned about the ROTE DREI in March 1946, when he had recalled how a Swiss Bundespolizei officer named Maurer had visited Berlin in 1944 to update his counterparts, and had reported the 'suppression' of the transmitters in Lausanne and Verrieres, mentioning the suspected existence of an emergency wireless in Lugano, and naming the network's six leading participants as 'Punter, Nikole, Sissy Dubbendorfer, Foote (tech expert for the group), Agnes Zimmermann, Robinson'.[3]

These six were probably Otto Púnter, a Swiss Communist and source of long standing; Leon (or his son Pierre) Nicole, who acted as cut-outs with the Swiss Labour (Communist) Party; Rachel Dúbendorfer, code-named SISSY, who would turn up in the GRU's Canadian spy ring exposed in September 1945 by the defector Igor Gouzenko; Allan Foote, himself; his German girlfriend from Munich, Agnes Zimmermann; and the elusive spymaster Henri Robinson, who perished in prison after his arrest in Paris in December 1942.

Described by his interrogator as a 'cold-blooded, ruthless, convinced' Nazi, Kopkow was also a 'strong opponent of Bolshevism and a strong Anglophile'. He had been arrested in Lubeck in May 1945 and revealed himself to have been the SD's principal expert on Soviet espionage. He had joined the state police in 1934 in East Prussia and in August 1938 had transferred to the Gestapo's *Referat* IIA3, where he was responsible for interviewing German technicians returning from employment in the Soviet Union. This experience had given him a detailed knowledge of the Soviet security apparatus, and in the autumn of 1939 he had been moved to IIA2, where he supervised penetration operations intended to counter sabotage by Russian-trained

Polish groups in Danzig. By 1942 he had been promoted head of the *Referat* and acquired an unrivalled knowledge of Soviet espionage across Europe.

MI5's close post-war liaison between the Bundespolizei, specifically Inspector Charles Knecht, revealed that the Abwehr had taken a close interest in the ROTE DREI, and that Hermann Haenseler had supervised the Swiss intervention.

While Foote was detained, and with no method of transmitting his information to, or even seeking advice from, Moscow, Rado had decided unilaterally to pass the material to the British through an MI6 officer at the Geneva consulate, Victor Farrell, who was in touch with one of his own organization, Alexander Abramson. Code-named ISAAK, Abramson was a Lithuanian employed by the International Labour Office (ILO), was head of the Russian information section, and Dübendorfer's cousin. Captain Farrell was an experienced MI6 officer, designated 42222, having served pre-war in Budapest, Prague and Vienna. This link between MI6 and the ROTE DREI would be misinterpreted after the war with the suggestion that the flow of information was in the opposite direction, and MI6 was manipulating the Soviet spy ring. In reality, Rado knew the value of Rössler's material and did not want it to be wasted.

In September 1944, after ten months in Swiss custody, Foote had been released on bail and in November he crossed the frontier covertly near Annemasse and travelled to Paris to make contact with Colonel Novikov, head of the Soviet military mission. During his fortnight in Paris he was reunited with Rado and accompanied him and another veteran Soviet agent, Leopold Trepper, on a flight to Cairo, en route to Moscow. However, Rado confided to Foote that he was nervous about his likely reception in Moscow, having admitted he had been in contact with MI6, so he went missing, leaving Foote to complete his journey with Trepper. Rado later changed his mind, having had his application for political asylum refused, and reached Moscow, where he was sentenced in December 1946 to ten years' imprisonment. He would be released in November 1954, to return to Budapest the following year.

Early in March 1947, after lengthy interviews with a counter-intelligence officer, Vera Poliakova, Foote had been given a new assignment, as an illegal in Argentina, and he was escorted to Berlin on the first leg of his journey, where he was issued with alias documentation in the name of a German, Albert Muller, born in Riga but living at Grellenstrasse 12 in the Soviet zone. Once he had established his 'legend', Foote was to continue to South

America on an assignment to supervise Soviet operations in the United States.

Regarding the eighteen months he spent in Moscow, Foote explained that he had been trained for various missions, first to Mexico, then China as a Canadian, but both plans had been dropped. He considered his training in micro-photography and radio techniques, undertaken at No. 40 School at Skhodnya, and at 36 Leninskaya, as redundant since he felt he knew rather more about the subjects than his instructors. Finally worn out, Foote had hatched a plan to contact the British and seek repatriation to be reunited with his brother, sister and brother-in-law, who all lived in East Grinstead.

Much of Foote's version of events, relating to his activities in Lausanne, were verified from other sources, such as Flicke, the German cryptographer who had worked on the intercepted messages and read much of the Swiss radio traffic, including some transmitted by Foote. At the end of the war Flicke had retained copies of the traffic and shared it with the Americans, apparently in the hope of finding a publisher for his memoirs, *War Secrets in the Ether*.[4]

Foote's story, as related to MI5 between 1947 and 1949, when a sanitised version was published as *Handbook for Spies*, attracted the interest of the FBI, CIA and Canadians because of the number of Soviet spies who had resurfaced in North America.[5] In particular, Dübendorfer's name had turned up in Montreal, in contact with her ILO colleague Hermina Rabinowicz, and a Soviet diplomat, Sergei Kudriavtsev (formerly Alexander Erdberg of the pre-war trade delegation in Berlin); Annie Becker in Beverly Hills; LOUIS in San Francisco; and William Helbein and Tibor Gergely in New York. All had links to the ROTE DREI and the suspicion was that the GRU intended Foote to transit through Argentina to develop the reconstituted network in which he had played a key role during the war.

Although Foote wanted to work for a British intelligence service, he was considered an unreliable adventurer by his case officers, and eventually he found a job in the Ministry of Agriculture's fisheries department as a regular civil servant, his usefulness as a walking encyclopedia of Soviet espionage exhausted.

* * *

The second great intelligence windfall of the immediate post-war era was the British recovery of details of a Gestapo investigation conducted during the Second World War. The treasure trove of documents recovered from the organization's headquarters in the Avenue Louise in Brussels were captured by British troops. Although most of the building's archive was seized intact, the sheer volume of files was so great that it would take almost two years for Allied intelligence personnel to sift through the material and find a large quantity of papers relating to the Sonderkommano ROTE KAPELLE that, under the leadership of Karl Giering, had conducted a lengthy investigation into a Soviet espionage network operating across Europe. According to the German analysis, when eventually Soviet diplomatic missions had been established in Europe, the OGPU had found it convenient to run deniable clandestine operations independently of the 'legal' *rezidenturas*. This expedient enabled networks to be managed during the war in Nazi-occupied Europe after the Soviet diplomatic and trade missions had been withdrawn. The result was the establishment, under a flimsy commercial cover, of a network in direct radio contact with Moscow. A joint Abwehr–Sicherheitsdienst investigation based in Brussels uncovered a network that stretched from Geneva to Berlin and those files became the foundation of lengthy post-war studies conducted by MI5 and then the CIA.[6]

The Gestapo's counter-espionage enquiries, which would have a domino effect, leading detectives from one conspirator to another, had begun with the detection of clandestine radio traffic in June 1941, which was monitored, traced to Brussels, but not read. During the night of 12/13 December 1941 Abwehr IIIF counter-intelligence investigators, guided by radio direction-finders, raided 101 rue des Attrebates in the Etterbeck district of Brussels and arrested an illicit wireless operator who gave his name as de Smets. In fact, de Smets was Lieutenant Anton Danilov of the GRU, who had been posted to Paris as an assistant military attaché in 1938, and had subsequently worked in that capacity in Vichy. In mid-1941 he had moved to Brussels to work for a more senior GRU agent, Viktor Guryevitch, as a communications expert. Danilov had been transmitting late at night as the Germans burst into the house and, in a fierce struggle, he was injured and overcome. Also recovered was a collection of 500 past messages to and from a figure code-named KENT that should have been destroyed, and served to assist a Funkabwehr cryptanalyst in breaking the Russian CAESAR cipher system.

Unaware of Danilov's arrest, several of his accomplices called at the house during the following day and one, Mikhail Makarov, was detained. Another visitor, Leopold Trepper, who was well-equipped with authentic German permits, managed to talk his way out of trouble and alert the rest of the network.

Although Danilov himself gave minimal co-operation, and would be executed two years later, the widow who was the principal tenant in the building, Rita Arnould, immediately turned informer and revealed her role as a courier and wireless operator in a ring headed by Viktor Guryevitch. The other occupant in the house, also a member of Guryevitch's cell, was Sofia Posnanska, a Polish Jewess who had been one of Trepper's subordinates in Paris in 1940 and had received cipher training in Moscow before the war. Rather than collaborate with her captors, she committed suicide in St Gilles Prison in Brussels. Meanwhile, Arnould betrayed a forger's workshop concealed in her house and, from passport photographs recovered in this Aladdin's cave of espionage paraphernalia, identified Trepper and Guryevitch as the key figures at the heart of the Soviet organization.

Eight months later, on 30 July 1942, the Abwehr radio direction-finders closed in on the attic of a house in Laeken, where they found Johann Wenzel, a German Communist from Danzig who had been trained as a wireless operator in Moscow and was in Belgium illegally, having been expelled as an undesirable in October 1937. At that time Wenzel had been studying engineering but early the following year he had slipped back into Brussels. After his arrest Wenzel refused to help his German interrogators in any way, but their study of the messages found beside his transmitter, which had been warm when the German investigators had burst into the house, led them to a hitherto undiscovered spy ring at the very heart of the Reich. After eight weeks of torture in Berlin, Wenzel was returned to Brussels and installed with a guard and his radio equipment in an apartment in the rue Aurore, where he co-operated fully.

Once the Sonderkommando had mastered Wenzel's ciphers, the Abwehr's principal cryptographer, Dr Wilhelm Vauck, succeeded in decrypting around two hundred of the ROTE KAPELLE signals that had been intercepted and recorded. On 15 July 1942 Vauck tackled a message from the 'Direktor', Moscow, dated 10 October 1941 and addressed to a certain KENT, one of several texts that disclosed data of the highest significance to the counter-espionage investigators:

KL 3 DE RTX 1010-1725 WDS GBT FROM DIREKTOR
TO KENT PERSONAL: Proceed immediately Berlin three

addresses indicated and determine causes failure radio con-
nections. If interruptions recur take over broadcasts. Work
three Berlin groups and transmission information top priority.
Addresses: Neuwestend, Altenburger allee 19, third right; Coro
Charlottenburg, Frederiastrasse 26a second left, Volf-Friedenau,
Kaiserstrasse 18 fourth left. Bauer. Call name here 'Eulenspiegel'
Password: 'Direktor'. Report before 20 October. New plan repeat
new in force for three stations GBT AR KLS RTX

The Gestapo promptly established the identities of the occupants of the
three suspect addresses, who were placed under surveillance. They were
Harro Schulze-Boysen of the Air Ministry; Arvid von Harnack, a respected
academic; and Adam Kuckhoff, a film producer. Another of these compromising messages, decoded by Vauck, referred to Saalestrasse 36, the Berlin
address of a young woman named Ilse who was also of some importance. A
signal dated 28 August 1941, decrypted retrospectively, made it clear that Ilse
was her true name:

An important agent known as ILSE will in the future be designated under the cover name ALTE ...

Gestapo enquiries showed Ilse Stoebe to be working for Theodor Wolff
at the Reich Foreign Ministry, and before the war she had been a correspondent for various Swiss newspapers. Accordingly, she was arrested in
Hamburg and under interrogation she revealed that she had been the
mistress of Rudolf Herrnstadt, the notorious *Berliner Tageblatt* journalist
who had defected to Moscow in 1933. Despite the seniority and sensitivity
of her post, Ilse had kept in touch with Herrnstadt, who became a senior
GRU officer supervising clandestine air drops into Germany, and had even
allowed her address to be given to GRU parachutists as a safe-house. Before
her execution on 22 December 1942 Ilse had implicated the network's three
most important members: Harro Schulze-Boysen; Arvid von Harnack,
the university lecturer who ran a widespread organization with sources in
both the Abwehr and Kriegsmarine; and Rudolf von Scheliha, a diplomat
in the Foreign Ministry's information section. Once Ilse Stoebe had named
Schulze-Boysen and von Harnack, their entire network amounting to eighty
sub-agents was rounded up and either hanged or beheaded without delay.

The subsequent Gestapo investigation concluded that von Harnack and Schulze-Boysen, both Communist activists for many years, had only been recruited by the GRU quite recently, in 1941. They had been given a wireless transmitter by Alexander Erdberg, of the Soviet Trade Delegation in Berlin before its withdrawal in June 1941, but they never achieved direct contact with Moscow, as intended. In August 1941 Viktor Guryevitch had given them another set, but again they failed and instead had relied upon couriers to pass messages to the Soviet embassy in Stockholm and to Wenzel in Brussels.

Among those exposed as members of the ring were Herbert Gollnow, an Abwehr liaison officer at OKW headquarters responsible for supervising clandestine air operations on the Eastern Front; Leutnant Wolfgang Havemann of naval intelligence; and Horst Heilmann, an Abwehr cryptographer who was having an affair with Schulze-Boysen's wife, Libertas. All were interrogated and then hanged at Ploetzensee prison. Von Scheliha, a more experienced Soviet agent, suffered the same fate. He had been recruited while serving at the German embassy in Warsaw in 1934 and had been paid for his information through a Swiss bank.

The next step in the Sonderkommando's investigation took place in November 1942 with the arrest of Konstantin Effremov, an experienced, thirty-two-year-old GRU officer and chemical warfare expert who had been operating in Western Europe under student cover since about 1936. Trained as an engineer, Effremov travelled on a genuine Finnish passport issued in the United States in the name of Jernstroem but, shortly before Wenzel's arrest, had prudently decided to switch to a new identity. Effremov had run a sizeable network of Soviet sources in Holland and had lived for a period before the war in Zurich. He had arrived in Brussels in September 1939, ostensibly as a student enrolled at the Ecole Polytechnique, to run an independent network but he used Wenzel as his radio link and in March 1942 he had been instructed to meet Trepper. Thus he acquired a considerable knowledge of the rings operating in Belgium and Guryevitch's contacts in Holland. Through one of his many contacts he had been put in touch with a corrupt Belgian police officer, Chief Inspector Charles Mathieu, who had access to Belgian travel documents and had proved useful in the past. However, Mathieu was a German informant, and he arranged for Effremov to be arrested when they met in on 22 July 1942. Under pressure, and anxious about the fate of his young wife in Russia, the Ukrainian had agreed to co-operate with the Abwehr and divulged enough information to compromise Trepper, alias Jean Gilbert, in Paris, headquarters of his commercial cover, Simexco.

A German raid on Simexcco's office caught one of the company directors, Alfred Corbin, who revealed that he had recently recommended a dentist to 'Gilbert'. Surveillance on the surgery eventually led the Abwehr to arrest Trepper on 5 December 1942 as he prepared to have his teeth treated. Once in German custody, Trepper agreed to collaborate, apparently motivated by the very justifiable fear that the Soviets would execute his entire family if they learned of his arrest. Indeed, Trepper not only betrayed his controller, Henri Robinson, but also agreed to transmit to Moscow as a double agent.

Trepper's capture came only a fortnight after the arrest in Marseilles of Viktor Guryevitch and his mistress, Margarete Barcza. Unwisely, Guryevitch had opened a branch of Simexco in Marseilles after he had fled from Belgium following the arrests there, and once Effremov had started to help the enemy the Simexco cover was compromised. Guryevitch was escorted to Berlin for interrogation, where he admitted his GRU code name KENT, and in March 1943 agreed to transmit to Moscow from Paris as MARS, under the Sonderkommando's control.

On 21 December 1942, acting on a tip from Trepper, the Germans trapped Robinson at his apartment in Paris, where they recovered a huge cache of documents hidden under the floorboards, including copies of the network's past radio traffic, a virtual archive of Soviet illegal activity in Europe dating back to the 1920s.

Born in 1897 in Germany, his father a Russian Jew, Robinson had studied in Geneva during the First World War and became closely associated with the Communist Youth International. In 1936 he was working alongside the Soviet military attaché in Paris before being placed in charge of all the French and English networks the following year, but he lost Moscow's confidence during the purges. Upon the outbreak of war he was ordered to subordinate his activities to Trepper, and reluctantly obeyed. There was no love lost between the two men, and their mutual hostility was later to be exploited by the Germans. According to Horst Kopkow of the SD's Amt IV,

> Robinson had been very stubborn under interrogation and they had never learned very much about his early career from him. At the end, however, he did admit that before the war he had acted as

courier and liaison officer between various Russian organizations in Switzerland, France and England. He had provided the Germans with his contact address in London, but this Kopkow was unable to remember ...[7]

After six months' of interrogation in France, Robinson was moved to Germany where he appeared before the same Luftwaffe court-martial as Harro Schulze-Boysen, convicted of treason and hanged at Plötzensee prison. Kopkow recalled that Robinson had only started to talk after his mistress and their illegitimate son had been implicated by Schulze-Boysen and arrested. Allegedly, his wife was executed and his eighteen-year-old son, who had lived with him in Paris, was sentenced to two years' imprisonment,

Kopkow's post-war interrogation was supervised by MI5's John Gwyer, who drafted a lengthy report into Robinson, anxious to trace any links between the ROTE DREI in Switzerland and England. When the Robinson papers were examined in London in March 1947 an MI5 officer, Michael Serpell, spotted a draft message addressed to Moscow dated 20 February 1941:

> Lange, Glou [corrupt text] 2 ecrire et signer Albert. Lieu Albert Hall, heure 11 et 17 signes Esquire et ticket metro Paris 07742, lui Esquire et metro Paris 07743. How do you do, Albert? Bob rendez-vous via Ellen.[8]

This signal caught Serpell's eye because of the reference to the Royal Albert Hall, and he found that it had been followed by another dated 18 March 1941:

> <u>Lange</u>: Ernest WEISS. Pad. 7501. Sheilla, femme du Prof. Vous avez raison, c'est bien difficile de se rapeller de tout, mais je pense que les renseignements envoyes vous souffiront pour reprendre la liaison. Vous pouvez toujours me pouvez des questions si quelque chose ne va pas.[9]

A check on the London telephone number Paddington 7501 showed it to have been registered to a German music hall pianist, Ernest Weiss, who had lodgings at 88 Kensington Church Street. According to his MI5 file, Weiss had been born in Breslau in December 1902 but had come to England in May 1932 as an exchange student from Breslau University to study at the London School of Economics. In 1940 he had been interned briefly in Huyton as an enemy alien, and then in April 1941 recruited into the Pioneer Corps to serve with the Royal Engineers. Commissioned, he was appointed a railway transport officer in Eastern Command but was invalided out of the army because of a heart condition in November 1945. He had become a naturalised British citizen in July 1946, and toured the country's variety theatres in a music hall piano act called Marek & Vyse with an Austrian, Roman Marek. As a sideline he also contributed articles to various magazines such as the *Economist* about the economics of Britain's railway transport system.

Weiss was placed under intense physical and technical surveillance by MI5 for two months and, in the absence of any evidence of his participation in espionage, he was interviewed in January 1948. Anxious that he might lose his British citizenship, Weiss confessed that he had been recruited as a Soviet spy by Hans Demetz, a school friend in Cologne in 1931 who, incidentally, had been mentioned by Krivitsky, as a GRU agent. As a Jew, Weiss was anxious to leave Germany, and Demetz had introduced him to his first controller, HARRY I, who had passed him on to HARRY II in Switzerland in 1935. Finally, he met Henri Robinson at a rendezvous at St Helier in Jersey in September 1937, but insisted he had broken off contact with Robinson after a final meeting in Paris in July 1939. This apparently sincere assertion seemed to be contradicted by mysterious large payments into his London bank account, some from Switzerland, which he could not explain.

Weiss acknowledged that his principal role had been as an intermediary between Ilse Steinfeld, who was secretary to the *Berliner Tagebltat* correspondent in London, Philip Scheffer. Weiss's task was to collect material from Steinfeld, who monitored the journalist's activities, and pass it on to a team of couriers who were seamen working on ships calling at the London Docks.

Weiss's account, as given to his MI5 interrogators, cleared up at least two pre-war cases of Soviet espionage and shed new light on Russian tradecraft. Weiss also acknowledged having played a role in the handling of Robert Switz, a spy who had been caught in France.

The case had begun when the FBI was informed that William Disch, a designer working on classified naval contracts in the Arma Engineering

Corporation, had reported an approach for information from Solomon Kantor, a former colleague who was a well-known Communist as well as a talented draftsman. Disch duly entrapped Kantor, who in turn led the investigators to Moishe Stern, an intermediary responsible for taking Disch's documents and photographing them in the Amtorg building. Surveillance on Stern revealed his connection with another mysterious figure, Robert Gordon Switz, who was to become a key figure in the expanding Soviet network of illegals.[10]

Switz had been born in New Jersey to wealthy parents of Russian origin and had been educated in France. He was a Communist idealist and, after his recruitment, had been trained in Moscow. In 1931 he was back in New York, working for Stern by running a source in the US Army. His contact was Robert Osman, a former Young Communist League activist who had been posted to Panama with the rank of corporal. His parents had also been Russian immigrants, and he supplied Switz with copies of documents he routinely typed while on administrative duties as an office clerk. Osman was compromised when his mail drop in New York failed, and a package full of incriminating papers was returned by the Post Office to the army in Panama and traced to Osman. In August 1933 Osman was sentenced to twenty years' hard labour, but his conviction was overturned and a new trial ordered when the eminent lawyer Louis Waldman took up his case. Osman's second trial led to his acquittal when Waldman demonstrated that the accused could not have mailed the package to the mail drop in New York. He showed that, far from being an active Communist agent, his client had been the unwitting dupe of Frema Karry, his Russian girlfriend, who had disappeared at the time of Osman's arrest. Waldman also learned that Osman's principal contact was a man known to him as 'Harry Duryea', but when, coincidentally, a photograph of Switz appeared in *Time* magazine on 26 March 1934, following his arrest, Osman recognized Switz as Duryea. In fact, Switz had fled to Paris as soon as Osman had been taken into military custody, and had resumed his activities there, this time running a network of sources in the French army and in the War Ministry, assisted by his recently acquired American wife, Marjorie Tilley. Both were arrested by the French police in December 1933 and, after months of interrogation, they confessed to having participated in a Soviet espionage ring. Furthermore, under interrogation they implicated dozens of others, including Lydia Stahl, a veteran Soviet intelligence officer.

The confession of Robert and Marjorie Switz earned them their release in 1935 but it had also implicated more than two hundred suspects, including several with access to the French Ministry of War's research into chemical and germ warfare. Six of those who were caught in the first wave of arrests also incriminated others in return for lighter sentences, and the French Deuxieme Bureau was more than satisfied when only ten suspects were convicted *in absentia*, having evaded capture. The Stern-Stahl-Switz Group, as it came to be known in western security circles, was to prove a mortal blow to the Soviet apparatus, particularly in the United States, where Stern was obliged to make a swift departure for Moscow, via Canada.

Lydia Stahl had been one of the founders of the Soviet illegal network in the United States. Born in Rostov in 1885, her husband had been a member of the nobility who had lost his estates in the Crimea during the revolution. The family had emigrated to New York, where Lydia's husband had started a new career as a stockbroker, and she had studied medicine but, after the death of her only son in 1918, she had returned alone to Paris where her interest in photography, and her American passport, made her an attractive target for Soviet recruitment. After taking a course in law, Stahl had returned to New York, where she worked with Stern until 1932, when she re-established herself in Paris and liaised with the Switzs after Osman's arrest had prompted their hasty exit. In March 1934 Lydia Stahl, who declined to co-operate with the French authorities, received a four-year prison term and upon her release resumed her activities in the United States. One of those closely associated with Stahl in both the United States and France was Alfred Tilton, a Latvian who had been the GRU's illegal *rezident* in New York, operating under a commercial front, that of a shipping office in Manhattan.

Under interrogation by the French and MI5, Switz and his wife had described a visit to London and a meeting in Kensington Gardens in September 1933 with a Soviet controller, HARRY II, and his companion who was identified by MI5 as Weiss. The incident was also recalled by Weiss, who had read a newspaper story relating to the couple's arrest two months later.[11]

The second espionage case that Weiss admitted having been involved with concerned Major Wilfred Vernon and an Irishman, William Meredith. Both were Communist Party members and employees at the Royal Aircraft Establishment at Farnborough. Weiss recalled that in May 1936 he had accompanied HARRY II to Farnham, where he had met Vernon and Meredith and acted as an interpreter for HARRY II, who spoke poor English. According to Weiss, both sources had been talent-spotted as spies by a CPGB activist, Dorothy Woodman. Having been introduced to the pair, Weiss bought a Wolsey Hornet to drive down to Hampshire to hold meetings with Vernon and collect film negatives of files he had photographed with a Soviet-supplied Leica camera. This arrangement continued until August 1937 when Vernon's home was burgled and the police discovered that he was in possession of a large quantity of unauthorised classified documents, including blueprints for the Avro Anson, a new twin-engined maritime reconnaissance aircraft.[12] Although Vernon was prosecuted under the Official Secrets Act and both men lost their jobs, the authorities had not realised that the pair were not careless employees, but Soviet spies. The only person Vernon had confided in was his defence counsel, D.N. Pritt, who was himself a Soviet asset, too. Subsequently Meredith, who was a co-inventor of the automatic pilot, had continued his spying, and had supplied details of a new aircraft bombsight manufactured by Smith's Industries at Cheltenham.[13]

When in 1948 Weiss revealed his participation in the Farnborough breach of security, MI5's embarrassment was acute, as Vernon was by then an elected Labour Party Member of Parliament, a fact that MI5 was keen to avoid mentioning to the FBI.

Although Weiss remained a not entirely reliable resource for MI5, it was never able to definitively identify HARRY II. Nevertheless, the Weiss case gave the analysts working on the Robinson papers a certain respect for the Sonderkommando's wartime investigation, and the strict compartmentalisation exercised by what clearly had been the British branch of the ROTE KAPELLE.

* * *

Because illegals operate in a hostile environment, without the benefit of the protection from the Vienna Convention that gives diplomats immunity from criminal prosecution, their illicit activities, travel and communications are conducted under special conditions designed to insulate them from unwelcome attention.

Naturally illegals have to communicate with the Centre to receive instructions and transmit their reports, but this contact is strictly regulated so as to avoid compromise. Typically, personal meetings will be avoided, and messages or funds will be exchanged through elaborate dead drops managed through a system of remote signals.

Illegals may often have to travel, either for periods of home leave in Russia, or to attend debriefing sessions in environments considered relatively free of hostile surveillance. To facilitate their movement across borders the members typically were issued with false passports, usually acquired through 'tomb-stoning', a technique involving bogus applications being made in countries such as Canada, Australia, Eire and New Zealand, usually in the names of long-dead children, thereby creating 'dead doubles' and exploiting a universal weakness in the passport system, which cannot reconcile birth records with deaths. In transiting to and from the countries in which they operate, illegals will seek to cover their movements by switching travel documents during their journey.

Illegals may require access to large amounts of cash, so another characteristic is possession of ingeniously designed concealment devices in which incriminating paraphernalia, such as money, passports and communications equipment, can be stored safely. Occasionally illegals may have to make contact with a courier or handler, and in those circumstances the expedient of an old-fashioned recognition password, known as a parole, is adopted. Management of a major surveillance operation is fraught with risk as illegals will have undergone a lengthy period of training, often lasting several years, which will include exercises intended to expose interest of a hostile security apparatus. Sometime referred to as 'dry-cleaning' (*proverka* in Russian), the objective is to spot evidence of an opponent without adopting behaviour that would betray an individual's true role. Jumping on and off trains and similar techniques designed to shake off an unwanted watcher may achieve that objective, but will also self-incriminate.

Nevertheless, surveillance is at the heart of any counter-intelligence operation, so a variety of sophisticated techniques are employed to, for example, keep a dead drop under observation through the use of remote sensors or a closed-circuit video camera, thus avoiding the necessity to deploy personnel that could be compromised.

The SVR *rezidentura* in New York, embedded inside Russia's Permanent Mission to the United Nations, maintained an additional electronic capability staffed by technicians in a compartmented unit code-named IMPULSE. Prior to 1981 it was known that the IMPULSE branch could intercept the FBI encrypted, frequency-hopping communications, and even when the appropriate countermeasures had been taken to prevent leaks, the FBI's local operations were still vulnerable to energy mapping, an ingenious method of tracking the movement of sophisticated comms equipment, and identifying neighbourhoods in which they were concentrated. Even though the SVR could not access the content of the signals, their existence was sufficient to warn of the FBI's presence in locations of interest. If the telltale signs of hostile activity were detected, the SVR preferred to err on the side of caution and abort a planned operation, such as a rendezvous or brush-pass contact.

* * *

During the Cold War the NKVD's global reach was partially exposed by the successful exploitation of the VENONA traffic, which enabled Anglo-American cryptographers to glimpse a parallel illegal apparatus that operated separately from the conventional legal *rezidentura*. In addition, in March 1947 Allan Foote had disclosed his appointment as the NKVD's new illegal *rezident* in the United States.

Information from another defector, Reino Hayhanen, in May 1957 led the FBI to the current illegal *rezident* in New York, Willie Fisher, but he was a professional of the old school and made no admission until he was exchanged in a spy swap for the U-2 pilot F. Gary Powers in February 1962. Meanwhile, in January 1961, an illegal network in London was exposed and led to the arrest of the local illegal *rezident,* Gordon Lonsdale. He too would be swopped in April 1964. Thus, during much of the Cold War, the Allied counter-intelligence community knew of how the KGB's elite Line N Directorate S-operated illegals, but could not gain an inside track until an illegal based in Hartsdale, New York, Rudi Hermann, became a reluctant double agent run by the FBI. Code-named AT LAST, because of his unique quality, Hermann was coerced into co-operating in May 1977 and revealed his true identity as Ludek Zemenek, a Line N professional who had transited through Toronto, where he had spent seven years with his wife Inga and children developing his 'legend' as a professional photographer before moving to the United States in 1968. His adopted identity of Hermann turned out to be that of a Wehrmacht soldier killed in the war on the Eastern Front.

During his three years under the FBI's control, Hermann was able to compromise several other Soviet assets, among them a Canadian academic, Hugh Hambleton, employed by NATO as an analyst. A long-term Soviet spy, thought to have been recruited by his Communist parents, Hambleton would be arrested in England in June 1982 and sentenced to ten years' imprisonment.

Eventually, following the arrest of one of his sons who was charged with shooting a police officer in California, Hermann became disillusioned and returned to his native Czechoslovakia, where he claimed to have duped the FBI and operated as a triple agent.

A country in which émigrés are encouraged by the government to retain their links, instead of adopting the American 'melting pot' approach, Canada has always been considered a very benign environment in which Soviet and Russian illegals could operate, or transit across the porous border into the United States. Another Soviet illegal, twenty-five-year-old Stephen (Istvan) Ratkai was arrested in Canada by CSIS in June 1988 after he had been exposed by a pregnant US Naval Investigative Service (NIS) double agent, Donna Geiger. Born in Canada and brought up in Budapest, his father's native country following his mother's suicide, he was identified as an illegal in May 1987 as he collected information from Lieutenant Geiger at a rendez-vous in the lobby of the Newfoundland Hotel, St John's.

Ratkai's arrest was the culmination of a relatively short double agent operation in which he met Geiger, posted to the US Naval facility at Argentia, and sold him classified material relating to SOSUS submarine tracking technology for $2,000 on three occasions from May 1987. The case had begun when Geiger posed as a disaffected naval officer short of money, and in December 1986 walked aboard the *Akademik Boris Petrov*, a Soviet ocean-ographic research vessel docked in St John's to hand over some supposedly secret documents and offer 'a business relationship'. Two months later, she received a positive response in the mail, and this led to her first rendezvous with Ratkai in a St John's carpark.

In February 1989 Ratkai pleaded guilty to attempted espionage and in March 1989 received two concurrent terms of nine years' imprisonment. Although the CSIS investigation of Ratkai did not lead to the public exposure of a wider network, it did illustrate the KGB's opportunism in exploiting the young man with a troubled family background who, born in Nova Scotia, had been brought up and educated in Canada and Hungary. Fluent in English, without a trace of an accent, Ratkai had been deployed on his KGB mission to operate under his own name, a rare variation on the illegals' orthodoxy. Perhaps more importantly, the case had developed from a relatively routine, low-level 'dangle' aimed at the crew of a Soviet survey ship, and was not the culmination of a tip from a mole or defector.

In May 1996, Ian and Laurie Brodie, who had been living in Canada under assumed identities, actually two children from Ontario who had died young in 1966 and 1965 respectively, were identified as Russian illegals by CSIS and arrested on immigration charges at their apartment in Roehampton Avenue. Lambert, who had arrived separately in Canada, and married in 1991, had been working for Black's Photography in the suburb of Markham, and his wife was employed by an insurance company. They were later exposed as Dmitri V. Olshevsky and Yelena B. Olshevskaya, and deported to Moscow in June 1996, having spent an estimated six to eight years undercover in Canada. The lengthy CSIS counter-intelligence operation code-named STANLEY had been prompted by Vasili Mitrokhin's treasure trove, the source which had compromised other KGB assets, such as George Trofimoff and Robert Lipka who both fell victim to FBI entrapments orchestrated by Special Agent Dmitri Droulimsky posing as an SVR officer in an effort to have suspects incriminate themselves. CSIS also benefited from another Mitrokhin tip relating to a Directorate S illegal, but despite extensive surveillance, he was never seen to engage in espionage.

In November 2006 a Russian travelling on a Canadian passport in the name of Paul William Hampel was arrested as he tried to board a flight in Montreal, and was found to be carrying false documents, a large amount of various currencies, encrypted SIM cards, three mobile phones, two digital cameras and a shortwave radio. A CSIS investigation revealed Hampel's background in Dublin where since July 1997 he had run a business consultancy, Emerging Markets Research & Consultancy Ltd, with a declared capital of a million Irish Punts, which operated in the Channel Islands, Belgrade and Cyprus. A skilled photographer, Hampel had published a well-illustrated, seventy-six-page book, *My Beautiful Balkans,* in 2003 and promoted it with a website, www. mybeautifulbalkans.com, which was registered to a rented basement apartment in Somerfed Avenue, Montreal. In his book Hampel described himself as a travel consultant and former lifeguard. A month after his arrest, Hampel was deported to Moscow, but was never charged with espionage.

Hampel was found to have acquired three successive Canadian passports after he applied for them in May 1995, May 2000 and April 2002. His last application, listing a modest, three-storey apartment block in St Jacques Street, Montreal, as his address, had been supported by a 1999 Quebec driver's licence and a forged 1971 Ontario birth certificate recording that Hampel had been born in Toronto on 11 December 1965. All this circumstantial evidence pointed to Hampel's role as a Directorate S illegal, although in the absence of a confession CSIS remained unaware of the precise nature of his mission.

* * *

In June 1982 the MI6 station in Tehran, headed by Ian McCredie, acquired an unexpected source, Vladimir Kuzichkin, the Line N illegal support officer at the local KGB *rezidentura*, who had been under consular cover since his arrival in 1977. Code-named REDWOOD, Kuzichkin had served in Iran for the past five years and was motivated to approach the British because of a disagreement with his *rezident*, Leonid Shebarshin. Some 6ft 6in tall, Kuzichkin was an improbable intelligence officer as he stood out in any crowd, towering well above the average height of Tehran's inhabitants, and was hardly inconspicuous. However, his value to MI6 lay in his knowledge of the influence exercised by the Soviets over the Tudeh party. His decision to flee Iran was prompted by the imminent arrival of a KGB security inspection, which Kuzichkin feared would conduct an audit and expose the loss of sensitive documents that had been in his custody.

After his successful exfiltration through Turkey, REDWOOD, who had the unusual KGB background of having played in a rock band in Moscow, went on a lecture tour of Allied intelligence agencies to explain the inner workings of Directorate S, regarded as an elite that exercised total security and hitherto had never experienced a defection.

During his debriefing, Kuzichkin had much to say, and had described his principal agents, KONRAD and EVI, a husband and wife team operating on Federal German documentation. In fact, KONRAD was a forty-one-year-old Latvian aeronautical engineer, Karl Kruminsch, and his wife, whom he had pretended to meet and marry in Denmark, was really Katarina Nummerk, an East German former kindergarten teacher. They had been staged through Finland and had intended to settle in Islamabad calling themselves Michel and Ursula Geschwinnt but, having been rejected by both the Pakistani and Indian authorities, and failing to land a job with the Swiss company Global-Car in Iran, KONRAD had found a job with Pasavant Werke, a West German company in Tehran.

Compromised by Kuzichkin, the couple was arrested in September 1981 at Zurich airport as they tried to board a flight to Vienna, carrying Federal German passports. They were tried seven months later on charges of engaging in espionage since 'at least 1978' and Kruminsch was sentenced to three years' imprisonment, while his wife received two and a half years. According to the Swiss prosecutor's seventeen-page indictment, Kruminsch had been a KGB agent for the past eleven years and had run, and financed, his activities through Zurich, having undergone four years of training in Moscow and East Berlin. They had entered Switzerland several times since 1978, and EVI had renewed her passport at the Federal Republic's embassy in Tehran. To protect Kuzichkin as the source, it was suggested that some discrepancy had been spotted during the passport renewal process. This expedient was also intended to undermine the KGB's confidence in its fake documentation.

Kuzichkin's apparently promising career in Directorate S had unexpectedly come to a full stop in June 1982, following what had looked like an improvement in his prospects. In June 1980 Vladimir Golovanov had been arrested in the act of meeting a Swiss illegal, code-named SHAROV, who managed a local transport company. Golovanov had been withdrawn hastily via Damascus, leaving Kuzichkin the senior Line N officer in Tehran. His appointment as head of Line N was confirmed by Yuri Drozdov, the new head of Directorate S, and he continued to manage KONRAD, EVI and a new, low-level Iranian illegal, VAGIF, who had been infiltrated into the country from Kuwait. However, in mid-1981 KONRAD's performance had deteriorated, and Kuzichkin had arranged a rendezvous with him in Moscow in June to find out the cause of the problems he had experienced in servicing his dead letter drops. Kuzichkin flew home in the usual way, ostensibly on leave, but KONRAD neither showed up for the meeting nor left the routine signals in the prearranged sites in Western Europe to indicate that he too was en route for Moscow.

This incident, followed by Kuzichkin's accidental loss in late May 1982 of an undeveloped film containing vitally secret documents in the *referentura*, sealed his fate and caused him to choose defection to the British in favour of confession and harsh punishment.

The advantage of investing in illegals is that they can be expected to undertake tasks that cannot be fulfilled by members of a legal *rezidentura* without the risk of attracting hostile surveillance from the local security apparatus. Some are mundane, such as surveying for dead drop sites, signal sites and other operational locations, and preparing photographs of them and writing descriptions for personnel unfamiliar with them. Other missions may include servicing existing drops and acting as an intermediary or 'cut-out' so as to avoid contaminating another party. In addition, illegals can talent spot and cultivate potential sources without arousing the suspicion inevitably attached to someone working under diplomatic cover.

Naturally, an illegal may never knowingly come into contact with classified information, or may never learn the content of material collected from a dead drop and then delivered to another contact at a subsequent rendezvous. However, this by no means diminishes the importance of the role of the illegal.

At the end of the Cold War western security and intelligence agencies had accumulated a significant amount of information about Directorate S methodology, but little was known about how the SVR had adapted Directorate S, inherited from the Soviet era, to cope with modern challenges. Previous attempts to study illegal operations have foundered because of the high level of training and security instilled into the professionals. On at least one occasion an effort was made to have the management of a source, actually a double agent, transferred to an illegal. In March 1959 the FBI had launched SHOCKER, an operation to dangle a US Army non-commissioned officer in front of Boris Polikarpov, a Soviet naval attaché in Washington, DC. Under the FBI's supervision Sergeant Joe Cassidy began to sell supposedly classified material relating to the development and production of nerve gas, a commodity that was bound to be attractive to Moscow. As well as misdirecting the Soviets about American research, SHOCKER served to enhance the status of an existing asset, Dmitri Polyakov, who was assigned the task of managing Cassidy.

Another advantage was the exposure of an illegal, code-named PALMETTO by the FBI, who was spotted servicing a dead drop filled in December 1970 by Cassidy at a site in Tampa Bay, Florida. Having already identified Cassidy's Soviet handler, Mikhail Danilin, the FBI hoped to entrap him outside the 25-mile travel limit applied to Soviet diplomats, but instead the surveillance spotted an unidentified figure, a target code-named PALMETTO. A check on his Volkswagen rented in Miami revealed that the driver was a Mexican, Gilberto Rivas y Lopez, holding a Canadian driver's licence. Further research showed him to be an academic employed as a professor teaching anthropology at the University of Minnesota.

Originally recruited in 1963 as a left-wing college student, Rivas undertook a tour of the American south-west in 1967, collecting information about military bases. In 1971 he returned to the United States to gain a doctorate at the University of Utah and then study at the University of Texas in Austin. Throughout the period from 1970, PALMETTO remained under physical and technical surveillance, but he was eventually pitched by the FBI when the Department of Justice ruled that an illegal wiretap had probably compromised the prospects of a future successful prosecution. Reluctantly, in 1978 the FBI pitched Rivas and his wife, Alicia Castellanos, at a motel in Minneapolis, but they declined to co-operate.

The PALMETTO case cost the FBI dearly, as in August 1977 a Cessna 172 surveillance aircraft tracking Rivas as he drove to Canada had crashed into a lake in bad weather, killing two special agents, Trenwith Basford, aged thirty-three, and the pilot, sixty-year-old Mark Kirkland. A year later, with Rivas back in Mexico, and Danilin transferred to Ottawa, the case was terminated. The FBI had run PALMETTO for twenty-three years, without a leak, and thereby demonstrated the organization's ability to resource and manage quite sophisticated, long-term counter-espionage operations.

Chapter IV

GHOST STORIES

GHOST STORIES was the code name suggested by an intelligence analyst based in the BACK ROOM suite of rooms occupied by the New York Field Office's counter-intelligence squad, who had been asked to provide a selection of suitable cryptonyms. The first on her computer-generated list was GHOST STORIES, which was then chosen. The operation itself, supervised by Alan Kohler, had its origins in the recruitment by the FBI of a SVR officer, Aleksandr Poteyev, code-named DUMB LUCK.

Born in Belarus in March 1952, and the son of a decorated war hero whose unit had been credited with destroying thirty-seven German tanks during a four-day battle in September 1944, Poteyev transferred from the Red Army, where he had served with Soviet special forces in Afghanistan, winning the Order of the Red Banner, having been attached to two special groups, designated ZENITH and CASCADE. He joined the KGB in 1975, serving in Minsk and then Moscow. As an FCD 1st Department officer he was posted to Mexico City and then Santiago de Chile. His last overseas assignment was to New York in 1995, when he was recruited by the FBI shortly before his departure in 1999, his request for an extension having been declined. Fortuitously, after his return to Moscow he was unexpectedly transferred into Directorate S as deputy chief of the 4th (North and Latin America) Department.

By January 2000 a major operation was under way involving hundreds of FBI special agents, the famous Special Surveillance Group watchers, numerous vehicles and at least one helicopter. GHOST STORIES also involved the surreptitious entry of homes, the installation of covert listening devices, the monitoring of communications and the examination of computer equipment in the homes of suspects. Much of the operation was supervised by a veteran FBI officer, Rick DesLauriers, originally from Longmeadow, Massachusetts, who had joined the organization in January 1987 and had served in Birmingham, Alabama, before being transferred to New York and then promoted deputy assistant director of the Counterintelligence Division at headquarters.

The first illegal to be placed under surveillance was Vicky Pelaez, who was watched in Peru from as early as January 2000 (which coincides with the beginning of the CIA's long relationship with Poteyev). Aged fifty-five, Pelaez was a Peruvian journalist married to Juan Lazaro in 1992, by whom she had one son, Juan, a talented pianist.

Born in Peru, she worked for a TV news programme *Frecuencia Latina* and in 1984 was kidnapped with her cameraman Percy Raborg by the Tupac Amaru Revolutionary Movement (MRTA) for seventeen hours. This episode established her reputation as a tough, feisty newswoman. Later married to Juan Lazaro, she was employed in New York City as a columnist for *El Diario La Prensa*, and acquired American citizenship. She made no attempt to conceal her admiration for leftist causes, especially for Fidel Castro and Hugo Chavez, and was a vocal critic of American foreign policy. While under audio surveillance, Pelaez was heard to remark to her husband, 'we are living with the enemy'.

Some of the evidence illustrating her active involvement in espionage would be disclosed by the FBI but, understandably, only the bare minimum so as to protect the organization's sources and methods. The trick was to balance the requirement to adduce sufficient evidence to indict the suspects, without revealing their full hand. Nevertheless, this public domain material does create a compelling picture of what happened on specific occasions over the decade in question.

On 14 January 2000 Pelaez was under observation and videotaped as she met a Russian illegal support officer in a public park in Peru, who handed her a package containing money. After the rendezvous she telephoned her husband in Yonkers, New York, and reported 'All went well.' On 20 February 2002 she returned from Peru and was recorded discussing with her husband money hidden in her suitcase. On 8 January 2003 Lazaro was recorded by the FBI as he told Pelaez that he would send a message written in invisible ink with her on an imminent trip to Peru. On 6 May 2003 the FBI recorded Lazaro telling Pelaez he was receiving radio transmissions from 'over there'. On 23 February 2003 the FBI recorded the couple counting a large sum of money and Pelaez was heard discussing having eight of ten bags, having divided the remaining bags so they would not be too bulky. They then discussed whether, after accounting for certain expenses, they had '72,500' or, as they later determined, 'seventy-six'.

On 10 September 2007 Pelaez and Lazaro were taped as he complained about Moscow's reaction to some of his recent reporting:

> LAZARO: They tell me that my information is of no value because I didn't provide any source … it's of no use to them.
> PELAEZ: Really?
> LAZARO: Yes. They say that without a source … without stating who tells you all of this … it isn't … your report isn't …
> PELAEZ: [Interrupts] Put down any politician from here!
> LAZARO: I'm … I'm going to give them what they want. But, I'm going to contain what I'm telling them … If they don't like what I tell them, too bad … but, [unintelligible] work because they like it … they're [unintelligible]. They say their hands are tied. On the inside, they don't even care about the country …
> PELAEZ: So … why do they have you? If they don't care about the country … what do we have Intelligence Services for?

Although Pelaez would her deny all knowledge of her husband's clandestine activities, the FBI regarded her from the outset as a willing co-conspirator who was equally complicit in espionage. On 8 January 2003, shortly before Pelaez took a trip to Lima, the FBI recorded a conversation in their home, with Lazaro saying, 'When you go to Peru. I am going to write in "invisible" … and you're going to pass them all of that in a book', to which she replied, 'Okay'. He went on, 'I'm going to give you some blank pieces of paper and it will be done there … about everything I've done.' This dialogue was interpreted by the FBI to mean that Pelaez was being instructed by her husband to pass a report written in secret writing, or invisible ink, to his controllers, from which she did not demur.[1]

If Pelaez was the first of the network to be compromised, her husband was the second. Juan Lazaro's true name was Mikhail Vasenkov, a professional intelligence officer who, aged sixty-six, retired from the SVR on 1 January 2006 and flew to Lima to collect his $80,000 annual pension. The next year, on 25 August, he attended another rendezvous in Peru where he was handed more money by a Russian diplomat.

The FBI traced Lazaro to Lima where, according to local records, he had arrived from Spain on a Uruguayan passport in March 1976. While in Peru he worked as a photographer and karate instructor, and adopted the identity of Lazaro, a child who had died at the age of three. After his marriage to Pelaez they lived in 17 Clifton Avenue, Yonkers, with his seventeen-year-old son Juan, and stepson Waldo Masical, a thirty-eight-year-old architect, from a previous marriage. Lazaro had a PhD in political science and taught Caribbean and Latin American studies. In a conversation in his home recorded by the FBI, Vasenkov told his wife that his family had moved to Siberia 'as soon as the war started' in 1941.This seemed proof, if any was really needed, that Pelaez could not have had much doubt about his family background, although in later years she would deny any previous knowledge of her husband's Russian past.

At the time Pelaez and Lazaro were placed under surveillance, the FBI and CIA had just received the vital physical evidence that implicated Bob Hanssen as KARAT, and there was anxiety that the mole might compromise yet another FBI asset, Colonel Sergei Tretyakov, a Line PR officer who had been the SVR's deputy *rezident* in New York since April 1995, operating under diplomatic cover on the eighth floor of the Permanent Mission to the United Nations at 136 East 67th Street. His *rezidentura* amounted to some sixty officers, covering the wide range of KGB specialisms, supported by about twenty-five secretaries, all of them KGB wives. Born in Moscow, he had been brought up in Tehran where his father, also a KGB officer, had been posted under trade delegation cover.

Eventually, in October 2000, aged forty-four, he moved out of his Riverdale apartment in the Bronx, to be granted political asylum in the United States, having supplied his FBI handlers with large amounts of information over an (as yet undeclared) period of time. He was credited with having passed some 5,000 SVR cables, more than a hundred SVR intelligence reports, and his information had resulted in 400 separate items of actionable intelligence circulated within the US intelligence community. Allegedly, he had been urged to defect in December 1999 while meeting the FBI during a family vacation in Las Vegas, but had opted to remain in place.

Reportedly, the catalyst for his decision to collaborate with the FBI had been the death in January 1997 of his mother Revmira, which meant he was no longer vulnerable through the intimidation of his family. Another motivating factor may have been the loss of the family savings, amounting to $25,000, in the collapse of the Russian banks in 1994.

A graduate of the KGB school at Medvedkovo, Tretyakov had previously been posted in January 1990 to the KGB's *rezidentura* in Ottawa, and while he underwent a lengthy debriefing he gave his interrogators an insight into how the SVR had adapted to the post-Soviet era. As a very senior SVR officer he enjoyed access to files and to individuals of great interest to the FBI, as he later described in *Comrade J*, his autobiography, co-authored with Pete Earley.[2] Eventually Tretyakov settled with his wife Helena, nineteen-year-old daughter Ksenia and their Persian cat Matilda, in Jacksonville, Florida, where he choked to death in a kitchen accident on 9 July 2010.

The son and grandson of KGB officers, Tretyakov never revealed precisely how long his co-operation with the FBI had lasted, but the SVR would have assumed the worst when compiling the mandatory damage assessment. This document would have identified every colleague and every *rezidentura* source likely to have been compromised by the defector, and in those circumstances anyone considered tainted would have been withdrawn to Moscow. As deputy to two *rezidents,* Valeri Koval, formerly in Mexico City, and then Sergei Kutafin, and close to the Washington *rezident* Vitali Dominratsky (who had previously served in Ottawa), Tretyakov was in a position to inflict lasting damage on the FCD. Such a major disruption can have a lasting impact on any clandestine organization and terminate many careers, but one likely consequence is that the SVR switched much of their operational activities to a compartmented illegal network, details of which would have been tightly held by Directorate S and therefore unknown to Tretyakov whose career had been in the 1st (America and Canada) Department of the KGB's elite First Chief Directorate.

The Russian reaction to Tretyakov's defection was to enhance the SVR's illegals organization, which, by its nature, was thought to be protected from the routine surveillance that diplomatic cover attracted.

* * *

As the GHOST STORIES investigation developed, the FBI drew more and more of the illegals network into its surveillance operation. Some of the individual members had links to each other, but for others the only connection was the Line N, Directorate S, illegals support officers based in New York under diplomatic cover who serviced the dead drops. Remote, technical coverage of the drop sites then provided further leads.

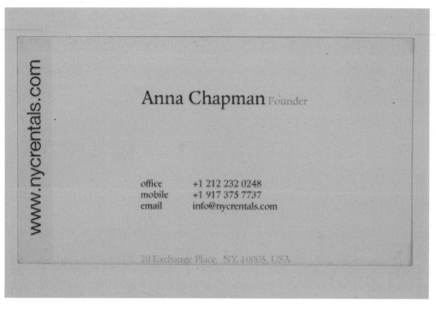

Anna Chapman's business card at the time of her arrest.

Andrey Bezrikov, alias Donald Heathfield

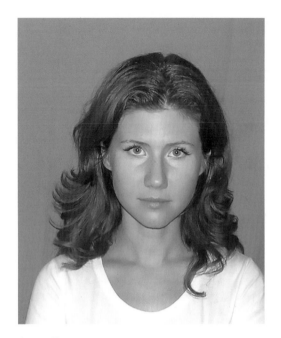

Anna Chapman

Anna Chapman at Starbucks' with "Roman", the FBI agent provocateur.

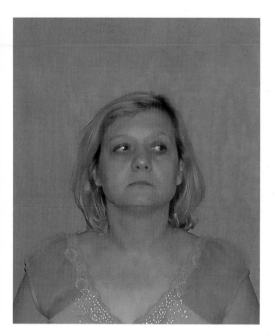

Elena Vavilova, alias Tracey Foley.

The FBI handcuffs used to restrain Anna Chapman at her arrest

Anna Chapman's Toshiba laptop which she gave to "Roman from the Consulate".

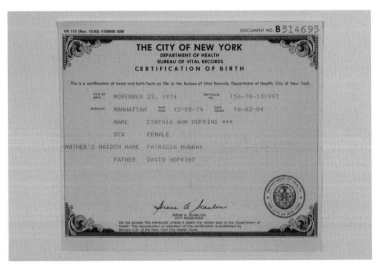

Cynthia Murphy's (authentic) birth certificate.

Ostensibly innocent computer image of flowers in which the SVR concealed a secret message, a technique known as steganography.

The discarded beer bottle used as a signal to indicate a dead-drop where money had been cached near a highway rest-stop in upstate New York.

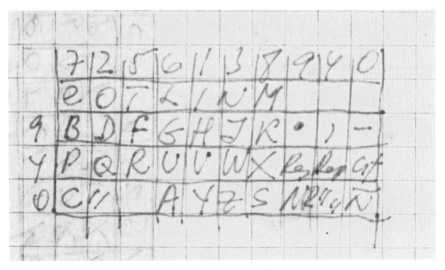

Juan Lazaro's cipher crib, photographed in his home by the FBI.

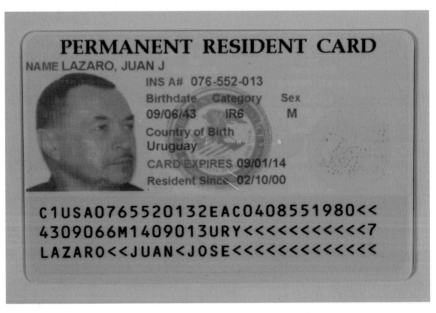

Juan Lazaro's U.S. permanent resident card issued legitimately under his alias.

Richard Murphy's university identification card.

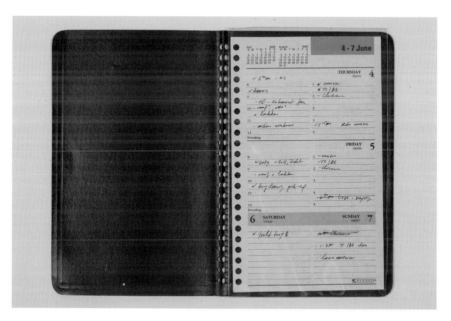

Richard Murphy's daily diary for June 2009, as photographed by the FBI during a covert entry into his home.

Sony ICF shortwave radio recovered from Donald Heathfield's' home and used as an emergency one-way channel of communication with Moscow.

A Sony Mavica digital camera recovered from Donald Heathfield's home by the FBI.

Virginia driver's license issued to Mikhail Kutzik under his alias Michael Zottoli.

Rock used to indicate a cache of money left in May 2004 near Wurtsboro, New York, by Pavel Kapustin, and collected by Mikhail Kutzik in June 2006.

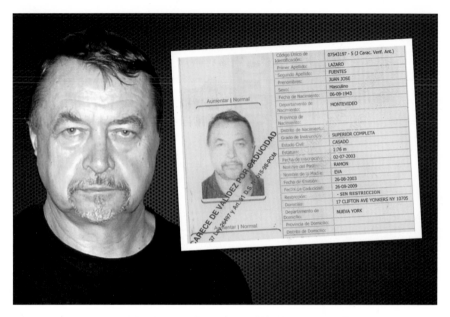

The genuine Peruvian identity card issued to Mikhail Vasenkov, alias Juan Lazaro.

Lydia Guryev, alias Cynthia Murphy.

Mikhail Kutzik, alias Michael Zottoli.

Cache: Metsos Cache Site on 17 MAY 2004

FBI photo of the Wurtsboro cache site.

Covert FBI surveillance camera catches Pavel Kapustin as he exchanges carrier bags with an SVR courier in the pedestrian underpass at a rural New York railway station.

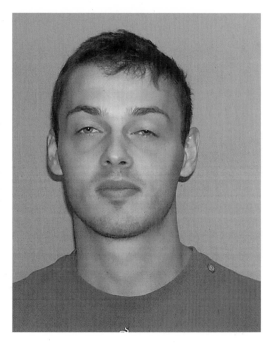

Mikhail Semenko, the Arlington travel agent who operated under his own name but was compromised by his contact in May 2010 with an SVR Illegals Support Officer from the New York *rezidentura*.

Murphy and Zottoli meet in Brooklyn in March 2010 while under FBI surveillance.

Murphy and Zottoli engage in an intense, two-hour conversation at Tillie's Coffee Shop in Brooklyn, during which he is passed $9,000, unaware that the FBI's Maria Ricci is sitting at a neighbouring table.

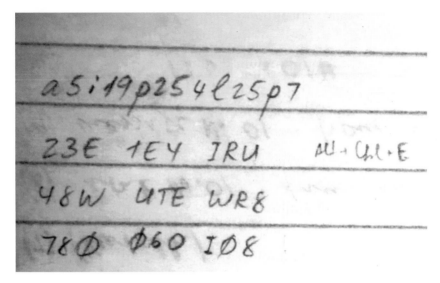

Murphy's note of his communications password found during an FBI search of his home.

In April 2009 Richard Murphy receives a bag of $300,000 in cash from an SVR Illegals Support Officer in a pedestrian underpass at the North White Plains railway station while under covert FBI CCTV surveillance.

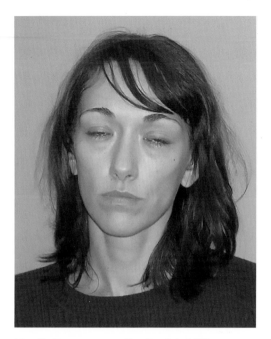

Natalia Pereverzeva, alias Patricia Mills.

The genuine U.S. passport issued to Vladimir Guryev in the name of Richard Murphy.

The FBI congratulates the fifteen agents and analysts who worked on the Hanssen case.

(L to R) Jack Platt, Nigel West, Dan Mulvenna and Brian Kelley.

If there was a single individual who acted as a controller for some members of the network, often taking on the role of paymaster, it was Pavel Kapustin, alias Christopher Metsos. Aged fifty-eight, the former Vermont ski instructor had travelled as a tourist on a false Canadian passport issued by the Canadian consulate in Johannesburg. The FBI soon established that the real Metsos had died in Canada at the age of five.

On 24 February 2001 the FBI watched Metsos meet Richard Murphy at a restaurant in Sunnyside, New York. This rendezvous served to incriminate Murphy and his wife, Cynthia. His real name was Vladimir Guryev, and he had moved from a Hoboken apartment, which was searched surreptitiously by the FBI on 27 July 2005, to a large three-bedroom home in 31 Marquette Road, Montclair, New Jersey, which had been bought in 2008 for $481,000. He was married to Cynthia, with whom he had two daughters, Katie, aged eleven, and nine-year-old Lisa. He had gained an International Business Degree from NYU's Stern School of Business, and an MBA from Columbia. While his wife worked, Murphy developed culinary skills and was known for the quality of his bread baking. He had lived in the United States since the mid-1990s and had studied economics at the New School in New York. The FBI established a static observation post next door to his home, at 29 Marquette Road, and during the July 2005 search copied a diskette containing a text message that referred to Murphy's radio signals ('radiograms') to Moscow:

> Pls make sure your radioequipment for RG rcptn is in order. We
> plan to send a couple of test rgs ...[3]

Murphy's wife, who alleged her maiden name had been 'Cynthia A. Hopkins', was actually Lydia Guryev, aged thirty-nine, who worked as an accountant in Manhattan for Morea Financial Services, a tax advisory and wealth management firm, where she earned a salary of $135,000 a year. Although the couple owned a green 1998 Honda Civic, she took the 66 bus into work in lower Manhattan every day. One of her clients, and also a target, was the New York financier Alan Patricof, a political donor to Bill Clinton, and a friend of Hillary's who in 2008 had been appointed national finance chairman of her presidential campaign.

Cynthia reported her introduction to Patricof with whom she had held 'several work-related meetings' and had been assigned his account, on which she would work for three years. This elicited an enthusiastic response from Moscow, which confirmed Patricof:

> is checked in C's database – he is clean. Of course he is very interesting 'target'. Try to build up little by little relations with him moving beyond just [work] framework. Maybe he can provide [Murphy] with remarks re US foreign policy, 'rumors' about White House internal 'kitchen', invite her to venues (to [major political party HQ in NYC, for instance) ... etc. In short, consider carefully all options in regard to Patricof.[4]

The FBI surveillance on the Murphys fell largely to Maria L. Ricci and later Derek Pieper. She had studied English at Columbia and then worked as a lawyer before joining the Bureau in 2001. Her very first assignment had been GHOST STORIES. Pieper was a graduate of Boston University's Law school who joined the FBI in 2004 after working for the US Attorney in New York and then the city's anti-corruption unit, the New York Department of Investigation. Both would remain with the operation, concentrating on the Murphys, until their arrest.

On 23 September 2004 the FBI recorded a conversation between the Murphys in which Cynthia told Richard that his documents would not bear the scrutiny required for him to apply for a government job. Accordingly, he should cultivate sources who did enjoy access to targets such as the White House.

As for the Murphys' principal tasks, it seems that an initial objective had been 'direct penetration' of US government institutions, but apparently their documentation was unlikely to withstand much scrutiny in the post-9/11 era, as was emphasized to Cynthia:

> C reminds you that placing a job in Government (direct penetration into main object of interest) is not an option because of vulnerability of your vital records' docs.[5]

Instead, Moscow urged Cynthia to adopt a strategy of indirect penetration by talent spotting, with a view to cultivating students applying to join the CIA. Accordingly, she was directed to

Strengthen … ties w. classmates on daily basis incl. professors who can help in job search and who will have (or already have) access to secret info

and to

report to C[enter] on their detailed personal data and character traits w. preliminary conclusions about their potential (vulnerability) to be recruited by Service.[6]

In accordance with her instructions, Cynthia supplied Moscow with lists of potential candidates for recruitment who required a check on the SVR's database. On one occasion she was directed to drop one contact as the person concerned was already working for another Soviet bloc

foreign spy net[work] … avoid deepening contact with them for sec[urity] reasons.

On 3 October 2006 the FBI covertly opened Murphy's safe deposit box, which was found to contain a forged birth certificate falsely identifying Murphy as having been born in Philadelphia.

Some of the FBI personnel deployed on GHOST STORIES remained with their targets for the full ten years. Ricci came to know the couple well, albeit from a distance, although she was very familiar with the inside of their home, which she had entered surreptitiously on five different occasions, and was acquainted with the code to the keypad of their automatic garage opener.

In 2009 Murphy flew to Rome, where he received an Irish passport that he used to travel to Moscow. There he and Cynthia were instructed by the SVR to collect information relating to a new Strategic Arms Limitation Treaty, Afghanistan, and Iran's nuclear programme. Four American government officials were identified by name as targets, and emphasis was placed on issues that would arise during President Obama's summit scheduled for July. Evidently Moscow

needs intels (related to this [sic] topics) which should reflect approaches and ideas of [Russia] policy team members' [XXXXXXXXXX] Try to outline their views and most important

Obama's goals which he expects to achieve during summit in July and how does his team plan to do it (arguments, provisions, means of persuasion to 'lure' [Russia] into co-operation in US interests).[7]

Moscow's area of intelligence requirements was not restricted to political reporting, and in the autumn of 2009 Cynthia mentioned that she had access to information about the gold market. The Centre responded with enthusiasm, indicating that her material had been circulated to the appropriate ministries:

Info: on gold – v. usefull [sic], it was sent directly (after due adaptation) to Min[.] of Fin[ance], Min[.] of ec[onomic] development.[8]

In April 2009 Murphy exchanged messages with Moscow about a rendezvous with a Line N support officer when he would receive $300,000, of which he should keep half, and pass on the remainder to another illegal. He was also to relay a memory stick to MIKE. The brush contact was to take place at a weekend at the North White Plains train station, which was described as deserted and free of video cameras.

C [Center] plans to conduct a flash meeting w. A to pass him $300K from our experienced field station rep (R). Half of it is for you. Another half is to be passed to young colleague (known to you) in fall '09 – winter '10 …
    Place: North White Plains train station (Harlem Line), quiet and deserted on weekends. No surveillance cameras. R – male in early 30s, dark brown hair …
    Scheme of flash meeting: … A and R meet in lower part of the stair case, in a dead zone. R hands over and A gets pack w. money (A's BN [Barnes and Noble} bag stays in your hands, A hides pack w. money into his tote).[9]

Among other things, the group known to the FBI as the New Jersey Conspirators was told that Murphy could definitively recognize 'Mike' by having the following exchange with 'Mike':

'Excuse me, did we meet in Bangkok in April last year?

> Reply: 'I don't know about April, but I was in Thailand in May of that year.'[10]

Sure enough, on 6 June 2009 the FBI watched Murphy at the White Plains train station encounter the SVR illegal support officer designated MIKE, accredited to the UN Mission, and be handed cash and a memory stick. After the meeting Murphy received a message from Moscow confirming that no hostile surveillance had been detected in the vicinity.

> Flash meeting: well done. A good job. Well done. R. and our tech people in NY didn't notice anything suspicious.[11]

This encounter was considered a breakthrough by the FBI because, for the first time, Murphy could be positively linked to a Russian government official, thereby overcoming the 'probable cause' legal hurdle required for an indictment. Furthermore, by following the money, MIKE's cash would contaminate another spy, Michael Zottoli.

On 26 September 2009 Murphy received a message from Moscow containing instructions on where and when to rendezvous with Zottoli in Brooklyn and provided their recognition phrases. He then met Zottoli at the designated street corner in Brooklyn and the two men walked to nearby Fort Greene Park, where they sat together on a bench for about ninety minutes, during which Murphy gave his companion a small package. Two days later, on 28 September 2009, Murphy sent a signal to Moscow confirming the successful payment to Zottoli.

On 18 October 2009 Murphy received a message from Moscow directing him to collect information about international affairs vital to Russia, detailing American attitudes and any comments made by American political and economic commentators, preferably those not already in the public domain but known to the State Department, government and influential think tanks, and

> to send more info on current international affairs vital for R, highlighting US approach and providing us w. comments made by local expert (political, economic) scientist's community. Try to single out tidbits unknown publicly but revealed in private by sources close to State department, Government, major think tanks.

When Murphy queried these instructions, he was reminded:

> You were sent to the USA for long-term service trip. Your education, bank accounts, car, house, etc. – all these serve one goal: Fulfill your main mission, i.e., to search and develop in policy making circles in US and send intels [intelligence reports] to C [Center].[12]

In anticipation of Murphy's planned visit to Moscow, the Centre transmitted a series of messages relating to his travel:

> [W]e expect A to arrive to C in February ...
>
> [L]et us know A's itinerary: date and time of docs exchange (including reserve ones) en route to and from C; duration of his stay in C. (for business issues we need 2–3 days). A's route (old one): USA–Europe (Rome) on US passport; exchange of docs – in Rome. Than [sic] Rome–Milan by train. In Milan A. takes flight SU-286 (combined Aeroflot-Alitalia flight). We'll provide A w[ith] two-way e-ticket Milan-Moscow-Milan,
>
> We confirm that A's docs'll be in Rome by Jan.23, so A may plan F[lash] M[eeting] with C's repr[esentative] for documents exchange any day after that time.
>
> Meeting place in Rome (same) – MP 'Stan' (at the show-window of the shop 'Libreria', address Via Illiria, 14 tinder address pointer of the house, subway Station San Giovanni)[.]
>
> Transit passport (old one) – Ireland ...
> • Name Doherty Eunan Gerard;
> • d.o.b ...
> • nationality irish;
> • d. of issue 30 Jul. 01, exp. date 30 Jul. 2011;
> • place of issue Dublin;
> • ... purpose of the visit – business-trip. Legend – interpreter or IT specialist (at A's [sic] discretion) 'by invitation' of [Russian Executive] ... (the print-out copy of invitation will be in the envelope w[ith] transit docs).[13]

When the FBI checked on the passport details it was discovered that they matched a part-time fireman in County Donegal who lived in Ballyloskey,

Cardonagh, and confirmed that he had once visited Moscow on a three-week holiday with his wife and three children in 2005. In anticipation of his trip he had mailed his passport to the Russian embassy in Dublin to acquire a visa.

In a message dated 28 January 2010, Moscow Centre told Murphy that Centre would 'buy [an] e-ticket (using [Murphy's] Ir[ish] passport data),' and that he could access a copy of documents related to the ticket in the drafts folder of a particular email address if necessary. The SVR also explained that the discussions at Moscow Center would involve the 'usual stuff,' including 'intel[ligence]'.

Soon afterwards Moscow also instructed Murphy to make a cash purchase of an ASUS EEE PC 1005HA-P laptop, and to bring it to Moscow later in the year, having destroyed the receipt. He was then ordered to fly to Rome, where he would receive a false Irish 'transit' passport in the name of Eunan Gerard Doherty, and take the train to Milan for a flight to Moscow, posing as an interpreter for an information technology meeting. He was to be given the passport at a rendezvous:

> Password (C's rep [representative]) – 'Excuse me, could we have met in Malta in 1999' (key words: Malta, 1999).
> A's rep[ly] – 'Yes indeed, I was in La Valetta, but in 2000' (key words: La Valetta, 2000).
> A's recognition sign: *Time* magazine in A's hands (title to be seen from outside).
> Sign of danger: '*Time* magazine in A's left hand (title to be seen from outside).[14]

On 19 January 2010 Lydia reported to Moscow that she was contemplating a post with a firm of lobbyists that would give her access to American and foreign government officials, but she expressed concern that this could lead to an extended screening check on her background. Two days later, the SVR replied that the section responsible for fabricating documents had expressed full confidence, noting that such checks did not 'dig too deep'.

> C[entre] is interested in N's getting this position which would expose her to prospective contacts and potential sources in the US government. Keep us informed of developments.[15]

On 9 February 2010 Murphy used an alias, David Hiller, to purchase an ASUS EEE PC 1005HA-P laptop from Adorama Electronics on 18th Street. A fortnight later, on 21 February he flew on Continental Airlines from Newark to Rome, returning on 3 March 2010. A covert search of his luggage at Newark Airport revealed that his laptop had been switched for an identical model, but with a different serial number.

Murphy and Zottoli were then observed on 7 March 2010 as they met at a payphone on the corner of Vanderbilt and DeKalb Avenues in Brooklyn, and then strolled to Tillie's, a nearby coffee shop, where they shared a table for almost two hours. Parts of their conversation were overheard, and the men discussed problems that had been experienced in Seattle when using their laptops to communicate with Moscow. 'This should help.' Murphy said. 'If this doesn't work we can meet again in six months,' and also said, 'They don't understand what we go through over here.' The conversation was overheard by Maria Ricci, who, coincidentally, had chosen to sit in Tillie's and watch out for Murphy's arrival in the street. To her astonishment, Murphy and Zottoli took shelter from the cold in the same café, and the FBI officer took the opportunity to video the encounter.

Two days later, on 9 March 2010, Murphy sent a message to Moscow confirming that he had given 'M' the laptop, two flash drives, and $9,000 in cash. He also reported that Zottoli had complained about 'hanging and freezing before completion of a normal program run' and that his wife Patricia's travel documents would no longer allow her to leave the United States on her current papers. A recent change in the country's entry requirements had created a problem that needed Moscow's attention.

In 2009 the FBI monitored Cynthia's communications when she complained to Moscow about her proposal to put the $400,000 house in New Jersey their name:

> We are under the impression that C. views our ownership of the house as a deviation from the original purpose of our mission here. We'd like to assure you that we do remember what it is. From our perspective, purchase of the house was solely a natural progression of our prolonged stay here. It was a convenient way to solve the housing issue, plus to 'do as the Romans do' in a society that values home ownership. [W]e didn't forget that the house was bought under fictitious names.[16]

In reply, the Centre identified her mission as the cultivation of people with links to policy-makers.

On 31 March 2002 the FBI watched Murphy meet Metsos in a restaurant in Sunnyside, New York, where Murphy complained about his frustrations, Metsos was heard to reply 'Well, I'm so happy I'm not your handler.' He was then seen to pass a bag of money to Murphy, saying 'there's forty [corrupt] black bag.' The FBI interpreted this encounter as Metsos the paymaster delivering $40,000 to Murphy.

Just over two years later, on 16 May 2004 the FBI watched as Murphy met Metsos again, in the same restaurant, where he was given an orange bag containing money.

On 30 May 2004 the FBI intercepted a telephone conversation between Murphy and Zottoli at which they agreed to meet on 19 June at 3pm. Mikhail Kutzik, alias Michael Zottoli, was a forty-three-year-old SVR officer who was married in June 2005 to Patricia Mills. He had arrived in Chicago from Canada on 15 June 1995 and worked from October 2007 to March 2009 at Premier Global Services, a telecommunications firm in Bellevue. During that period the couple lived in a Bellmont Court apartment on Capitol Hill with their two young sons, Kenny and a younger child. A surreptitious search of their home made by the FBI on 17 February 2006 went undetected.

Zottoli gained a bachelor's degree in business administration from the University of Washington Bothell in 2006 and held a black belt in karate. He had moved from Seattle, where he had driven a blue BMW and worked for an investment bank, to the River House apartments in Arlington, northern Virginia, in 2009. When asked about his background, Zottoli claimed to have been born in Yonkers, New York, but had been brought up in Taiwan where his father had been in the construction business. Mills would say that she was a Canadian, but her Social Security number had been allocated to someone else.

Concerns about the weakness of Mills' alias documentation was reported to Moscow on 9 March 2010 following a tightening of the regulations by the new Department of Homeland Security, the new agency created in the aftermath of the 9/11 attack:

> Neither can his wife leave the US because whatever papers she has now are no longer sufficient for travel, because as of this year the doc requirements for entry from the US to wherever she needs to go have changed. M needs your advice on the situation and his options.[17]

The FBI learned that the real Zottoli had been born in Yonkers, but had died eighteen months later and is buried in Fairfield, Connecticut.

Zottoli's wife was Natalia Pereverzeva, alias Patricia Mills, who arrived in the US in 2003, and had moved from their high-rise apartment in Seattle to northern Virginia with their two sons, aged one, and Kenny, aged three. While living in Chicago, she had conducted an affair with Metsos.

While Zottoli was under observation on 17 May 2004, he was seen to empty a drop already compromised by Metsos. A month later, on 19 June 2004 Zottoli and his wife, who had flown in from Seattle-Tacoma airport, went to New York's Central Park. Although Murphy was there too, they were not seen to make contact with each other. Zottoli then returned to his hotel and telephoned Murphy. During a brief conversation they agreed to hold another meeting the next day. Accordingly, at 4pm the following afternoon Zottoli went to the subway entrance at Columbus Circle and was seen to meet Murphy, who wore a backpack, and accompany him into Central Park, where he handed Zottoli a red museum paper bag containing cash. Four days later, on 24 June, Zottoli and Mills flew back to Seattle from Newark.

On 17 April 2005 the FBI watched Metsos meet Richard Murphy at a restaurant in Sunnyside, New York, and pass him an ATM card and a PIN number so he could withdraw cash.

On 5 June 2006 Zottoli and Mills flew from Seattle to New York and collected a package concealed at a remote site at Wurtsboro, New York. Four days later, on 9 June, Zottoli was filmed in his hotel room in Washington, DC, as he removed and hid a full money belt. He later divided the money into several wallets.

These events, often separated by many months, were caught on camera by the FBI and served to establish a firm link between Metsos and his four subordinates, Zottoli, Mills and the Murphys. All five knew each other, but had the means to communicate with Moscow independently of one another.

During the ten years of GHOST STORIES' duration, the FBI monitored four types of communication with 'C', the abbreviation for 'the Centre', as the SVR's headquarters were known. Firstly, there was an encrypted internet channel; then there was a short-range laptop-to-laptop link and, for emergencies only, a one-way shortwave broadcast from Moscow. This latter, slightly antiquated technique, proved unsatisfactory in Chicago, because of poor reception conditions, forcing the agents to relocate to the coast where the atmospherics were more favourable. Finally, some of the spy ring routinely received instructions over the internet using steganography, a method of concealing messages in an ostensibly innocent website page.

The FBI learned about the steganography technique from computer diskettes copied during the covert searches conducted in 2005 and 2006 on the three homes in Boston, Seattle and Hoboken. The diskettes had been encrypted, but FBI technicians gained access to the stored data, and to a hundred deleted text messages that had been uploaded and downloaded to and from ostensibly innocent websites that were actually controlled by the SVR.

The SVR spies Anna Chapman and Mikhail Semenko were equipped with the latest generation covert communications, which transmitted and received messages over short distances over the ad-hoc wireless systems installed in their laptops. These encrypted transmissions, exchanged anonymously over a range of only a hundred feet, were almost impossible to intercept and were also supplied to Richard Murphy and Michael Zottoli in March 2010.

According to the FBI, some of the network received instructions through one-way voice messages broadcast from the notorious 'numbers stations', which constantly transmit spoken, apparently random numbers on a short-wave frequency. This technique has the advantage of being impossible to decrypt unless an interceptor knows the precise time a particular text is to be sent, and is in possession of the encryption key. Significantly, the SVR spy Donald Heathfield was found to have a shortwave radio in his home, and Juan Lazaro possessed a Realistic DX-440 receiver.

Monitoring of current signals and the recovery of past messages was a priority for the FBI as these texts betrayed the tasks assigned to individual agents. Some of their external targets for cultivation and recruitment were assigned cryptonyms such as PARROT, CAT and FARMER, as happened with a message dated 3 December 2004 when Heathfield confirmed the cultivation of an academic contact:

> During the seminar at [deleted] Dv made contacts w. [deleted] working for [deleted] in [geographical location of facility, name omitted]. He works on issues of strategic planning related to nuclear weapon development. Dv. had conversations with him about research programs on small yield high penetration nuclear warheads recently authorised by US Congress (nuclear 'bunker-buster' warheads).

Agree with your proposal to use FARMER to start building network of students in DC. Your relationship with PARROT looks very promising as a valid source of info from US power circles. To start working on him professionally we need all available details on his background, current position, habits, contacts, opportunities, etc ...[18]

On 23 September 2005 Heathfield reported having 'established contact' with a person described as a former high-ranking senior national security official, and a message in 2007 from Moscow indicated that Heathfield had suggested at least six other targets:

Got your note ... and signal ... No info in our files about E.F., BT, DK, RR ... Agree with your proposal to use FARMER to start building network of students in DC. Your relationship with PARROT looks very promising as a valid source of info from US power circles. To start working on him professionally we need all available details on his background, current position, habits, contacts, opportunities, etc. Plus, you should observe our security rules and recommendations in working with contacts. ... Agree with you [sic] proposal to keep relations with CAT but watch him.[19]

CAT was later identified as Professor Leon Feurth, a former State Department diplomat who had served in Europe and worked for the Bureau of Intelligence and Research. He had then worked on the staff of the House Intelligence Committee, and in 1985 was appointed national security adviser to Senator Al Gore. After the 2000 election Feurth joined the Elliott School of International Affairs at George Washington University, but retained his links with the Democratic Party. According to the FBI's analysis, Feurth was judged to be an influential figure and therefore a target for cultivation.

Of greatest interest was Directorate S's attempt to exploit modern technology by loading the agents' laptops protected with a twenty-seven character password. While access to the portal was gained simply by typing ALT + CTRL + E, the algorithm itself was exceptionally complex. However, it was the private wi-fi system, which had the advantage of enabling individual agents to exchange messages over very short range with handlers out of eyesight, that was employed by Chapman.

On 16 May 2004 the FBI watched Metsos attend a rendezvous at Forest Hills train station in Queens with an SVR Line N officer, who handed him an orange bag of money that he then passed to Richard Murphy at a restaurant in Sunnyside, New York. The SVR officer was identified as a diplomat accredited as a second secretary at the Russian Permanent Mission to the United Nations. A few hours later, Metsos went to the restaurant in Sunnyside, where he was recorded handling his 'cut' to Murphy, remarking that 'you will meet this guy, tell him Uncle Paul loves him … he will know … It is wonderful to be Santa Claus in May.'[20]

The following day Metsos cached a large sum of money at a remote location in the vicinity of Wurtsboro, New York, where Michael Zottoli would retrieve it two years later on 5 June 2006. The site was located by FBI special agents, who had fitted a GPS tracking device to his car, and a package wrapped in duct tape was found at a depth of 5 inches, indicated by a partially buried beer bottle. Having photographed the contents, the package was reburied but monitored remotely by a video camera concealed on a power transformer.

In the meantime, a fortnight after Murphy received the orange bag of money from Metsos, Murphy met Zottoli in Manhattan and passed the money on to him.

Five years later, in June 2010, the very same SVR officer would be seen communicating with a young man in Washington, DC. The contact turned out to be twenty-eight year-old Michael ('Misha') Semenko, who worked as a travel agent for the Travel All Russia travel agency in Arlington, where he sold customised tours of Russia. When, in the autumn of 2009, the agency moved to Clarendon, Virginia, he went too, having returned briefly to Russia, ostensibly to replace his student visa with a work visa. Increasingly desperate for a visa, Semenko was forced to approach the US Army and join up, but at the last moment found an acquaintance who was prepared to sponsor his visa so he could work in the travel industry.

He had first come to the United States in the autumn of 2005 to attend Seton Hall University in New Jersey for work on his master's degree in diplomacy and international relations as well as Asian studies. He also spent a year at the Harbin Institute of Technology. Previously, he had studied Chinese at the Amur State University in Blagoveshchensk, and had spent almost two years in China teaching English. He graduated from Seton Hall in 2008, having worked as an intern for the World Affairs Council in Washington,

DC and been a staffer with the Conference Board in New York City. He was fluent in English, Mandarin, Russian and Spanish, and had owned a Mercedes S500 sports car.

He lived alone in the Rahill Apartments, Arlington, where he had sub-let number 33 to an acquaintance, Michael Gaynor, until 1 July, and had moved in with a friend nearby temporarily. He had found the apartment through a friend, Mark Grueter, whom he had met when the latter had spent a year in 2001 as a Peace Corps volunteer working as the adviser of a Model United Nations Club at Amur State University. He made one final visit to Russia in April 2010.

On 27 May Semenko attended a New America Foundation debate about American and Chinese approaches to capitalism and introduced himself to the chairman, Steve Clemons, a senior fellow at the influential think tank. This was one of many similar events Semenko attended, and he made formal applications to join the Carnegie Endowment for International Peace as well as Clemons' New America Foundation. On 9 June he sat in the audience of the World Affairs Council to listen to James S. Robbins, the *USA Today* columnist who had served in the George H. Bush administration as a special assistant to the Undersecretary of Defense for Policy in the Office of the Secretary of Defense. Once again, Semenko had produced a business card and asked about job opportunities at the American Foreign Policy Council.

A few days earlier, on 5 June, the FBI had been watching as he carried a bag into a crowded restaurant on Wisconsin Avenue in north-west Washington, DC. Ten minutes later a car with a Russian diplomatic licence plate entered the restaurant's carpark, circled the area, and parked. The driver was identified as the same SVR illegal support officer who had been spotted on 16 May 2004 at Forest Hills station, New York, attending a brush pass rendezvous with Metsos. Moments later the FBI detected an encrypted wi-fi channel that operated for twenty minutes. After the car had driven away, Semenko emerged from the restaurant.

Thus, according to the evidence made public by the FBI, the surveillance on Metsos had initiated after he had been contaminated by his contact with Richard Murphy back in February 2001. Metsos had then unwittingly led the FBI to Mills and Zottoli, and to his SVR support officer in New York, who inadvertently compromised Semenko. This was classic counter-espionage tradecraft, but required really exceptional patience. It also served to high-light the efficacy of accurately identifying Directorate S personnel buried deep in diplomatic cover.

***

The fourth married couple to be identified as members of the network were Donald Heathfield and Trace Foley. He was really Andrey Bezrikov, aged forty-nine, who lived at 35B Trowbridge Street, Cambridge, Massachusetts, and was married to Tracey Lee Ann Foley, really Elena Vavilova. A surrep-titious search of their home made on 29 July 2006 by an FBI unit headed by Peter Strzok, went undetected.

Heathfield had graduated from Harvard's John F. Kennedy School of Government in 2000 and worked as a sales consultant for Global Partners Inc., a Cambridge-based international management consulting firm, and then for his own venture, Future Map Strategic Advisory Services, regularly attending business conferences in the United States, London and Oxford. His own consultancy business had a website, www.myfuturemap.com, and he promoted his own software program, which claimed to assist corporate decision-making. He also contributed a chapter to a book on scenario plan-ning, *Scenarios for Success: Turning Insights into Action*, edited by Bill Sharpe and Kees van der Heijden, and published in 2007. This was essentially a nineteen-page monograph entitled *Building a Comprehensive Strategic Future Management System: A Future Map Approach*, which he had presented at an Oxford University seminar. Heathfield was one of ten contributors, and his non-controversial text was intended to establish his credentials in his particular, slightly esoteric field.

In January 2001 The FBI's Peter Strzok searched his bank deposit box and found photographs of Tracey taken when she was in her twenties. The film manufacturer was Tacma, a Soviet company.

In one of his messages to Moscow, Heathfield accounted for his expenditure:

> Got from Ctr. 64500 dollars, income 13940, interest 76. Expenses: rent 8500, utilities 142, tel. 160, car lease 2180, insurance 432, gas 820, education 3600, payments in Fr 1000, medical 139, lawyers fees 700, meals and gifts 1230, mailboxes, computer supplies 460, business (cover) 4900, trip to the meeting 1125.[21]

The deposit box also contained an ingenious trap, an envelope glued lightly to the interior, a classic telltale that would indicate any unauthorised disturbance.

The real Donald Heathfield's father, Howard William Heathfield, had died in 2005 aged seventy, and his newspaper obituary published on 25 June noted that his son had predeceased him in 1963. Actually, Bezrikov was from Krasnoyarsk in Siberia and had attended Tomsk University between 1978 and 1983, where he had met Elena, and then had transferred to a university in Moscow. He was fluent in French and English, but spoke both with a detectable foreign accent.[22]

In Canada, Heathfield had studied economics at York University in Toronto, starting in 1992, and then moved to Harvard, where he gained a master's degree in public administration at the Kennedy School of Government. He had also attended a summer course at the London School of Economics. In 1995 the family moved to Paris, where Don took an MBA at the École des Ponts. His wife Elena shared his home in Trowbridge Street and worked as a local realtor, first for Channing Real Estate, and then for Redfin. She travelled on a false British passport and had two sons by Donald: Tim, a twenty-year-old student at George Washington University in Washington, DC, born in Toronto, who had been an intern in China in 2008, and Alex, aged sixteen. However, according to the FBI surveillance teams, the marriage was a sham and both partners conducted affairs with each other's knowledge and consent.

On her real estate website Elena claimed to be a native of Montreal who had worked in human resources in Toronto before opening her own travel agency in Cambridge that specialised in organising groups visiting the French wine regions. She listed her interests as her family, gourmet food, ballet and travel in Europe and Asia. In reality she had been brought up in Tomsk and had attended a prestigious German-language high school. She had also toured Japan with a group of other Soviet students. On 3 October 2004 FBI microphones in their home had recorded an incriminating conversation held between Foley and Heathfield in which they had discussed covert communications with Moscow:

'Can we attach to files containing messages, or not? Let's say four pictures ...'

In early 2010, in anticipation of her visit to Moscow scheduled for March, Foley received her elaborate travel instructions from Moscow Centre:

> Itinerary to M [Moscow] for D: Paris – Wien (by train) Mar 18 in Wien exch[ange] docs for British pass[port] – [Moscow] (Mar 19, flight OS 6010. Very important: Sign your passport on page 32. Train yourself to be able to reproduce your signature when it's necessary. 2. Pls be aware that you just visited Russia (see stamps on page 14 – entry – Mar 16 departure Mar 17). If asked, we suggest you use the following story: You flew to Moscow on Mar 16 from London for example flight SU 211 to participate in business talks (your business is international consultancy seminars – pls, copy sample of your husband) on invitation by Russian Chamber of Commerce ... In the passport you'll get a memo with recommendation. Pls. destroy the memo after reading. Be well.[23]

As regards the actual tasks assigned to Heathfield and Foley, a message dated April 2006 listed them as: the use of the internet by terrorists; US policy in Central Asia; problems with US military policy and 'western assessments of [Russian] foreign policy'. In May 2006 the pair responded to Moscow by submitting reports on such topics as 'turnover at the head of the CIA' and the 2008 US presidential election, the information having been 'received in private conversation with [redacted], former legislative counsel for US Congress, specialist in [redacted], member of faculty in economics of [redacted]. Has contacts within Congress and policymakers of Washington.'[23]

* * *

The Heathfield sons, Tim, born in June 1990, and his younger brother Alex, born in Toronto in June 1994, asserted they had been unaware of their parents' true Russian nationality, later tried to appeal their loss of Canadian citizenship, and in 2014 filed an affidavit describing the family's interest in international travel. However, the Canadian Security Intelligence Service countered that Timothy at least had been indoctrinated into the SVR when his parents revealed to him their true allegiance, a conversation in their Boston home captured on tape by the FBI. After a protracted legal battle Alexander won the right in December 2019 to his Canadian passport.[24]

* * *

Apart from Anna Chapman, the last member of the GHOST STORIES network to be identified was Alexei V. Karetnikov, a twenty-three-year-old living in Redmond, Seattle, who had worked for Microsoft for nine months as a software tester. He had entered the United States under his own name in the summer of 2008 to work as an intern for Microsoft. He then returned to Russia for a year, but took up a full-time job with Microsoft in October 2009. According to his Facebook social media profile, he had attended Physics and Mathematics Lyceum 30 High School in St Petersburg until 2004, had graduated from St Petersburg State Polytechnic University, and also had undertaken some code writing for NeoBIT, a software company based in Bucharest. Following his arrest on 28 June, Microsoft conducted an internal review to assess any damage he had done, but could find none. Having admitted to being in the United States illegally, he was deported by order of an immigration judge on 12 July.

* * *

The final component of the Directorate S espionage offensive aimed at the United States began in London in 2001 with the arrival of Vasili Kushchenko's eldest daughter, Anya. Her visit was to give her the opportunity to embrace a truly western lifestyle, and in September she was taken by her then English boyfriend, Charlie Hutchison, to a rave party in the city's Docklands. A trainee lawyer, Hutchinson enjoyed a fling with Anna before Alex Chapman introduced himself. At the time Anna was studying economics at the People's Friendship University of Moscow, where she had a boyfriend, Vyacheslav Serkov, but she was making regular visits to London and Chapman flew to Russia to see her. Within five months, in March 2002, they would be married, starting a process through which she would acquire legitimately a British passport in her married name. Their delayed honeymoon, two weeks in Egypt and a fortnight in Zimbabwe, was paid for by her father.

Alex Chapman had been educated at Bradfield College in Berkshire, a leading public school, but had dropped out aged sixteen and found work in a recording studio. Together the married couple moved into a rented flat in Stoke Newington, a socially deprived area of north London, and she began a series of low-paid jobs, at NetJets in Battersea, which leased and sold aircraft into the Russian émigré community, and at the small business section of the Barclays Bank branch in Ealing. It was when she joined a Mayfair hedge fund, Navigator Asset Management, registered in Wigmore Street, that she started to socialise with a group of wealthy investors. The business was headed by a Maltese financial adviser, Nicholas Camilerri, who had met her in Cipriani's, a popular West End restaurant. Her seductive good looks ensured she received plenty of attention and eventually, with her marriage failing, she moved into a small apartment near Marble Arch and advertised for a flatmate. That companion turned out to be Elena Savitskaya, a waitress at the Lanesborough Hotel at Hyde Park Corner.

Chapman's relationship in 2007 with Laurent Tailleur, a French playboy, with whom she lived briefly at his large home in Elm Park Road, Chelsea, having been introduced by Camilerri, was ended by her after a few months but led to her development of a real estate website that she launched in Moscow, advertising property across the Russian Federation.

In retrospect, Chapman's five years in London served to transform the naïve tourist into a confident manipulator who used her men friends as stepping stones up the social ladder to the point where she was familiar with many of the capital's most exclusive nightspots, such as Tramp and Annabel's. Whether this was part of a plan, to ingratiate herself with English society and access people of influence, or whether she was subsequently recruited by her father's SVR colleagues because she made the opportunity happen, remains moot. Certainly she moved from Chapman to Tailleur, at very different ends of the social spectrum, without much apparent effort. The only evidence of her involvement in anything disreputable seems to be her unexplained role in the registration of a charity, Southern Union Limited, at her husband's former address in Gibson Gardens, Stoke Newington. Allegedly Southern Union had been created to assist Zimbabwean expatriates in the transfer of funds to Harare at favourable rates. Reportedly Kushchenko had served at his country's embassy in Nairobi with the rank of vice consul, and had then lived in Zimbabwe.

One of the company's named directors, Steven Sugden, would later complain of identity theft and deny any knowledge of the business, while a Russian-speaking Zimbabwean entrepreneur with the same name was linked to the company. In December 2012 Sugden would be charged in Harare with offences relating to his application for two Zimbabwean passports under false names. The proprietor of the Thorn Tree Lodge, a resort in the Harare suburb of Glen Lorne, Sugden would marry his co-owner, Tarryn Crundall, in Cape Town.

Chapman's arrival in the United States in 2010 was an attempt to expand PropertyFinders Inc., which she ran from her two-bedroom apartment at

20 Exchange Place in downtown Manhattan. Four days before her arrest she purchased the web domain name www.NYCrentals.com from a website broker for $23,500. In reality her hectic social life and self-promotion on the internet was a cover for her apparently new role as an illegal. Her lifestyle included attendance at numerous parties, a visit to The Venetian in Las Vegas in January 2010 with her then boyfriend Bill Staniford, owner of a real estate website, www.PropertyShark, and a fling with Russell Terlecki, another real estate broker and the co-owner of a tequila brand and a sportswear business. Perhaps coincidentally, his business accountants employed Cynthia Murphy.

A former US Marine, Staniford was a graduate of the University of Texas and a Republican Party supporter with political ambitions who had made his fortune trading real estate data. Chapman had introduced herself to him in January 2010 at his office, but they did no property business together. Instead she spent plenty of time at his upper east side apartment. Perhaps also of interest to Chapman was his past military service as a Marine Corps cryptographer stationed in 1992 in Panama and involved in signals intelligence collection against Colombia, Nicaragua and Peru.

Russell Terlecki, who she was also dating, was originally from Hamilton, New Jersey, and joined Sotheby's International Realty in 2010. He lived in Navesink, New Jersey, and commuted across to Manhattan, where he met Chapman.

Meanwhile, Chapman was also seeing Michel Bittan, a sixty-year-old Jewish businessman originally from Casablanca who had lived in France and Israel before emigrating to the United States and making his real estate fortune in New Jersey. He lived in a mansion in Englewood, New Jersey, and also owned two restaurants in Manhattan.

Chapman's fourth and last American lover was John Altorelli, a partner of the Dewey & LeBoeuf law firm, which would collapse in 2012 in a major financial scandal. Altorelli, having separated from his third wife, allowed Chapman to move into his apartment on West 37th Street and hosted parties there to introduce her to his circle of wealthy friends and clients. When he was squiring her around fashionable restaurants in New York his income was estimated to be $3.5 million, with his firm billing his clients some $35 million annually.

All four men, of course, were unaware that, thanks to Poteyev, Chapman had been watched by the FBI from the moment she had landed at Kennedy Airport in 2010. However, that surveillance had not shown Chapman to have had any direct contact with anyone in the SVR, for her covert communications were conducted from public sites anonymously, over an ad-hoc wireless network to a contact nearby also using a laptop. Because of her apparent isolation from any other illegal, and as she was never seen to commit an overt act of espionage, as required by the criminal statutes covering money laundering and failing to register as the agent of a foreign government, the FBI prepared a contingency plan to entrap her if the need arose.

The first time the FBI observed Chapman communicating remotely with her Line N handler was on 20 January, when she sat in the window of the Starbucks coffee shop on East 47th Street and was linked to another computer in the vicinity for twenty minutes. This ingenious, almost untraceable method of exchanging messages in real time would be just one of the channels of communication adopted by the SVR. Originally designed by Microsoft to allow gamers to compete against each other from different rooms in the same house, the SVR had adapted it to the needs of two people establishing a secure, encrypted link without risk of interception. While the FBI possessed the technical means, if within range, to detect the creation of a private wireless local area network, it could not access the covert electronic messages without changing the individual laptop's Media Access Control functions. Accordingly, the SVR had developed a near-perfect method of short-range secure transmitters.

* * *

Another manifestation of the west's exploitation of Poteyev's information was the identification of Sergei Yakovlev, alias Antonio de Jesus Amurett Graf, a skilled illegal, supposedly a businessman based in Madrid, who personified the need for Directorate S to adopt plausible 'legends' for its case officers. Yakovlev travelled on a Portuguese passport issued against a Brazilian birth certificate, and part of his role was to manage an important NATO source, Herman Simm.

Born in May 1947 in the north of Estonia, Simm had joined the police in 1967 and by his country's independence in August 1991 had risen to the rank of colonel, and later would be appointed director-general of the police board. In August 1995 he was transferred to the Ministry of Defence as head of analysis in the defence policy division, and then in 2001 promoted to the ministry's security department, a post he resigned in November 2006 when he continued as a part-time government adviser.

In reality Simm, who married Heete, a senior Soviet police officer, had been a KGB source from his recruitment in 1985 and since independence had been holding up to four secret meetings a year with two successive case officers, later identified as Valeri Zentsov and then Sergei Yakovlev. According to Simm's detailed confession, he had been contacted by Zentsov, a thirty-nine-year-old former KGB colleague code-named VALENTIN, while on holiday in June 1995 in the Tunisian resort of Sousse. Thereafter the recruitment was completed by the SVR *resident* in Tallinn, and Zentsov, who had been born in Berlin, attended a further fifteen times, in ten different countries, and supplied a large quantity of classified material in return for a monthly retainer of $1,300, with occasional bonuses.

Zentsov announced his retirement at a meeting in Helsinki in November 2001, and his replacement as Simm's handler was the bearded Yakovlev, whose first rendezvous took place in the railway station of a Tallinn suburb. This was followed by a series of fourteen meetings conducted outside Estonia. In addition, Simm communicated through a telephone pager registered in Prague, and serviced dead drops with discarded juice cartons containing memory cards and flash drives. When Estonia joined NATO in March 2004 Simm created the National Security Authority within the defence ministry to handle classified documents and issue security clearances, giving him the widest possible access to all types of sensitive NATO and EU reports. As the designated custodian of classified material, and authorised to travel on his diplomatic passport overseas as a courier visiting other NATO and EU countries, Simm enjoyed unrestricted access to thousands of secret documents.

However, while meeting Yakovlev in Stockholm in March 2008 he sensed hostile surveillance, and later claimed to have broken off contact at a final meeting in Riga in June. However, on 16 September he had received an emergency warning from Yakovlev about an illness, a familiar, semi-transparent signal used by Directorate S, but nevertheless an egregious breach of tradecraft. In the call, made directly to Simm's mobile, and recorded by the Kaitsepolitsei (KaPo) Yakovlev claimed to be in Turkey. Three days later Simm was arrested by the KaPo outside his home in Saue, and a search of his summer home in the country revealed a collection of classified documents, a list of dead drops, concealment devices and a one-time cipher pad. Pages bearing coded instructions in Yakovlev's handwriting were examined and found to have the illegal's DNA.

A 141-page NATO damage assessment of the estimated 3,000 documents passed to the SVR concluded with the opinion that as a spy Simm had been the 'most damaging in Alliance history', having sold secrets 'including installation, maintenance, procurement and use of cryptographic systems'. He was also found to have 'compromised a wide range of NATO intelligence reports and analyses'.

At his trial in February 2009 Simm pleaded guilty to charges of treason and was sentenced to twelve and a half years' imprisonment, to be served in solitary confinement at the grim post-Soviet era prison at Tartu, and fined $1.3 million. His guilty plea meant there would be no public disclosure of any evidence that might indicate precisely when, and on what information, the KaPo's Alexander Toots had initiated a mole hunt code-named WHITE KNIGHT. In consideration of his co-operation, Simm's wife, who was strongly suspected to have been his co-conspirator, escaped prosecution. Simm, who admitted that he hoped to be freed in a spy swap, had his application for early release turned down in November 2019.

Obviously, the prime concern of those engaged in the Yakovlev investigation would have been Poteyev's safety, and it is likely that the KaPo was indoctrinated into the case only at a late stage when there was less risk of a leak. One of the cover stories subsequently circulated was that Yakovlev had made an unsuccessful recruitment pitch to a Lithuanian official in southern Europe who had promptly reported the approach, prompting a counter-espionage investigation.

Created in 1991, the KaPo had been handicapped from the outset by employing staff contaminated by past links to the Soviet KGB or Estonian KGB. Some had opted to move to Russia, but others had stayed in the hope of concealing their pasts. For example, Vladimir Veitman had been a KaPo technical officer of sixteen years' experience with the Estonian KGB, and after his arrest in August 2013 he acknowledged having been recruited in 2002 for the SVR by a former colleague, Nikolai Yermakov. In passing, Yermakov had casually mentioned to Veitman that his direct superior in the SVR was their old friend, Valeri Zentsov. Veitman, whose daughter was married to an American and lives in the United States, would be sentenced to fifteen years' imprisonment. Another of Veitman's KaPo colleagues, also recruited by Yermakov, was a technician, Uno Puusepp, who had joined the organization in November 1991 and had retired, undetected, in April 2011, moving to Moscow in 2017. The son of a KGB officer, Puusepp had been recruited in 1996 and later boasted that he had tipped off the FSB to several KaPo operations and assets, among them the former FSB officer Valeri Ojamae, and Igor Vyalkov, a former airport border guard at Sheremetyevo-2 who was arrested in September 2002. In December 2004 Colonel Vyalkov was convicted of having spied for Estonia since 2001 and was sentenced to ten years' imprisonment.

In celebrating Puusepp's long-term penetration of the KaPo, the FSB released a list in December 2014 of officers who, it was claimed, had remained in Estonia after independence to assist Russia. They were Valeri Titov, Aleksandr Repkin, Tatyana Valtbach, Alexei Posledov and Vladislav Preitlov. All had been named in 1991 as among thirteen former KGB staff considered unsuitable for employment, but they had been hired anyway.

In February 2012 further evidence of hostile penetration of KaPo emerged with the arrest at Tallinn airport of Aleksei and Viktoria Dressen, both Estonians of Russian heritage, as she tried to catch a flight to Moscow while carrying classified material on a memory stick. Born in 1968 in Riga, Dressen was convicted of spying for the FSB in July 2012 and sentenced to sixteen years' imprisonment, and his wife received six years, to be followed by five years' probation. He had joined the police in 1991 in Viljandi and in 1993 had transferred to the KaPo. Despite some minor disciplinary issues, Dressen had been promoted and in 2007 was appointed to head the political extremism section. At the trial the prosecution alleged that Dressen had been approached to spy for the FSB in 1998, but had only agreed to do so in 2001, and that his wife had acted as his courier. However, the Russian Interfax news agency would later report that he had been an FSB asset for twenty years. His handler was identified as Evgenni Tyashikun, a senior FSB officer later promoted to be the organization's deputy head in the Moscow oblast.

Dressen had come under suspicion in 2007 when he had been placed under surveillance, and coincidentally he had suffered a demotion when he had performed poorly during the April rioting in Tallinn over the controversial relocation of a Soviet war memorial. This incident had provided the KaPo with a convenient pretext to limit Dressen's access, and thereby mitigate the damage he was suspected of inflicting.

In September 2015, having been stripped of their Estonian citizenship, the Dressens were exchanged at the Kunichina Gora frontier post on the Piusa river bridge for Eston Kohver, a forty-three-year-old KaPo officer who had been lured to the border area and then abducted at gunpoint by the

FSB in September 2014. Kohver, who had joined KaPo in 2010, had been investigating cross-border cigarette smuggling and was intending to meet a potential informant when he was ambushed and seized in a forest close to the village of Miikse. Disarmed of his Taurus service pistol by a group of FSB men equipped with stun grenades and radio jammers, Kohver was dragged onto Russian territory and then incarcerated at Lefortovo in Moscow where, in August 2015, he was sentenced to fifteen years' imprisonment on a bogus charge of espionage.

The scale of KaPo's penetration problem became evident following the promulgation of a law in 1995 that offered immunity and anonymity for KaPo personnel willing to incriminate themselves and declare their previous KGB connections. A major purge followed, together with the establishment of new recruits who had undergone training in the west. This cadre of reliable professionals would be responsible for ferreting out several Russian moles run by former KGB Estonians working for the FSB or SVR. These relatively low-level spies did not merit support by illegals, given the porous nature of the Russian frontier and the lack of visa requirements for ethnic Russians living in the Baltic states. Their tasks were also quite limited, usually related to reporting on NATO activities at the Amari, Emetsa and Vovu airfields, and the military exercise area at Párnu. In contrast, Simm had been handled by a high-value illegal for eight years.

While languishing in prison Simm complained that he had been abandoned by the SVR, and he must have been disappointed when the Dressens were freed separately in a very obviously choreographed abduction designed very specifically to give Moscow leverage in negotiating the release of a convicted criminal. Upon his arrival in Moscow the jubilant Dressen was welcomed by Viktoria and their son Daniel, who had already emigrated from Estonia when she was freed.

In the same month that Simm was sentenced, February 2009, another spy was arrested, this time in Poland. The GRU illegal, Tadeusz Juchniewicz, was the forty-one-year-old proprietor of a hunting rifle accessory shop who had been living in the country for at least a decade. A search of his home had revealed a large amount of sophisticated communications equipment, which suggested direct radio contact with Moscow. He had been kept under surveillance by the Polish security service (ABW) for six months, and then detained in secret until he was put on trial in Warsaw in October 2010, where he was convicted and sentenced to three years' imprisonment and a fine of

$13,000. According to the prosecution, Juchniewicz had used his business to joining hunting clubs where he could cultivate senior Polish military personnel. He was paroled from prison in Wloclawek in November 2011.

Any impartial review of the events of 2008 suggests that the rate of attrition suffered by Moscow during the early months of the year was not coincidental, and more likely a direct consequence of western agencies seeking to exploit the advantages offered by Poteyev and Shcherbakov. Herman Simm, it will be recalled, thought he detected hostile surveillance in March 2008, when Aleksei Dressen was already under suspicion. Juchniewicz had come under observation from August 2008, and the GRU chief, General Valentin Korabelnikov, was dismissed without explanation at the end of April 2009, at the age of sixty-three, after twelve years in his post. He was replaced by his deputy, General Alexander Shlyakthurov. One possible explanation for this chronology may be an inconclusive mole hunt, and certainly one that allowed Shcherbakov and Poteyev to survive undetected until June 2010.

During this critical period there were several other important, relevant incidents, one of which occurred in the Czech Republic, a NATO member since March 1999. In September 2009 a prison psychologist, Robert Razhardzho, fled to Russia as his relationship with another psychologist, a senior Czech army officer, Major Vladimira Odehnalova, came under investigation by the BIS security apparatus. With a background of Russian mother and an Indonesian father, Razhardzho had settled in the country in 1992 and was alleged to have been recruited by the GRU in 2003 while on vacation in Crete.

Thirty-nine-year-old Major Odehnalova's role as aide to three senior officers: General Frantisek Hrabal, the head of the president's military office; Josef Sedlak, the Czech representative at NATO headquarters at Mons; and the deputy army chief of staff and former director of military intelligence, General Josef Proks, caused all three to resign when the scandal became public.

On the evening of Razhardzho's disappearance he had taken his wife and two children to a pizza restaurant in Prague before driving to a former Red Army airbase, whence he was exfiltrated to Russia, leaving his family bewildered. The issue of how Razhardzho made such a timely escape is unresolved but, like other former eastern bloc countries, the new democratic administration in Prague had encountered difficulty in creating a security agency uncontaminated by the previous regime. Not surprisingly, when the

BIS had been established in 1994, many of its staff had been profession-als drawn from the military counter-intelligence service that had pledged allegiance to Moscow. Reportedly, the BIS investigation of Razhardzho had taken five years, and was nearing its conclusion.

Perhaps the most remarkable of the counter-intelligence investigations ini-tiated in 2009 was that of the Hungarian politician Bela Kovacs, who would be elected to the European Parliament in May 2010. When the Hungarian Constitutional Protection Office (AH) completed its enquiries in September 2014 an application was made successfully to have the MEP's immunity lifted so he could be prosecuted.

Born in Hungary in February 1960, the illegitimate son of a Soviet soldier, Kovacs was adopted by a couple who were posted to the Hungarian embassy in Tokyo, where he learned Japanese and English. He completed his studies in Moscow University and in 1986 married a Soviet journalist, Svetlana Istochina, who was seven years his senior and in possession of an Austrian passport acquired during an earlier marriage.

At his trial in Budapest in July 2018 the immensely wealthy, pro-Kremlin Kovacs denied charges of espionage, but he retired from parliament in July 2019.

Chapter V

Take Down

Once the decision had been taken in Washington, DC, to close down GHOST STORIES to provide leverage for Vasilenko's release from prison, thirty FBI Special Agents assembled at the New York Field Office, where they were briefed on what was to be a carefully timed and co-ordinated operation to be mounted with the intention of scooping up the entire illegals network simultaneously on Sunday, 27 June 2010. Altogether, an estimated one hundred Special Agents had been indoctrinated into the investigation, without a hint of a leak, and the plan was to detain everyone before any warnings could be issued.

The biggest obstacle to the plan was the lack of any evidence of an overt act, as required by the money laundering, espionage and foreign agent registration statutes, committed by three players: Mikhail Semenko, Alexei Karetnikov and Anna Chapman. In these circumstances, and in the absence of sufficient time to wait for the trio to incriminate themselves, the FBI adopted a high-risk strategy of entrapment, setting up Semenko and Chapman to undertake tasks that would justify their arrest. Both Semenko and Chapman were in the United States legitimately and were in possession of authentic travel documents and visas, which meant they were not in violation of even the immigration law. The expedient chosen by the FBI was to insert an *agent provocateur* into their routine and persuade them to alter their behaviour so as to provide the FBI with a pretext for arrest. The problem with this tactic was the necessity to exploit password information from the CIA's source inside Directorate S, Aleksandr Poteyev, which would certainly compromise him in a way that the SVR could not fail to notice.

In a worst-case scenario, in which the SVR indulged in a savage purge to rid the organization of past and present traitors, the CIA felt an obligation to warn Shcherbakov of an imminent crisis, and to offer him exfiltration, too. Accordingly, arrangements were made independently to alert both men who, of course, had no clue of the other's role as a CIA asset.

The trick was to execute all the arrests at precisely the same moment, having successfully entrapped Semenko, Karetnikov and Chapman. In all three cases there was an element of a gamble, as any one of them might, at any moment, contact Moscow for guidance during what had to be a false-flag ruse. The plan called for both Semenko and Chapman to be given a pre-agreed emergency code word, and then directed to follow instructions that would provide the FBI with the pretext for an arrest. Details of the code word procedure had been disclosed by Poteyev, so when Chapman was called in New Milford, Connecticut, at the weekend home of her current American admirer, the celebrated lawyer John J. Altorelli, she hardly hesitated when the authority of the code word was invoked for her to be ordered back into Manhattan to attend a special rendezvous at which she would receive instructions for an urgent assignment.

When the plan was initiated, the FBI inserted one of their own, a Russian-speaking special agent who introduced himself as 'Roman, from the consulate' and used Poteyev's secret password to summon her to a single meeting on Saturday, 26 June at a Starbucks coffee shop, not far from her Exchange Place apartment, on 47th Street at Eighth Avenue, where she had been observed on ten different Wednesdays between 20 January and June 2010. These electronic *trefs* (clandestine rendezvous) were conducted very professionally, and the FBI was conscious that on one occasion, in April 2010, the Line N case officer had been seen to arrive in his minivan and park nearby, but had aborted the dialogue, having suspected hostile surveillance.

All the usual protocols had been followed, so Chapman's suspicions had not been aroused. However, all the previous *trefs* had taken place every other Wednesday – never on a weekend – for the past five months, although their location had varied. Sometimes it had been the Barnes & Noble bookshop on Greenwich and Warren Streets in Tribeca, or occasionally the Starbucks near Times Square, but she had not held a face-to-face meeting before.

The caller, who had identified himself only as a member of the Russian consulate, had telephoned at 11am to arrange an urgent meeting later that same day, but when Anna returned his call at 12.20pm she had explained she was out of town and could not make it until the following day. The Russian emphasized the urgency, and forty minutes later Chapman called again, agreeing to meet at 4pm the same afternoon, saying she was returning to the city for the purpose.

The encounter took place at 4.30pm as Chapman was seated next to the window, overlooking the street corner, and the man introduced himself as Roman, in Russian, as having come from the consulate and the person to whom she had spoken earlier, but the rest of their conversation was conducted in English so as to avoid attracting unwelcome attention. To prove his *bona fides*, Roman used a certain code name for Chapman that only she and her Directorate S handlers knew. Nevertheless, she was apprehensive, and said she could not talk to him until she knew more about him. He promptly reciprocated, explaining that he was an illegals support officer, operating under diplomatic cover at the consulate, working for the same department as her. Apparently satisfied, she asked if he might have been followed to the meeting, but he reassured her that his counter-surveillance measures had taken up the past three hours. He also told her that he knew she should be travelling to Moscow in two weeks, 'to talk officially about her work'.[1]

When asked if all was well with her regular Wednesday rendezvous, Chapman complained that she had experienced serious connection problems with her computer. Indeed, she even entrusted Roman with her silver Toshiba Protégé R-500 laptop that, she complained, needed to be fixed or examined in Russia. Having agreed to take care of the problem, the man disclosed that he had a task for her, and handed her a passport, explaining that it needed to be passed to another illegal operating in New York under alias. Roman described how Chapman should carry a copy of *People* magazine and meet her contact, a woman, the following morning at 11am. For a parole, or recognition system, the woman was to say, 'Excuse me, haven't we met, in California last summer?' to which Anna would say, 'No, I think it was in the Hamptons.'

> Finally, Roman asked her, 'Are you ready for this step?'
> 'Shit, yes,' was her enthusiastic reply.

Once the delivery had been made, he instructed, Anna was to signal success by pasting a US postage stamp, upside down, on the side of a city street map directly outside Starbucks. Having accepted the assignment, the couple departed, at about 5pm. His parting words were, 'Your colleagues in Moscow, they know you're doing a good job. So keep it up.'

Although she was unaware of it, Chapman had been under intensive surveillance throughout the encounter, with FBI personnel outside the café, watching for any unanticipated Russian intervention, and inside, posing as regular Starbucks customers, although some had been equipped with covert video equipment so a permanent record of the episode could be retained. For instance, the young man seated directly across from her who appeared to be texting, was actually using his Blackberry 9630 as a camera. The FBI's objective, of course, was to entrap an espionage suspect that hitherto had not made any overt criminal act, and thus far proving her to be an unregistered foreign agent would be a difficult prosecution. However, the moment she accepted the forged passport, knowing it to be illegitimate, took her beyond the threshold needed to prefer charges. Her conversation had been equally incriminating, and from the FBI's perspective the issue was now down to timing an arrest, and that would be decided at the highest levels. Her conversation and behaviour had been sufficient to justify an arrest, and acquisition of her laptop was an unanticipated bonus that would doubtless also offer further damning evidence of criminal offences.

An hour later, at 6pm, Chapman undertook what appeared to be a counter-surveillance routine by entering several stores in Brooklyn. First there was a CVS pharmacy, then a Verizon shop, then a Rite Aid pharmacy, before returning to the Verizon outlet. When she left, for the second time, she discarded her bag in a garbage bin, together with her receipts and packaging that indicated she had bought a Motorola mobile phone, identifying herself on the customer agreement as 'Irine Kutsov of 40 Fake Street', and two TracFone international calling cards. Clearly the visit to two pharmacies, without a purchase being made, suggested a counter-surveillance routine. Chapman had tried to establish, without being too obvious, that she was seeking to spot if she was under observation. However, the very thought that *any* twenty-eight-year-old woman could walk through two pharmacies without being tempted to buy something, or even ask for assistance about a particular product, beggared belief. Using all their experience and professional skills, the FBI watchers discreetly retrieved the bag, thus allowing her calls to be intercepted. Having acquired the mobile's number, it was simplicity itself for the federal authorities, already armed with a Foreign Intelligence Surveillance Act warrant issued by the FISA court in Washington, DC, to monitor her outgoing traffic. Any number called would be logged and, if subsequent calls were carried over internet, microwave or satellite channels they would also become the target for monitoring, perhaps in real time, with the actual conversations recorded. Aware of this global capability, refined since the terrorist atrocities after September 2001, and improved by greater inter-agency co-operation, the SVR had trained Chapman to take certain precautions, but her lapse in tradecraft by so casually discarding her mobile phone details saved the counter-intelligence mole hunters hours of work. Through her negligence, Chapman had given the FBI instant access to the one method of communication she truly trusted. Furthermore, even though she paid in cash, Chapman could be linked to the bag and its contents forensically.

Chapman also dumped the charger, suggesting she was not intending to retain the mobile phone, and made several calls to Moscow, including one to her father in which she reported her contact with Roman, a man she described guardedly as 'someone from the past'. Evidently he was able to quickly check on what had happened, for his advice half an hour later was that she might be compromised and therefore should act entirely innocently and report the approach to the police. She was also to hand in the passport, alleging that a stranger had left it on her table in the coffee shop. As Chapman listened to these instructions, she made one further, devastating disclosure, 'Father, I also gave him my laptop ...'

These conversations, and the troubled, eloquent silences, all recorded under the terms of the FISA warrant, would suggest that Chapman had become anxious about the unexpected approach from Roman, and perhaps had undergone serious misgivings about the wisdom of having spoken to him so candidly, not to mention handing over her laptop. There must have been consternation in Moscow, but the speed with which Vasili responded implies that he was already deeply implicated in the entire operation. The best course, it was decided, was to bluff it out and have Chapman try and insulate herself from the mysterious, unknown figure of Roman, the man who seemed to have been so incredibly well informed.

Chapman remained under surveillance until the following day, when instead of attending the meeting at 11am, she waited until 1pm and went to the New York Police Department's 1st Precinct station house in Ericsson Place, lower Manhattan, where she gave an abbreviated account of her encounter with the unknown Russian. Her largely male audience, who appreciated her skin-tight clothing and the glimpse of her green thong peeping above her bare midriff, took possession of the passport and quickly recognized that this was a matter for the federal authorities. Accordingly, the police called the FBI New York Field Office and a special agent, identifying himself as a

Brooklyn detective named Joe, kept her occupied for five hours as she leafed through police mug shots.

Joe had listened to Chapman's version of what had happened the previous day, and had pretended to take notes as she described her account with the stranger in Starbucks. As she finished, Joe asked whether this was 'spy stuff', a characterisation with which she readily agreed. Feigning mystification, Joe asked her to look at some photos of men he said were known 'spies'.

Joe's real purpose, of course, was to delay Chapman until she could be formally arrested without causing any political embarrassment to Dmitri Medvedev, who was then returning home to Moscow after his official visit to Washington, DC and then the G8 and G20 summit in Toronto. As soon as his aircraft had cleared US airspace, the decision was taken to take Chapman into custody. The door of the interview room was thrown open and Christie, a woman FBI Special Agent, seized her wrist, spun her around while deftly snapping handcuffs on her wrists, and then submitted her to a humiliating internal examination to ensure she was not carrying any concealed contraband.

Completely unprepared for this dramatic development, Chapman was confronted by Joe, who gave her some hideous news. Her conduct amounted to espionage and the FBI knew all about her activities for the SVR. Aghast, Chapman asked what was likely to happen next. Joe's blunt reply was simple:

> 'You are looking at forty years' imprisonment. But before you say anything, go next door and look at yourself in the mirror. Then imagine what you will look like in forty years, when you are released, aged sixty-eight. Don't say a word. Just look.'

A few minutes later, ashen-faced, Chapman emerged from the adjacent room, apparently having contemplated the prospect of several decades in an American federal penitentiary. Reportedly she asked simply, 'What do you want to know?' Thereafter she was detained in isolation at the Metropolitan Detention Centre in Brooklyn, her request for low-calorie food respected.

* * *

Meanwhile, in Washington, a very similar false-flag entrapment was being conducted by another FBI *agent provocateur* who had introduced himself to Semenov on the evening of 26 June at a meeting that was arranged in a downtown restaurant during a call to his mobile phone. As with Chapman, the FBI stand-in gained Semenko's confidence by mentioning a code word that should have been known only to the spy and his SVR handler, and the two men agreed to rendezvous later the same evening on a street corner at 10th Street and H Street in north-west Washington, DC. Having met and exchanged the customary greeting, they moved into a nearby park and sat on a bench where, almost immediately, Semenko began to complain about problems with his laptop communications.

Once again, the undercover agent seized the opportunity and thus allowed the FBI to score a second unimaginable coup by casually asking if he would like the laptop checked out. The answer was 'yes' and he passed it over. Although the surveillance was imperceptible, even to the professional Line N eye trained to spot the clues, both men were surrounded by FBI personnel and they recorded the scene with a BlackBerry. To gain his trust the FBI officer, who recorded the conversation on a concealed device, mentioned an earlier meeting with an SVR handler, on 5 June, thereby demonstrating the depth of his knowledge. Apparently impressed, Semenko then dropped his guard and confided that he had been trained by, and received his instructions from, 'the Centre'. He claimed that his communications training had lasted only a week, although he had previously undergone a course lasting a fortnight, and that he had been directed only to hold face-to-face meetings in the safety of the New York consulate.

In another parallel with Chapman's entrapment, Semenko was asked to undertake an assignment, the delivery of an envelope containing $5,000 in notes, to a dead drop under a footbridge in nearby Arlington County Park. This procedure was very characteristic of the routine adopted by the FBI mole Robert Hanssen who had finally been arrested in February 2001 just as he had filled a drop site beneath a bridge in Foxstone Park, a large secluded public space in Vienna, northern Virginia. The site was covered by remote cameras, and Semenov was recorded as he fulfilled his task, having placed the money in an envelope concealed inside a newspaper. This act alone would be considered sufficient by the Justice Department lawyers supervising the operation to justify his arrest. The drop, Semenko was instructed, should take place precisely between 11 and 11:30am, and he obeyed the directions, unaware that the area was covered by covert surveillance cameras. He was arrested at 8am on Sunday morning, the very first to be taken into custody.

By the time the arrests were made, Shcherbakov and Poteyev were already on their way, separately, to the United States. Reportedly Poteyev, whose thirty-one-year-old daughter and son Vladimir, who worked for Rosoboronexport, were already in the United States, fled Russia by taking a train to Minsk on Friday, 25 June and then using a genuine passport containing details of an innocent visa applicant to the US embassy named Dudochkin, to reach Frankfurt in Germany.[2] During his journey he sent a farewell text message to his wife Marina, which enabled her to play the role of a victim until she could join her husband:

> Try to take it calmly. I am leaving not for some time, but forever. I didn't want to, but I had to. I am starting a new life and I will try and help the children.

In Shcherbakov's case, his daughter was already living in the United States, but his son, employed by Russia's Federal Drug Control Service (FSKN), had to be exfiltrated too.

When the Murphys were arrested at their home on Sunday evening, 27 June, the FBI recovered two maps of Costa Rica, which suggested the couple might have been planning to flee the country.

At Heathfield's home the FBI recovered a dozen computers and a short-wave radio, together with details of a bank deposit box that was found to contain cash and passports. He had planned to leave the country for a vacation in Moscow on Sunday evening.

Naturally, with an operation of this size and complexity there was always a chance, however well planned it was, of some aspect miscarrying, and the problem encountered by the FBI was the absence of Metsos, who had eventually turned up in Cyprus on 17 June, staying with a red-headed companion at the Atrium Zenon Hotel in the southern coastal resort of Larnaca for twelve days.

Metsos was to be arrested on an international arrest warrant to face charges of money laundering on Tuesday, 29 June at Larnaca airport as the couple tried to board a flight for Budapest carrying one-way tickets. His laptop, Canadian passport and several memory sticks were confiscated by the local police, but he was granted bail of €27,000, which was paid in cash the following day. Upon his release from custody to face an extradition hearing a month later, he checked into the Achilleon Hotel Apartments, only to vanish, probably over the 'Green Line' into Turkish-controlled Northern Cyprus. At the time the porous border, with five official crossings, was irregularly patrolled by UN peacekeepers, supported by occasional Turkish anti-smuggling mobile checkpoints, so there were plenty of informal rural routes between the two territories.

Accordingly, the FBI issued a fugitive notice alleging conspiracy to commit money laundering and being an unregistered agent, and published a wanted poster that included a list of his aliases: Christopher R. Metsos, Pavel Kapustin, Gerard Martin Kelleher, Diego Cadenilla Jose Antonio, Luis Miguel Alarcon-Correas, Patrick Allen Woolcocks, Peter Michael Franklin, Graham Douglas Cox, Pavel Gukov, Sean Proinnsias, with various dates of birth: 16 June 1956, 7 April 1954, 17 November 1959, 20 October 1955, 21 June 1956, 17 March 1956, 9 October 1953, 27 April 1958, 1 June 1954, and 30 December 1954. When MI5 investigated the genuine British passport used by Metsos, issued to a Weybridge-based international sales executive for a broadcast equipment company, it was learned that Patrick Woolcocks had travelled to Moscow for a trade show in November 2003 and stayed at the Mezhdonarodnaya. Evidently the SVR had taken the opportunity to clone the document, probably when he had made his visa application.

According to Metsos' Cypriot lawyer, his client had told him that he had divorced some fifteen years earlier, and had a son living in Paris. He would not reveal any other details.

* * *

The final illegal to be compromised by Poteyev and rolled up by the CIA in the immediate aftermath of the GHOST STORIES arrest was Sergei Cherepanov, alias Henry Frith, who for the past twenty years had posed as a business consultant from New Zealand, employed by Frimor Consultores, a firm with an office at Calle Goya 47 in Madrid, in which his Spanish partner was Carlos Moreno who advised small enterprises on applying for state subsidies for training programmes. Cherepanov shared an apartment with an older lady, Carmen Valdezate, who was suffering from cancer. Although his New Zealand passport stated his birthplace on 9 November 1957 as Ecuador, and he had claimed an Ecuadorian mother, the real Lawrence Henry Frith had died at the age of fifteen months, in Waikato in March 1937, and Cherepanov had been born in the Soviet Union two years earlier, in 1955.

On 28 June, in co-ordination with the arrests in the United States, the moustached Cherepanov was approached outside his home by a British MI6 officer and offered the opportunity to co-operate. He pleaded complete ignorance of anything to do with Russian espionage, but fled to the airport early the following morning, only to resurface in Moscow where he was reunited with his wife Olga and son Andrei.

The implication of this chain of events suggests that even though Cherepanov had been under intensive surveillance for several months, if not years, there was an absence of evidence that could be adduced in a criminal trial, in circumstances somewhat reminiscent of the lack of much with which to charge Chapman or Semenko. Such an interpretation is supported by the unprecedented media briefings that accompanied Cherepanov's early morning vanishing act given by the CNI chief, General Felix Sanz Roldin. His somewhat unusual openness followed a precedent set in 2007 when details of Robert Flores, a Soviet mole, had been disclosed by his predecessor, Alberto Saiz Cortes.[3] In July 2010 Sanz circulated claims that Cherepanov had communicated with Moscow using his laptop and a flash drive containing an encryption program. Furthermore, as if to underline the depth of the compromise, both of Cherepanov's Line N support officers at the embassy, Anton O. Simbirsky and Aleksandr N. Samoshkin, were expelled, clear proof that they had incriminated themselves while under surveillance.

Given the fact that Cherepanov had been in place in Madrid for some twenty years, and the investment by Directorate S implied by the support required to sustain him, his former business partner remained mystified by what had happened, commenting that their firm had never been profitable and he had been surprised by the extent of Cherepanov's foreign travel, particularly to South America, which did not seem justified by the company's actual trading.

The message received by the SVR in authorising Cherepanov's very sudden withdrawal amounted to an acknowledgment that Poteyev's betrayal of Directorate S's assets had ranged far beyond the United States and Germany. Put simply, the SVR's worldwide illegal network had been a complete waste of time, money and personnel for more than a decade. This seemed especially true of illegals with a South American country somewhere in their legend, which might suggest that there had been a breach of security in Directorate S's 4th Department, the very section in which Poteyev had been promoted to in 1999.

Having released the very detailed, twenty-seven-page sealed complaint sworn by Maria Ricci dated 25 June against eight of the defendants, and her second affidavit, covering eighteen pages and dated two days later, the FBI intended another 'shock and awe' offensive designed to overwhelm any possible defence. Quite apart from the major charge, of acting as an unregistered agent of a foreign government, all the defendants could have faced money laundering and financial fraud indictments, one for each act of, for example, a house purchase or a car lease. The probable sentences would be counted in decades, and the prisoners knew it.

Both the FBI complaint documents made clear that the suspects had been watched over a very long period, and searches conducted years earlier had virtually eliminated any chance of pleas of innocence against the first eight. Thus the formal legal complaints became instruments of leverage for Vasilenko's freedom, amounting to eloquent, factual evidence of Russian espionage. Convictions would mean lengthy prison sentences and the possibility of some of the defendants seeking to make a deal, none of which would be in the interests of the SVR or, for that matter, the Kremlin.

Chapter VI

Negotiations

Having acquired the leverage for Vasilenko's release, the task confronting the CIA Director Leon Panetta was to open negotiations with his opposite number in Moscow, Mikhail Fradkov, without revealing his true objective. Both men were lifelong politicians, not intelligence professionals. Panetta was a seventy-two-year-old Roman Catholic Democrat first elected to the House of Representatives in 1977, and appointed to head the CIA in February the previous year. He had served as an intelligence officer briefly during his US Army service in 1964, and often joked that he enjoyed spy movies. Fradkov was of Jewish heritage, sixty years old, and a professional trade negotiator, having represented his county at GATT in Geneva. He would be appointed trade minister by Boris Yeltsin in 1997, and director of the federal tax police by Vladimir Putin in 2001 before becoming prime minister in 2004 and heading the SVR in October 2007.

The task before the two men was complicated as there was only one convicted American spy in Russian custody at that moment, namely Alexander Zaporozhsky, who was hardly a fair exchange for the ten incarcerated in the United States. The other putative spy, Alexander Sypachev, had been jailed in November 2002 for eight years in a maximum security labour camp on charges of having spied for the CIA for eight years, although he had not actually done so.

A Defense Ministry staffer, Colonel Sypachev had been convicted in 2002 of attempting to sell secrets to the CIA, but was due for release anyway. Allegedly he had offered information to the US embassy in Moscow in February 2002 and had been arrested by the FSB on 4 April in the act of delivering an envelope containing a classified, two-page report relating to the deployment of Russian intelligence personnel. From the CIA's standpoint, Sypachev had never been an asset, and reportedly had co-operated with the FSB.

Accordingly, in the absence of much in the way of bargaining chips, the Clandestine Service chief, Mike Sulick, who had headed the Moscow Station between 1994 and 1996, now run by Daniel M. Hoffman, approached his British counterparts for any additional candidates for inclusion. On his second tour in Moscow, having previously been posted to Helsinki and Tallinn, Hoffman had been educated in France and at the London School of Economics, and was fluent in French, Russian, Estonian, Finnish and Urdu. He had also served in Islamabad during the aftermath of the 9/11 attack, and in Iraq, but on this posting he had been declared to his Russian hosts. His task was to manage the Moscow end of the spy swap, liaising directly with the CIA's old protagonist, Aleksandr Zhomov.

MI6, then headed by Sir John Sawers, had suffered several losses in recent years, and two alleged assets were currently languishing in a labour camp. One was Igor Sutyagin, an academic who had been accused in 2004 of supplying secrets to his MI6 contacts in London, supposedly having been recruited in February 1998 while attending a conference held by Birmingham University's Centre for Studies in Security and Diplomacy, at Wast Hills House in King's Norton. Formerly the home of the Cadbury chocolate manufacturing family, the property had become a popular venue for seminars and similar events. The situation was delicate because the arms control expert had never enjoyed access to classified information and ostensibly had been hired by the publishers of a scholarly journal to peer review papers on disarmament submitted to the subscription-only periodical.

Having accepted the invitation to contribute to what appeared to be a legitimate academic journal, the forty-four-year-old Sutyagin was unaware that the entire enterprise was a commercial front for MI6. A member of the respected Institute of United States of America and Canada Studies in Moscow since 1989, Sutyagin had written dozens of articles on nuclear weapons and non-proliferation treaties, and was the co-author of a 693-page study, *Russian Strategic Nuclear Forces*. He was charged with passing information on nuclear submarines and weapons to a British company that the prosecution claimed was a cover for the US Defense Intelligence Agency (DIA).

At the Birmingham conference, Sutyagin had been approached by a couple calling themselves Sean Kidd and Nadia Locke who commissioned him, on behalf of a political risk firm named Alternative Futures, to participate in a consultancy agreement. However, after his arrest by the FSB in Kaluga in October 1999 Sutyagin was accused of having supplied classified information to the DIA in return for a regular retainer of $1,000 a month, from an organization that consisted of a small front company equipped with a fax and telephone answering machine, operated from a suite of rented offices in Leadenhall Street in the City of London. On the occasions Sutyagin visited the offices, a staff of four or five people were visible. In his defence, Sutyagin insisted that his contributions had been drawn from open sources, and never contained classified information. By the time his case had come to trial Kidd, Locke, their colleague Christopher Martin, and the company had disappeared. In December 2005 Sutyagin, having been sentenced to fifteen years' imprisonment, was transferred to a penal colony at Kholomogory, where he remained, content to serve out the remainder of his sentence and then be reunited with his wife and two daughters.

The fact that Sutyagin continued to protest his innocence of the FSB's charges of espionage made the situation especially delicate, for the addition of his name to any list of western assets would be interpreted by the FSB as confirmation of his guilt. The prisoner himself, of course, was not consulted on his inclusion, and would have refused his release if he had known the terms and their implications. However, as the Russian prisoners in the US judicial system could not be released without a determination of guilt or innocence before a court, the US Justice Department required a guilty plea to trigger the exchange, so the SVR reciprocated, and imposed the same condition, although in Moscow's lawless society the gesture was largely meaningless, and was intended to be face-saving.

The second, less complicated MI6 asset was Sergei Skripal, a GRU colonel previously based in Malta who had also served in Afghanistan, and been attached to the *rezidentura* in Madrid in July 1996 when he had been cultivated and recruited by Pablo Miller, an MI6 officer operating under business cover with the alias Antonio Alvares de Idalgo. Introduced by a Spanish CNI officer named Luis, who had been given the task of cultivating Skripal, Miller represented himself as an entrepreneur in the wine trade who was keen to export Spanish wine to Russia, an enterprise the Russian had mentioned to Luis.

Formerly an officer in the Royal Tank Corps and then the Royal Green Jackets, serving in Brunei, Ulster, Cyprus and Germany, Miller had graduated from Sandhurst and in 1982 gained a degree from Oxford in modern languages and history. After joining MI6 in 1990 he had been posted to Nigeria in 1992, and then Estonia from 1997 to 1999, and finally Warsaw in 2010 for three years. He was appointed OBE in June 2015, and upon his retirement moved to Salisbury and worked with two former MI6 colleagues, Christopher Steele and Christopher Burrows, in a business consultancy with offices in Berkeley Square and then Victoria. Their company, Orbis, would later gain worldwide notoriety because of Steele's role in writing and disseminating a series of reports during the 2016 US presidential election campaign containing derogatory information about Donald Trump.

In 1999, while based at the embassy in Tallinn, Miller had been compromised by Valeri Ojamae, a former Russian FSB officer who would be arrested at Moscow's Leningradsky railway station in March 2000 and sentenced in April the following year to seven years' imprisonment, after having been convicted of spying for Estonia and MI6. According to the Russian media, Ojamae had been run as a double agent against the British for a year, after he had been betrayed when he had volunteered his services to the KaPo in 1999.

* * *

Skripal was close to the end of his three-year posting to Madrid and was due to return to Moscow in September, accompanied by his wife Liudmila and daughter Yulia. While in Moscow, where he was assigned to the organization's personnel department, Skripal maintained contact with MI6 through a covert channel of secret writing but, three years later, in September 1999, at the age of forty-eight and diabetic, he retired and took a job with Moscow's municipal administration. In 2000, he went on a family holiday to Malaga, where MI6 had invested in a time-share apartment for him, during which he re-established personal contact with MI6, and this became the pattern of the relationship, with Skripal periodically visiting Malta, Spain, Portugal and Turkey where, according to his detailed confession, he would meet an MI6 case officer and receive around $3,000 in cash on each occasion.

In the spring of 2004 the GRU *rezidentura* in Madrid was engulfed in a scandal involving an embezzler, Yuri Burlatov, who had been caught stealing funds, and selling information to the Spanish CNI. A naval officer, Burlatov later died while in custody, apparently having hanged himself, but in December Skripal was arrested at his apartment in Krylatskoye, west of Moscow, and interrogated at Lefortovo. In August 2006 a military tribunal sentenced him to thirteen years' imprisonment and he was consigned to

IK-5, a grim penal colony near Pot'ma in Mordovia, 2,775 miles south-east of Moscow, with only a limited expectation of survival. Built during the Stalin era, the site is one of eighteen prisons in the area, none of which are marked on maps.

The person who had compromised Burlatov and Skripal turned out to be a Spanish CNI officer, Roberto Flóres Garcia, originally a Guardia Civil police officer from Pravia in the northern province of Asturias, who had joined the police in San Sebastian in 1991 but had transferred to CESID the following year. Within CESID's regional office in Intxaurrondo he came under the command of Colonel Enrique Rodriguez Galindo, a legendary counter-terrorism specialist who deployed his notorious 'Black Legs' against the ETA separatists. For the next seven years Flóres worked undercover, posing as a journalist, infiltrating ETA in the Basque country and successfully insinuating himself between those negotiating on behalf of the terrorists, a human rights group and a conflict resolution organization, Remembering Guernica, headed by Juan Gutiérrez, and the government. In his guise as 'Rafael Vera' Flores helped run a peace conference held at the Miramar Palace in San Sebastian in 1994, but by 1998 he had raised so many suspicions that his cover was endangered, requiring his withdrawal, and a posting first to Paraguay, and then to Peru.

In 1999, having proved himself an exceptional operations officer while targeted against ETA, he had been transferred to Lima in a liaison capacity as deputy to Juan Coll Real, the information attaché, where his identity had been revealed by a local newspaper, thus wrecking his future as a clandestine operator in the field. According to the Peruvian media, Flóres had been part of a conspiracy to influence the country's presidential election in May 2001 in which Alejandro Toledo defeated the incumbent Alan Garcia, and had collected information about trade unions and political parties. Specifically, Flóres, purporting to be a communications expert, had cultivated the opposition leader, his 'Peru Posible' movement, and members of his cabinet until his role at the embassy was exposed in June 2000 by a *La Republica* correspondent, Gustavo Gorriti, under the headline 'I was spying on Toledo'.

Upon his return in 2001 to the headquarters in Madrid known as 'La Casa', and increasingly resentful of being restricted to desk duties, Flóres had approached an SVR officer under counsellor cover at the Russian embassy, Petr Y. Melnikov, in December 2002 and sold the first of a series of computer memory cards on which he had stored vast quantities of data relating to Spanish counter-intelligence personnel and their priorities. In amongst this material was sufficient information to incriminate Skripal and Burlatov, but CNI detected a change in the *rezidentura*'s behaviour, and initiated a mole hunt that resulted in March 2005 with Flóres being placed under surveillance. An alternative explanation, and probably the more likely, is that the CIA tipped off the Spanish to a major leak. In any event, by then Flóres had long gone, having resigned a year earlier, in March 2004, to live in Tenerife, where he would marry Maria Jose Espinosa, the forty-year-old daughter of a distinguished, well-known local surgeon, Dr Luis Espinosa Garcia-Estrada, open his own intelligence consultancy business, the Conflict Resolution Centre, in the Calle Esquivel, and own two apartments. A journalist who had covered the Barcelona Olympics in 1992, Maria was a stringer in the Canaries for various agencies, including Europa Press, and had worked as a translator for the *Washington Post*.

Following his resignation from CNI, Flóres had travelled to Mexico to generate work and visited Cochabamba in Bolivia to attend a seminar entitled Business Leadership in Conflict Situations, in a failed effort to land an advisory role with the socialist President Evo Morales. His website, www. capacitador.com, boasted of his CNI credentials, but in his neighbourhood in Tenerife he was best known for having delivered unremunerated lectures about adolescent behaviour problems.

When Flóres's rented second floor apartment and garage in Calle Casa Azul, in the La Vera district of Puerto de la Cruz, were raided by CNI on Monday, 23 July 2007, thousands of classified documents were recovered, including deleted copies of two incriminating letters he had delivered to the SVR. In the first, dated December 2001, he had identified himself as 'a director of CESID' who was willing to 'collaborate', by providing a 'who's who' of the organization, in return for $275,000. The second letter, which was undated but thought to have been sent in 2002, offered to update the previous information and claimed he was about to occupy a position of responsibility in the new CNI (CESID's successor organization) that would give him access to material relevant to the Russians. Finally, a search of Flóres's bank accounts showed undeclared, unexplained income.

At his trial in Madrid in January 2010, during which Flóres denied the charges against him, the prosecution could demonstrate that he had been in unauthorised possession of classified material, but could not prove they had been passed to the SVR. In his defence, Flóres asserted that the two incriminating letters had been a component of an unapproved 'dangle' exercise designed to entrap the Russians, which was part of a monograph he was researching. Accordingly, he was convicted on the lesser change and sentenced to twelve years' imprisonment (later reduced on appeal to nine).

* * *

When MI6 came to nominate candidates for inclusion on Panetta's list, Skripal and Sutyagin deserved mention. Sutyagin was somewhat of a victim, and Skripal had been placed in jeopardy by CNI and not through any fault of his own. Thus, in both examples, it could be argued, and was, that MI6 had failed in its duty of care to both agents. In a business entirely dependent on reputation and trust, MI6 perceived an obligation to do whatever was necessary to remedy the predicament of both men.

* * *

Panetta's initial conversation on speakerphone with Fradkov, from his seventh-floor office at Langley, depended on the SVR being willing to admit that the arrestees were indeed theirs.

> I looked around the room. Our people waited as to what Fradkov would say because there was this silence … and then Fradkov said, 'Yes, they are our people'. And you could see all the jaws drop in the room. And the fact that he was acknowledging that they were Russian spies.

With four on his list, plus Vasilenko, added as an apparent afterthought, Panetta opened his bidding with Fradkov on 4 July, who responded with a demand that Aldrich Ames and Robert Hanssen be included in any swap. This counter-proposal was firmly rejected (as had previous, similar suggestions), so the offer defaulted back to an exchange of the ten in American custody for the four in Russia. At this point the Russians appeared unaware of the disappearance from Moscow of Poteyev and Shcherbakov, but at this late stage an unanticipated obstacle emerged.

In order for the ten prisoners to be freed, the Department of Justice required all to enter guilty pleas to the charges entered against them, and all but one was content to acknowledge their true names and origins. However, Lazaro alone exercised what he regarded as the necessary self-discipline and declined to make any admissions. At one moment he asserted that 'he would not violate his loyalty to the "Service", even for his son'. The solution to this impasse was the appearance in New York of a senior SVR officer who was ushered in for a private meeting with the spy. When confronted with a direct order from his superior, whom he knew and recognized, Lazaro reluctantly acquiesced and made the statement required by the lawyers. Although this individual has never been identified, there is speculation that he was the recently exfiltrated Poteyev, fulfilling his last operational role as a defector.

Curiously, Lazaro's wife Pelaez declared to the judge that she had never received any training as a spy, and had no intention of living in Russia. She said she had been promised $2,000 a month stipend, a visa and free housing, but she planned to return to her family's ranch in Peru. She would be granted bail of $250,000 and be released, to be monitored electronically at her home while her co-defendants were remanded in custody until the exact terms of the spy swap were agreed. After her guilty plea, which accepted deportation within seventy-two hours, Pelaez joined the other nine prisoners for their charter flight to Vienna, but she did not last in Moscow and in February 2011 flew to Peru to attend her father's funeral in the highlands city of Cuzco, having been employed as a journalist on the *Moscow News*.

During the visit she gave an interview to a local magazine in which she claimed ignorance of her husband's espionage, and said, 'I might never forgive him for not being straight with me.'

With the final formalities completed, a federal judge, Kimba M. Wood, sentenced the ten to time served, which was eleven days, and then ordered their deportation. They were then put aboard a bus to a New York airport and flown to Vienna.

Characteristically, while in custody Chapman complained about the quality of the prison food and, on the flight to Vienna, expressed concern about her Chanel handbag. Apparently unaware of the global publicity given to her arrest, she also asked if the British authorities would be informed that she held a British passport. An FBI officer broke the news to her that her passport had been confiscated and would not be returned.[1]

The spy swap in Vienna, watched over by the FSB's Aleksandr Zhomov and the FBI's Alan Kohler, attracted worldwide media attention, not least because the event harked back to the darkest days of the Cold War. Even at this late stage it was important to maintain the deception and offer misdirection about why the US authorities had agreed to the exchange. Two alternative cover stories were offered. One suggested that some of the illegals were planning to leave the jurisdiction anyway, and the FBI did not want to lose them altogether. Indeed, Heathfield and Chapman had planned an imminent departure, and FBI Director Robert Mueller acknowledged publicly the necessity of making the arrests while they were still in the country. The other, supported by the content of the FBI's complaint affidavit issued to justify the arrests, implied that the illegals were getting too close to Secretary of State Hillary Clinton, and so had to be closed down to avoid political embarrassment. This was the line peddled by Frank Figliuzzi, later appointed head of the Counterintelligence Division, who declared, 'Several were getting close to high-ranking officials. One had gone to work for a confidant of a US Cabinet member.' Neither explanation, of course, was strictly true.[2]

* * *

The last of the illegals to be deported was Alexei Karetnikov, who was flown back to Russia on 13 July 2010, but even at this stage the SVR seems not to have grasped how the organization had been hoodwinked. Firstly, the absence of the Shcherbakovs went unnoticed, but then Poteyev's disappearance was investigated and the scale of his deception became clear. At his subsequent trial held *in absentia* in Moscow in June 2011 Chapman gave evidence for the prosecution and described how the FBI undercover agent Roman had used the code word known only to Poteyev and her Directorate S handler, thereby ensuring his conviction. He was sentenced to twenty-five years' imprisonment, but by then had been safely resettled in a pair of neighbouring, newly built three-bedroom apartments on the fortieth floor of a Trump condominium on Collins Avenue in Miami, Florida, where he had registered as a Republican Party voter, and a four-bedroom house in Whitting Drive, Manassas, Virginia. During the proceedings, it was alleged that Poteyev had been recruited by his daughter, and that his son had also spied for the CIA. Like her brother, a graduate of the law school of Moscow's new, private International University, Margarita had supposedly been employed by the American Councils for International Education, a US organization sponsoring student exchanges, and studied for a master's degree at Eastern Kentucky University in Richmond, Kentucky. She then completed her doctorate in criminology at the University of Delaware in Newark. In 2014 she joined the Justice Studies Department at James Madison University at Harrisonburg, Virginia, to teach a course entitled 'Sex Offenders and the Death Penalty'.

The Russian media covering the trial reported that Poteyev had initially asked in May 2010 to visit his Ukrainian mistress in Odessa, where she had given birth to their baby, but permission had been refused. It was also speculated that Sergei Tretyakov may have identified Poteyev to his CIA contacts as a likely target for cultivation and eventual defection. No further mention was made of wife Marina, except to note that reportedly she had filed a police report in January 2003 concerning a violent burglary at their home in Moscow's Krylatsky Hills by three men masquerading as police officers.

Chapter VII
Aftermath

Although the Russian authorities went through a ritual of welcoming the returning illegals as heroes, and informed the media that they had been received by Vladimir Putin, who praised their courage, saying 'just imagine … you have to master a foreign language as your own, think and speak it and fulfill tasks in the interest of the motherland for many years without counting on diplomatic immunity'. He went on to predict, 'I am sure that they will have an interesting and bright life.'

Although Prime Minister Putin, who himself served as a KGB Line KR officer at the Dresden sub-*rezidentura* between 1985 and 1990 in a lacklustre career lasting sixteen years, gave an account of having sung patriotic songs with them, such as the SVR favourite, *From Where the Motherland Begins*, the public exposure of the network was more than just a very visible professional humiliation.

All the freed illegals were invited to participate in a nationwide tour of the country, but privately told that they could not continue to work for the SVR, although they would be found jobs in state industries. Chapman was offered a television programme and Heathfield accepted an academic post at Moscow's prestigious MGIMO university.

In operational terms, the costs were extremely high because everything that had been accomplished over the previous decade would have to be reassessed as having been tainted by the FBI's interference. Indeed, commentators in Moscow speculated that the financial waste may have amounted to $600 million, with some eighty other assets worldwide having been placed in jeopardy.

At the very least the SVR's group of illegals had been neutralised, with none of them ever being able to travel to or through a NATO country again in their lifetime. In terms of disruption, a major preoccupation for Directorate S would be the post-mortem damage assessment designed to determine the causes of the debacle.

Despite the gravity of the situation, it was clear that the SVR did not respond to the disaster in the United States by withdrawing all their illegals abroad immediately. Indeed, in Marburg, Germany, at eight o'clock on 28 October 2011 police mounted a dawn raid on a local suburban home and subsequently arrested two agents who had already sold one of their three cars and apparently were preparing to move abroad. One, forty-three year-old Heidrun Anschlag, was sitting in her study operating a computer linked to a shortwave radio. The other, her fifty-one-year-old husband Andreas, was arrested while on a business visit to Balingen. They were accused of having been moles for the past twenty-five years. He claimed to have been born in Argentina but educated in Austria before moving to the Federal Republic in June 1988 and studying engineering and plastics technology in Aachen. Two years later he had married his partner, Heidrun Freud, who had supposedly been born in Peru but had acquired Austrian citizenship, and they had a daughter. According to the investigation conducted by the federal German security service (BfV), Andreas joined an auto components manufacturer in 1998 but later moved the family to North Rhine-Westphalia and then to Rhineland-Palatinate. In his job he travelled frequently, and visited the Czech Republic, Spain, the United States, Portugal, and Brazil to see clients such as DaimlerChrysler, General Motors, BMW and Volkswagen. Their daughter, a medical student, was apparently unaware that her parents were Russian.

The BfV established that their authentic Austrian passports had been issued by a corrupt official on false biographical information and the declared places of birth, in Valentín Alsina, Argentina, and Lima, Peru, were bogus. In 1986 he had transited through Mexico City, where he had been registered in an apartment at Rio Papaloapan 13, and then moved in June to Wltwasserstrasse 31 in Aachen. Once again, a Russian illegal with a 'legend' back-stopped in Latin America had been compromised.

Andreas, who often mentioned his interests in travel, walking and deep-sea fishing, spoke with a detectable Russian accent, although he said he only knew German, Spanish and English. The BfV's search of the house revealed large sums of cash, including 33,000 Swiss francs and other currencies valued at €36,000. Other items recovered suggested that Andreas had been talent spotting potential recruits for the SVR by joining various policy discussion groups, and had identified various individuals as suitable candidates, including a recently retired director of German military intelligence and two other high-level federal officials.

In the couple's covert communications monitored by the BfV, their call sign was ALPENKUH-1 and Moscow responded with CRISTIANOFOOTBALLER. According to their meticulously maintained accounts, they received around $99,000 a year from the SVR for their espionage. However, in August 2011, following the GHOST STORIES debacle, they had been summoned to Belgrade to meet their Directorate S controller, LEONID, who warned of compromise and arranged an emergency extraction plan. In the event of exposure they were to telephone the Russian consulate-general in Bonn and identify themselves as 'Sasha and Oljia Rost'. A further rendezvous with the SVR was held in Rome during a brief visit between 28 September and 2 October, when further aspects of the couple's withdrawal was discussed, and they were promised a promotion upon their arrival in Moscow.

Following the meeting with LEONID, the Anschlags' pattern of behaviour changed dramatically. He told his employer that his marriage was at risk, so he wished to resign his job at the end of October 2011. He also cancelled his lease, telling his landlord that he was moving to Bulgaria or Romania.

At their trial in Stuttgart in February 2013 the prosecution alleged that between 2008 and 2011 the couple, code-named PIT and TINA, had received classified NATO material from an unnamed Dutch source. The pair were both convicted of espionage and Andreas was sentenced to six and a half years' imprisonment, with his wife receiving five and a half. However, Heidrun was released and deported to Moscow in November 2014, perhaps as part of a swap for an FSB officer, Colonel Valeri Mikhailov, who had been convicted in June 2012 of espionage and sentenced to eighteen years' imprisonment, to be served in Irkutsk. Her husband was released and deported in June 2015 having served half his sentence and paid a sequestration order for €600,000.

The spy who had supplied the Anschlags with secrets was subsequently revealed to be Raymond Poeteray, a sixty-one-year-old Dutch diplomat who was arrested at Schiphol Airport in March 2012 as he attempted to catch a flight for Bangkok carrying four computer memory sticks loaded with classified information. According to the Dutch security service (AIVD), Poeteray, who had served in Hong Kong, Seoul and Indonesia in a career with the Foreign Ministry dating back to 1978, had been selling military and political secrets to the Russians since 2008 to pay off his debts, and had explained the money, amounting to $94,000, had come from his profitable trading in jewellery that he had purchased abroad. Altogether it was estimated that he had met the Anschlags on twenty or thirty occasions, usually in Amsterdam, The Hague, or at a rendezvous close to the German frontier. At the end of his trial in The Hague in April 2013 Poeteray was sentenced to twelve years' imprisonment.

Prosecution evidence adduced at his trial suggests that when Poeteray held a rendezvous with Anschlag in Amsterdam on 14 February 2009 they were under AIVD surveillance. A search of his home in The Hague produced a gun and a collection of 450 classified documents.

Curiously, Poeteray had been the subject of adverse publicity some seven years before his arrest when he and his wife, Meta, had abandoned a child whom they had adopted while in South Korea. The couple, then based in Hong Kong as a vice consul, had placed their adopted daughter Jade in the care of the local authority, claiming they were unable to cope with their own two children and the ethnic Korean.

The arrest of Poeteray and the Anschlags, coming on top of the exposure of Cherepanov, proved to be just the beginning of a series of major setbacks for the Russians. No sooner had the Anschlags been taken into custody than another source, allegedly managed by the GRU, unwound in Canada with the arrest in January 2012 of a junior naval officer, Jeffrey Delisle, at his home in Bedford, Nova Scotia. At the time he was posted to the intelligence and communications facility HMCS *Trinity* located inside the shorebase at Stadacona in Halifax, Nova Scotia. He had originally joined the Canadian army in 1996 as a reservist, then signed up full-time in 2001, transferring to defence intelligence duties in Ottawa in 2006. He gained a university degree and was granted a commission in 2008. Delisle married his wife, Jennifer, in 1997 and they had four children in quick succession before she had an affair that, he claimed, had prompted his espionage.

In his confession to the RCMP's Sergeant Jim Moffat, Delisle, aged forty-two, admitted having walked in to the Russian embassy in Ottawa in June 2007 to sell classified material, which had included details of STONE GHOST, a signals intelligence computer database shared by the 'Five Eyes' partnership. As a threat assessment analyst, Delisle had been cleared for access to the most sensitive Allied intelligence sources, the product of which he downloaded onto a thumb drive, smuggled out of the top security building and passed to his handlers via a shared email address on a server based in Egypt, using the 'draft message' option, over a period of more than four years and being paid $3,000 a month in twenty-three instalments. He met one of his handlers, VICTOR, during a five-day trip to Rio de Janeiro's Rio Presidente Hotel in September 2011. Some of his payments would be traced to Western Union transfers made by Sergei Shokolov. Fedor Vasilev, Andrei Orlov and an account in the name of 'Mary Larkin', an Irish identity linked by the FBI to the GHOST STORIES investigation. In debt, overweight and diabetic, Delisle developed an addiction to video gaming that he financed by cashing his payments at a Money Mart. At his trial in February 2013 it was disclosed that the FBI's Frank Figliuzzi had formally alerted the RCMP to Delisle's espionage in December 2011, and he was sentenced to a dishonourable discharge and twenty years' imprisonment.

More was to follow, and perhaps other unpublicised betrayals may well have acted as the catalyst for the extraordinary and shocking events that followed as Vladimir Putin sought re-election in 2018.

* * *

Following Sergei Skripal's arrival from the spy swap in Vienna at RAF Brize Norton, he was driven to a London hotel with Sutyagin, where the pair were separated. In accordance with the established narrative, Sutyagin would be left in limbo, without explicit support from MI6, and he found work at the Royal United Services Institute for Defence Studies in Whitehall. His legal status remained uncertain as he was never handed the promised Russian presidential pardon, and his lawyer in Moscow could only elicit the FSB's official opinion that he was a 'fugitive from justice'. As his two daughters were at university, this meant that his family could visit him in London, but he could not return to Russia.

Meanwhile, Skripal was put in harness by MI6, undergoing a lengthy debrief at Fort Monckton, and then offered alias resettlement, as experienced by Oleg Lyalin, Vladimir Rezun, Vladimir Kuzichkin and Oleg Gordievsky.[1] All four had been issued with new documentation, suitably back-stopped, and identities that allowed them to live out their retirement free from the fear of retribution. The process had worked as planned for the Rezuns, both GRU officers who were relocated in a university city, but Kuzichkin did not fare so well, suffered a psychiatric collapse and died in 2007. Lyalin, who died in February 1995, had lived under MI5's protection for twenty-one years without incident, although the KGB had made one attempt to penetrate the Metropolitan Police Special Branch to trace his hiding place.

Gordievsky's resettlement had presented particular problems because of his ex-wife, Leila, who was the daughter of a KGB officer, and their two daughters Maria and Anna, who eventually opted to return to Russia. Although Gordievsky was provided with an alias identity, and a detached suburban house in the Home Counties, his contact with the foreign media meant his cover was semi-transparent.

The risk of an attack on defectors in Britain increased dramatically with the assassination of Alexander Litvinenko in November 2006 when he was poisoned by two former FSB colleagues, Andrei Lugovoi and Dmitri Kovtun, in the Millennium Hotel in Grosvenor Square. Litvineko had been granted asylum upon his arrival in London in November 2000 and six years later acquired British citizenship.

While not strictly a Russian intelligence defector formally under British protection, the forty-three year-old Litvinenko was paid a consultancy retainer by MI6 and it sponsored his visit to Madrid in 2005 to lecture at the CNI on Russian organised crime. After three weeks of hospital treatment, Litvinenko succumbed to a radioactive toxin, polonium -210, three weeks after it had been administered in a cup of tea.[2]

Skripal's resettlement posed some of the same challenges as Gordievsky in that he remained in Skype contact with his family in Russia, consisting of his elderly mother Yelena, his brother Valeri, and his son and daughter, who visited regularly. In 2011 MI6 funded Skripal's new home, chosen by Yulia, at 47 Christie Miller Road, Salisbury, for £260,000, and his wife Liudmila then joined them. Thereafter, Skripal's usefulness as an intelligence source was probably quite limited, considering that his interviews at Fort Monckton had been designed to extract just about everything he knew about the GRU, however out of date. Additionally, recent defectors are routinely circulated to allied intelligence agencies in a classic 'dog and pony' show to encourage co-operation, and reportedly Skripal visited Prague in 2012 and again in October 2014 at the invitation of the BIS Czech intelligence service. Soon afterwards, on both occasions, three and then two Russian diplomats respectively were expelled from the country, the implication being that Skripal had identified his former colleagues at the local GRU *rezidentura*, and their Czech hosts had taken the appropriate action. Similarly, Skripal was alleged to have visited Tallinn in June 2016, Madrid and also Bogota. Usually such assignments are limited to a study of local diplomatic personnel, or perhaps an assessment of local Russian organised crime, but occasionally defectors are deployed to encounter former friends and colleagues in a bid to persuade them of the advantages of defection. Such pitches are, of course, fraught with danger and often resented by the recipients of the approach, which would normally be an obligatory reporting matter. Failure to report would be open to misinterpretation, but the submission of a report might also engender sufficient suspicion to hinder a career.

By Russian standards, a degree of attrition following a defection is regarded as an occupational hazard, to be expected, but to aggressively pursue staff to persuade them to defect is quite unacceptable and might amount to justification for an extreme act to deter such behaviour.

Chapter VIII

Salisbury

On Monday, 4 March 2018 Sergei Skripal and his thirty-three year-old daughter Yulia collapsed in the centre of Salisbury suffering the effects of A-234, a third-generation, Russian-manufactured, military-grade Novichok nerve agent. Yulia had only flown in to England to join her father the previous afternoon, and had accompanied him on a visit for a drink at the Bishop's Mill pub on Sunday afternoon before lunching at Zizzi's Italian restaurant in Castle Street.

The Skripals had been living in the Wiltshire market town for the past seven years, and the local cemetery contained the grave of Sergei's wife Liudmila, who died of uterine cancer aged fifty-nine in October 2012, and his alcoholic forty-three year-old son Sasha, who died of liver failure in St Petersburg in July 2017. In the same year, Sergei's elder brother Valeri died in Yaroslav, east of Moscow.

After the attack Sergei Skripal remained in a coma for five weeks, and would not be discharged from hospital until May, when he was placed under MI6's protection. Meanwhile, an army decontamination operation, code-named MORLOP, dismantled his house and garage and took a year to declare the area safe.

As the police investigation unfolded it emerged that the front door handle of Colonel Skripal's home at 47 Christie Miller Road had been contaminated with the toxin, and three suspects, all GRU officers, were quickly identified, based on CCTV evidence and mobile phone records. The principal person of interest was Colonel Anatoli Chepiga, alias Aleksandr Petrov; and his companion, Dr Alexander Mishkin, alias Rusian Boshirov, a combat physician. Both men had flown into Gatwick two days before the incident, and had returned to Moscow on the same evening. A third suspect, forty-eight year-old General Denis Sergeyev, alias Sergei Fedotov, had also arrived on Friday, 2 March on a separate Aeroflot flight from Moscow, and departed on his return flight bound for Sheremetyevo at 1330 on Sunday. Examination of Yulia's email account suggested that it had been hacked regularly for the past seven years.

The three serving GRU officers had distinguished military careers, some details of which were publicly available. Chepiga, born in Nikolaevka in April 1979, had been educated at the Far Eastern Military Command Academy in Blagoveschensk, and then served with the 14th Spetsnaz Brigade at Khabarovsk, and fought during the second Chechen war in 2014. During three tours of duty in Chechnya, Chepiga received twenty commendations and in December 2014 received Russia's highest military honour, Hero of the Russian Federation, for an unspecified act of valour, probably in the Ukraine. His large apartment was on the twelfth floor of a GRU building near the organization's headquarters on Prechistenka Street.

Less public information was available on Sergeyev, who had been born in Usharal, Kazakhstan, in 1973 and had attended the Suvorov Military School in Ekaterinburg, graduating in 1990, and then passed out from the Military Diplomatic Academy in Moscow.[1]

Mishkin was born in 13 July 1979 in the village of Loyga, in the Archangelsk District in Northern European Russia, and studied in St Petersburg where he attended the S. Kirov Military Medical Academy. In late 2014 he was decorated Hero of the Russian Federation by Vladimir Putin, in recognition of his military service in the Ukraine. His apartment in Moscow, where he lived with his wife and two daughters, was in a GRU accommodation block,

The tradecraft adopted by the three included the extensive use of untraceable mobile phones using prepaid SIM cards, which revealed Sergeyev's movements in Moscow and his frequent visits to the GRU headquarters at Khoroshevskoe 67B, and to the GRU Academy at Narodnoe Opolchenie 50/1 in the north-east of the city, where he worked, and close to his apartment on Sorge Street, shared with his wife Tatyana and teenage son. During his weekend mission to London, Sergeyev posed as the manager of a courier business, a firm that when scrutinised was revealed to be a very flimsy GRU commercial front.

Although Sergeyev sent and received many secure encrypted communications over the weekend, he only made eleven telephone calls, all to the same unregistered number in Moscow, but identified online as 'Amir, Moscow'. He had taken a taxi from Heathrow to his hotel, but had gone back to the airport on the express from Paddington.

Scotland Yard's Counter-Terrorism Command conducted a lengthy enquiry and established a chronology of events, supported by an MI5 team led by the newly appointed deputy director-general, Ken McCallum, which placed Chepiga and Mishkin arriving at Gatwick on Friday afternoon, travelling to Victoria by rail, and then going straight to Waterloo, where they spent an hour before checking in to a shared room at the CityStay Hotel, a small budget two-star establishment in Bow, east London. At 1250 on Saturday afternoon they took the train from Waterloo to Salisbury, where they remained for an hour and a half before making the return journey and overnighting for a second time at the CityStay.

On Sunday the pair left Waterloo at 1020, arriving at Salisbury at 1148, and made the return journey at 1510, reaching Waterloo at 1645, and checking in at Heathrow at 1928. Thus, during a visit lasting from Friday afternoon to Sunday evening, the two GRU officers had made two trips to Salisbury where they had spent a total of five hours. The timeline suggested that the GRU men had walked straight to Skripal's home on Sunday morning, reaching it within ten minutes.

Even though Chepiga and Mishkin, still acting under alias, would later protest their innocence during a contrived television interview in Moscow, and claim to have been authentic tourists interested in the spire of Salisbury Cathedral, cutting short their visit because of inclement weather, their abnormal behaviour, and their reliance on classic tradecraft, marked them out as intelligence professionals equipped with an unusual choice of unregistered mobile phones. Their explanations sounded ludicrous to western audiences, but their purpose was merely to present a fig leaf defence, however implausible, just so there was a formal denial on the record.

Scotland Yard detectives found travel traces to show that Sergeyev had used the same alias to visit Britain in 2016 and March 2017, and that on the latter occasion Mishkin had also been in the country at the same time. All three held passports with very similar serial numbers, which were all issued in 2010 by the same office in Moscow. Sergeyev had visited Bulgaria three times, and a movements analysis revealed that all three men had credit card usage in France's Haute-Savoie, a travel pattern in the French Alps associated with the GRU's *Spetsnaz* Unit 29155.

Reportedly, 29155 was a covert group of Special Forces veterans commanded by General Andrei Averyanov and based at the 161st Specialist Training Centre in eastern Moscow.[2] Manned by personnel who had combat experience in Afghanistan and Chechnya, 29155 would become closely associated, through travel to Zurich, Geneva, Lausanne, Barcelona and Amsterdam, and distinctive mobile phone use, with computer hacking. In April 2018, four GRU officers, Alexei Minin, Oleg Sotnikov, Evgenni Serebriakov and Aleksei Morenets, were apprehended in The Hague as they attempted to circumvent computer security at a sensitive site, the headquarters of the Organisation for the Prohibition of Chemical Weapons (OPCW), which was located in Johan de Witlaan street, adjacent to their rooms in the Marriott Hotel.[3] All four were carrying Russian diplomatic passports, and had been met at Schiphol Airport by an accredited Russian embassy official. Two of the passports were issued on the same day, and had sequential numbers. Despite the wads of cash and espionage paraphernalia found by the Dutch defence intelligence service (MIVD) in their rented Citroen C3, including mobile phones and a digital camera containing a photo of a taxi receipt for Minin's journey from the GRU headquarters at Komsomolsky Prospekt 20 in Moscow to Sheremetyevo, the four were expelled once their diplomatic status had been verified.

At the time the OPCW had been one of several international facilities analysing samples of the toxin recovered in Salisbury, and study of the Russians' movements across Europe by train and plane disclosed their intention to target another research facility, the Spietz Laboratory, near Berne. Evidently the Swiss federal institute, which had also been entrusted with working on the same substance, was to be the subject of a 29155 mission, as suggested by an advance train ticket for 17 April from Utrecht to Berne.

While General Sergeyev stayed at a hotel near Paddington station, Chapiga and Mishkin had travelled to Salisbury by train twice, from Waterloo, and mobile phone analysis suggested the three may have held a rendezvous on the Thames embankment before going to the railway station.

Following the death in June of an Amesbury resident, forty-four year-old Dawn Sturgess, the local police recovered a receptacle, a Nina Ricci *Premier Jour* perfume bottle, which apparently had been used to carry the Novichok, and had been discarded in a rubbish bin. Sturgess's boyfriend, Charlie Rowley, had found the bottle and had unwittingly given it to her, with fatal consequences.

* * *

In September 2018 Chapiga and Mishkin were formally charged by Scotland Yard with conspiracy to murder, but as yet no further arrest warrants have been issued. However, in February 2020 prosecutors in Sofia announced that an investigation into two attempts on the life in 2015 of a local factory owner, Emilian Gebrev, his son Christo, and another Bulgarian, had resulted in warrants being issued against forty-one year-old Egor Gordienko, alias Georgi A. Gorshkov, a Russian diplomat accredited to the Russian Mission to the World Trade Organization in Switzerland, and two companions, Sergei Fedotov and Sergei V. Pavlov. On the night Gebrev was poisoned, possibly with a nerve agent seen on CCTV to have been sprayed onto the door handle of his grey Nissan in the underground car park of the Marinela Hotel, where he was dining in the tenth-floor rooftop restaurant, the three Russians had caught a flight from Sofia to Istanbul, where they changed planes and flew to Moscow. It was later speculated that Gebrev had made himself a GRU target because his business, EMCO, supplied weapons to the Ukrainian and Georgian governments. A month after the first attack, when Gebrev was recuperating at his home on the Black Sea south of Burgas, a second attempt was made.

Fedotov, of course, was the alias adopted by Sergeyev, and Pavlov has been unmasked as Sergei Lyutenko, a GRU officer whom MI5 established had previously visited London with Sergeyev from 26 February to 4 March 2017. The third, using the false identity of Gorshkov, was actually Gordienko who, like the others, had checked into the Hill Hotel, close to EMCO's offices. Nine days later he had flown back to Moscow from Greece.

Altogether eight GRU officers were identified by the Bulgarian authorities as having visited Bulgaria in what appeared to be four sequential missions. The first, in February 2015, had involved Sergeyev, Lyutenko and Gordienko staying in Sofia for a week. They left on 22 February and were replaced by another trio, Ivan Terentiev, alias Ivan Lebedev; Nikolai Ezhov, alias Nikolai Kononnykhin; and Alexei Kalinin, alias Alexei Nikitin. Finally, on 6 March, Vladimir Moiseev, alias Vladimir Popov, arrived and stayed until 11 March. Then, on 24 April, Sergeyev, Lyutenko and Gordienko returned, but left on the night of the murder attempt, 28 April, when Gebrev fell ill for the second time and went into a coma, nearly dying in Sofia's military hospital. Two days later, on 30 April, Sergeyev and Gordienko drove in a rented car to Belgrade, and flew back to Moscow.

Scrutiny of flight data later suggested that Sergeyev went back to Bulgaria on 23 May, landing at Burgas accompanied by another GRU officer, Danil

Kapralov, a combat physician who had adopted the alias Danil Stepanov. When they rented a car at the airport they disabled the GPS tracking system, presumably to avoid leaving a record of their movements. Finally, on 28 May, Gordienko flew back to Sofia, but only stayed two days, driving to Belgrade with Sergeyev to catch a flight to Moscow.

Of the eight suspects directly implicated, Moiseev had attracted some notoriety as the former *Spetsnaz* soldier and veteran of the 2008 war with Georgia who had been named as a conspirator involved in the plot to stage a coup in Montenegro in October 2016. The plan, foiled at the last moment by the local security apparatus in the capital Podgorica, was to assassinate the NATO-supporting prime minister, Milo Djukanovic, seize the parliament and install a pro-Moscow administration in the tiny Balkan state. In the criminal trial that followed in October 2017 two Russians, both described as GRU officers, were prosecuted *in absentia:* Vladimir N. Popov (who had posed as a photo-journalist but was really Moiseev), and Eduard Shishmakov, alias Eduard V. Shirokov, a former Russian assistant military attaché in Warsaw who in June 2014 had been expelled for espionage, having been incriminated by a Polish spy identified only as 'Lieutenant-Colonel Zbigniew J', deputy director of the Defence Ministry's education and publicity department, who in May 2016 was imprisoned for six years by a military tribunal.

Popov and Shirokov were convicted and sentenced to twelve and fifteen years' imprisonment respectively, but the Kremlin declined to extradite them. Instead, a senior SVR officer, General Leonid P. Reshetnikov, previously responsible for operations in Bulgaria until his official retirement in 2009, was removed from his post at Moscow's prestigious Institute for Strategic Studies without explanation.

Commenting on what he described as a failure by an over-ambitious GRU, Igor Sutyagin wryly observed on the bungled coup, 'It's embarrassing for everybody. You are not guilty if you fail. You are guilty if you fail and get caught.'[4]

The attempt on Emilian Gebrev's life marked a downturn in the Bulgarian government's already strained relations with Russia, and the episode continued to have an influence, as was demonstrated in January 2020 when two Russian diplomats were expelled from Sofia at forty-eight hours' notice for their involvement in the coup, and a newly appointed incoming military attaché was refused a visa.

From Scotland Yard's viewpoint, the incident had compelling significance, for it linked the attempt to kill Skripal in Salisbury to three identified GRU officers carrying state-sponsored false documentation, one of whom demonstrably was connected to another GRU-linked bid to kill Gebrev in Sofia three years earlier.

Chapter IX

Directorate S

The mainstream media reaction to the failed assassination in Salisbury was typical of the earlier almost universal misinterpretation of the GHOST STORIES coup, which represented the arrestees as incompetent 'sleepers' who had failed in their mission and had been tripped up by their own bungles. Once again, western analysts had fallen into the trap of 'mirror imaging', the tendency to judge Moscow by Washington standards. In particular, relatively little was understood about Directorate S, or the culture of *konspiratsia* that was its foundation. Put simply, the SVR, like its KGB predecessor, placed an emphasis on clandestine intelligence collection techniques in preference to reliance on what the west termed open sources. Because of an innate distrust of everything published in the west, the Kremlin's policy makers opted to believe their spies, and were prepared to invest heavily in an extraordinarily expensive illegals programme that would not be contemplated by their adversaries. Certainly the CIA and, to a lesser extent, MI6 had run non-official cover operations, but not on anything like the scale of Directorate S. Any cost–benefit analysis mitigated against the widespread use of such volunteers, the penalties for whom could be immense if caught. The CIA's euphemistic Office of External Development was haunted by the memory of Hugh F. Redmond, originally from Yonkers and ostensibly a representative of Henningsen and Co., a food import–export company based in Hong Kong, who had been arrested in Shanghai in April 1951 as he attempted to board a ship bound for San Francisco.

A former D-Day paratrooper with the 101st Airborne Division, Redmond died nineteen years later in a Chinese prison, still protesting his innocence. Redmond had enlisted in the US Army in July 1941 and fought in Normandy and Arnhem in 1944 before being wounded during the Battle of the Bulge in January 1945. When he was discharged in October 1945, he had been decorated with the Silver Star, a Bronze Star with Oak Leaf Clusters, and a Purple Heart. In July 1946, he had been enrolled in the War Department's

Strategic Services Unit, a clandestine organization headed by Colonel John Magruder, an Office of Strategic Services (OSS) veteran, and posted to Shanghai, where he had married a White Russian piano teacher named Lydia. Having arranged for her to leave China, Redmond had been detained with dozens of Americans, mainly missionaries.

Chinese news reports of his arrest claimed Redmond had been the organiser of a spy ring consisting of seven agents, and according to a 700-word indictment he had routinely used an alias, Jerome Strother, and a code name, EUCLID.

Almost nothing had been known about Redmond's incarceration, apart from his conviction and life sentence, until a fellow inmate at the notorious Ward Road Gaol was released to Hong Kong in July 1952, and further news emerged in March 1953, when a German prisoner was interviewed. Then in April 1954, a French priest, Alberto Palacios, reported having shared his cell in Shanghai's Rue Massenet prison. Five months later, in September 1954, Shanghai's Military Control Committee announced that Redmond had been linked to a spy ring that had been set up by OSS. Allegedly, the Chinese authorities had seized a large amount of incriminating material, including sixteen code books, six bottles of an ingredient for developing secret ink, hundreds of compromising documents, and a suitcase with a hidden compartment. Also convicted were five other men and two women, of whom Wang Ko-yi and Lo Shih-hsiang were executed in Redmond's presence.

By the end of 1955, twenty-eight of the forty-one Americans in Chinese custody had been released, but the State Department had seemed reluctant to make representations on behalf of Redmond's family. In January 1958, his mother, Ruth, was allowed a brief visit to his prison, a meeting arranged by the Red Cross and reported by the *New York Times*. Thereafter, they exchanged letters each month, and she made two further visits, in October 1962 and October 1963, but failing health prevented her from making further journeys. In 1968, the CIA, while maintaining the pretence that Redmond was simply an innocent businessman, arranged for an intermediary to pretend that a fund of $1 million had been accumulated from donations made by well-wishers and attempted to open ransom negotiations with Chinese diplomats, but nothing happened.

Finally, in July 1970, Beijing announced that on 13 April 1970 Redmond had died after having severed an artery in his arm with a razor. His body had been cremated and his ashes were handed over to the American Red Cross for burial in his native town, Yonkers, New York. Inevitably, Redmond's tragic experience, and his determination not to embarrass his country or the Agency, cast a long shadow over the deployment of NOCs.[1]

Redmond's harrowing incarceration contrasted sharply with the only two KGB illegal *rezidents* caught in the west, Willie Fisher and Konon Molody. Arrested in New York in June 1957, Fisher spent just four years in prison before he was freed in an exchange for the U-2 pilot F. Gary Powers in February 1962.

Fisher had entered the United States from Canada in November 1946, having sailed to Quebec on the SS *Scythia* from Cuxhaven. His US passport was in the name of Emil Goldfus, born in 1902 in New York, who had died at the age of fourteen months. After nine years in his post, Fisher had been betrayed by his assistant, Reino Hayhanen, who had been recalled to Moscow but had decided, while in Paris on his return journey in May 1957, to seek asylum at the US embassy. Under interrogation by the FBI, Hayhanen supplied enough information to identify Fisher who, in the absence of evidence of espionage, was arrested on immigration charges.

In a series of interviews Hayhanen gave the FBI full details of his background and training as a KGB illegal, describing how in September 1954 he had been assigned by the New York *rezident*, Mikhail Svirin, who operated under United Nations diplomatic cover, to an illegal *rezident*, whom he knew only as 'Mark'. He met Mark for the first time at a cinema in Flushing, Long Island, and thereafter was in contact weekly, fulfilling various minor routine tasks. Hayhanen had arrived in the United States in October 1952 via Helsinki and London, and established himself as a newly arrived Finnish immigrant seeking a job as a garage mechanic in Brooklyn, Newark and finally Peekskill.

An alcoholic, Hayhanen had been motivated to defect after he had performed poorly, moved in with a girlfriend, failed to make any recruitments, and had misappropriated $5,000, which he had been instructed to deliver to Helen Sobell, the wife of the imprisoned spy Morton Sobell. Once safely in American custody, he had helped the FBI find Mark's studio in Fulton Street, Brooklyn, a development that served to compromise the illegal *rezident*, even though he had taken the precaution of moving to a new hotel under yet another false identity.

Apparently confident that he would be exchanged, Fisher adopted an impressively professional attitude and declined to assist the FBI in any way whatever, beyond claiming (falsely) to be a Soviet citizen named Colonel Rudolf Abel.

Similarly, Molody, who had been arrested in London in January 1961, was swapped after just over four years in custody. However, during the first six months of his twenty-five-year prison sentence he was interviewed frequently by MI5's Charles Elwell, who attempted to negotiate a deal that might mean a review of his sentence, or even his release in a prisoner exchange, in return for his co-operation. Molody, who consistently refused to admit his real name, even though he acknowledged having been a Soviet intelligence officer since 1941, struck up a rapport with Elwell and confided that he had information to trade, but was interested in returning to Moscow and then escaping to the west with his son Trofim and daughter Lisa, if not his wife Galya. He also explained that even with full remission he was facing sixteen years in prison, which he could not contemplate, and in time he would lose any influence he had with friends in the Illegals Directorate as they moved on or retired.

Elwell's curious affinity with Molody was based partly on shared experiences. They had known each other briefly in July 1956 while studying Chinese at London University, when Elwell had adopted the alias 'Charles Elton'. Elwell also had first-hand experience of being imprisoned, as in March 1942 he had become a prisoner of war in Holland, having been caught landing agents on the coast, and he would not be liberated from Oflag IV-c at Colditz Castle until April 1945.

After interviewing Molody in Manchester's prison at the end of July 1961, Elwell reported on their conversation;

> I took the opportunity of telling Lonsdale that the only thing that really interested us was any names of Russian spies either active or inactive. Lonsdale said that he did not know the names of many and he thought it too risky to give us the names of those he did. Whereas he might just get away with telling us what he proposed to tell us, he would never be forgiven for betraying another spy. Even if he succeeded in escaping to the West he would be recorded as a traitor and his name put down on a list of those who would be assassinated.[2]

The two men developed a relationship of kinds, to the point that Molody suggested a writing partnership in which Elwell should ghost his memoirs, an offer he declined. Significantly, having proposed an elaborate exfiltration plan, Molody asked that details should not be shared with MI6 as he believed the organization had been penetrated. When pressed on this tantalising issue, Molody claimed that the KGB would have fully exploited information about his MI6 colleagues supplied by George Blake. Although he had met Blake in prison, and could not be absolutely sure of the organization's hostile penetration, he considered it highly likely. He also hinted at the existence of another spy whom he was prepared to reveal if he could be sure the KGB never learned of his betrayal. In addition, Molody requested resettlement in England and financial support amounting to £1,000 a year.

Molody had arrived in Southampton aboard the SS *America* in March 1955 on a Canadian passport in the name of Gordon A. Lonsdale, with the stated intention of undertaking a post-graduate course at London University. He had come under MI5 surveillance in May 1960 when one of his sources, Harry Houghton, had been identified as a spy on information shared by the CIA. Code-named REVERBERATE, Houghton had unwittingly led his MI5 watchers to his contact, Molody, who was code-named LAST ACT. He in turn was investigated and inadvertently compromised his communications support, Morris and Lona Cohen, who were based in suburban Ruislip, pretending to be New Zealanders Peter and Helen Kroger. In reality, they were both Americans who had fled New York in July 1950 after they had been implicated in the spy ring headed by Julius and Ethel Rosenberg. Until their true identities were established the couple were code-named KILLJOY by MI5.[3]

MI5's surveillance, Operation WHISPER, continued until January 1961 when Houghton, his co-conspirator Ethel Gee (code-named TRELLIS), Molody and the Cohens were taken into custody and their homes searched. A large quantity of incriminating espionage paraphernalia was recovered, but while Molody acknowledged his role as a KGB illegal, he divulged very little of substance. However, he did say, in casual conversation with Elwell, that he thought he had detected some surveillance in November 1960, which he had reported to Moscow, but had not been allowed to flee on the basis of his unconfirmed suspicion. It would take a further six months for Molody's true name and family background in California, where he had been brought up before the war by his aunt Tatiana Piankova, to be discovered by the FBI. Molody himself explained that he was reluctant to admit his name as this news would be interpreted in Moscow as evidence he had co-operated with his captors.

The FBI's research revealed that Molody had become an American citizen while he was living with his mother's divorced sister, who taught ballet dancing in Berkeley. A check in US immigration records showed that he had also been issued a legitimate passport in February 1938 in anticipation of his return to Europe, at the age of seventeen, Tatiana having described him on the passport application form as her son. The FBI learned that Molody's mother, Yekatarina, had been a well-known physician in Moscow, her home address still listed in the city's telephone directory as 16/20 Subovsky Boulevard, and that her third sister Anastasia had been arrested in 1949 in San Francisco as a suspected abortionist. Molody's first cousin, George Jaure (third aunt Serafima's son), was also traced by the FBI to the restaurant he owned in Santa Rosa and interviewed.

Molody would remain in prison until April 1964, when he was exchanged for Greville Wynne, an MI6 asset arrested in Budapest in October 1962. The Cohens would also be freed in a swap in July 1969 for a British academic, Gerald Brooke, who was serving a five-year sentence for smuggling anti-Soviet leaflets into Moscow.

Whereas the KGB developed and deliberately promoted a reputation for extracting its personnel, the CIA became increasingly risk averse, especially as Redmond's espionage became an issue when President Richard Nixon made his historic visit to Chairman Mao Zedong in Beijing in February 1972. The Chinese negotiators who arranged the meeting insisted as a precondition that Nixon acknowledge Redmond's true role as a spy.

Since that episode the CIA has understandably been discreet about its deployment of NOCs into denied territory, and this was the underlying sensitivity surrounding Valerie Plaime, who ostensibly dropped out of her CIA career to become a NOC in Europe. Plaime's role as a CIA analyst working in the Iraqi weapons of mass destruction task force became public knowledge when in 2002 her (then) husband Joe Wilson undertook a mission to Niger to look for evidence of the regime's illicit acquisition of uranium yellow cake. In the ensuing controversy, sparked by Wilson's own newspaper articles, Plaime's previous role as an NOC was revealed, although the disclosure by the columnist Bob Novak did not breach the 1979 Intelligence Identities Protection Act, the criminal statute designed to prevent the compromise of undercover personnel. The very unwelcome public debate about Plaime's CIA career drew unwanted attention to an aspect of covert intelligence collection, as did her 2007 memoirs, *Fair Game*, in which her co-author Laura Rozen circumvented the CIA's confidentiality rules and gave a detailed account of Plaime's clandestine missions.[4]

The concept of planting intelligence officers into an alien environment and leaving them to live completely artificial lives embedded in a foreign country is quite antithetic to westerners, so MI6 has rejected the Soviet model in favour of providing 'natural cover' for missions of short duration. With rather greater resources at its disposal, the CIA has a long history of posting NOCs overseas under a variety of commercial and journalistic covers. Indeed, it is no coincidence that when the CIA was created in 1947 it was joined by quite a number of FBI veterans who had served during the war in Latin America in the super-secret Special Intelligence Service (SIS). When the SIS had been established in 1942 all its overseas personnel were deployed under a variety of commercial covers before the US State Department eventually, and reluctantly, accepted the concept of 'legal attaché' posts in its missions abroad.[5]

* * *

The extent to which Directorate S lost its prestige over the 2010 arrests quickly became apparent during the course of a further FBI surveillance operation conducted from March 2012 by the New York Field Office against Evgeni Buryakov, a forty year-old Russian banker working on Third Avenue in Manhattan for a state-owned development bank, Vnesheconombank, under his own true identity. Information from a former Merrill Lynch oil analyst and ex-US Navy lieutenant, Carter Page, supplied to the CIA, suggested that in 2008 he had become the focus of an SVR recruitment operation, and he had identified his contact in New York as a consular official, Aleksandr Bulatov, who turned out to be an SVR officer. Page would remain a CIA 'operational contact' until 2013, and receive a positive assessment from his case officer.

Between 2004 and 2007 Page had lived in Moscow and had been Merrill Lynch's local deputy branch manager. In the following years Page, whose grandly titled consultancy Global Energy Capital failed, cultivated several Russians, including his future business partner, Sergei Yatsenko, of Gazprom. Based on the CIA's tip, Buryakov and his wife Marina came under the FBI's scrutiny, and both his rented, two-storey home in Leibig Avenue in the Bronx and his twenty-ninth floor office were the subject of FISA warrants.

The FBI placed Buryakov under intensive physical and electronic surveillance in March 2012, which revealed his frequent meetings with two SVR officers based at the New York *rezidentura*. One was Igor Sporyshev, the son of the FSB's General Mikhail Sporychev, who had worked at the Russian Trade Mission since November 2010, and the other was their SVR superior officer, Viktor Podobny, based with the Russian delegation to the United Nations since December 2010. As part of the FBI's counter-intelligence operation the Russians were handed large binders containing economic data relating to the oil industry, which also concealed miniature eavesdropping equipment. When the bulky files were stored in the *referentura* they recorded numerous compromising conversations, in one of which Buryakov acknowledged that he had acted in an undercover role for the SVR during his previous posting, which had lasted five years, in Pretoria. FBI analysis of the audio recordings concluded that the SVR's principal task was the collection of economic intelligence for the organization's Directorate ER.

Not all the transcripts compromised the SVR officers. In one recording, relating to an exchange in his office in Russian with Sporyshev, Podobny complained that his life was hardly comparable to James Bond's:

> I'm sitting with a cookie right now at the [...] chief enemy spot. Fuck! Not one point of what I thought then [corrupt] not even close. [corrupt] movies about James Bond. Of course, I wouldn't fly helicopters, but pretend to be someone else at a minimum.[6]

On another occasion, on 25 April 2013, a discussion was taped about the GHOST STORIES episode, when Podobny remarked to his twenty-seven-year-old subordinate Sporyshev, 'First of all, Directorate S is the only intelligence that is real intelligence, Directorate S,' to which his companion replied, 'It was.' This prompted Podobny to elaborate:

> I don't know about now. No some things remain, like Middle East, Asia, not everything has fallen. Look, in the States even the S couldn't do anything.
>
> They caught ten of them. And you remember what they were charged with: illegal cashing [of the money] the Center sent, that's all! And then Putin even tried to justify that they weren't even tasked to work, they were sleeper cells in case of martial law. They

weren't doing shit here, you understand. Maybe they had a directive not to do anything, if they were here 10 years or whatever … they were in the States in the sleeper mode only.

Well, they studied some people, worked out some exits, but they didn't get any materials … It would've been a lot prettier than just wrongly filled out immigration, false identity, and money laundering. Well, they got slapped with money laundering only because they were sending cash by mail. That is it. So, when we discussed that we need to work from different positions, I agree that untraditional is more effective but even the S cannot do anything here.[7]

A fortnight earlier, on 8 April, the FBI's covert microphones had also caught Podobny discussing the chances of recruiting Carter Page, explaining that Page

wrote that he is sorry, he went to Moscow and forgot to check his inbox, but he wants to meet when he gets back. I think he is an idiot and forgot who I am. Plus he writes to me in Russian [to] practice the language. He flies to Moscow more often than I do. He got hooked on Gazprom thinking that if they have a project, he could be rise up. Maybe he can. I don't know, but it's obvious that he wants to earn lots of money …

Sporyshev: Without a doubt.

Podobny: He said that they have a new project right now, new energy boom. He says that it is about to take off. I don't say anything for now.

Sporyshev: Yeah, first we will spend a couple of borrowed million and then …

Podobny: [corrupt] [laughs] it's worth it. I like that he takes on everything. For now his enthusiasm works for me. I also promised him a lot: that I have connections in the Trade Representation, meaning that you can push contracts [laughs]. I will feed him empty promises.

Sporyshev: Shit, then he will write me. Not even me, to our clean one.

Podobny: I didn't say the Trade Representation … I did not even indicate that this is connected to a government agency. This is intelligence method to cheat, how else to work with foreigners? You promise a favour for a favour. You get the documents from him and tell him to go fuck himself. But not to upset you, I will take you to a restaurant and give you an expensive gift. You just need to sign for it. This is ideal working method.[8]

Based on this evidence of a potentially incriminating relationship, the FBI's Gregory Monaghan interviewed Page on 13 June 2013, when he recalled meeting Podobny in January at an energy symposium held in New York and sponsored by the Asia Society. Thereafter, under the FBI's supervision, Carter continued to meet Podobny.

The FBI operation remained active until January 2015, when Butyakov was arrested and charged with being an unregistered agent. He pleaded guilty and was sentenced to thirty months' imprisonment and a $100,000 fine. When he was released at the end of March 2017 from the federal prison at Elkton, Ohio, Buryakov was deported to Moscow. His co-conspirators, who claimed diplomatic immunity, were quickly withdrawn from New York.

Meanwhile, Carter Page remained running his consultancy in New York, and in July 2016 was invited, apparently on the basis of his recent appointment as a foreign policy adviser to Donald Trump, to give a lecture to one of Moscow's new private universities, the New Economics School. When news of Page's controversially pro-Putin views became known in Washington, he was removed from Trump's panel of advisers.

* * *

All too often self-styled Kremlin-watchers had taken a single incident out of context, avoided the discomfort of seeing history through Soviet-era eyes, and ignored the Chekist mindset in which power, and the exercise of power, is itself the goal, however self-deluded or illusory that might be. By failing to recognize that the Russian Federation has a GDP comparable to South Korea or Spain, that the oil-dependent economy is in ruins, and that conditions outside the cities of Moscow and St Petersburg are recognizably Third World, western commentators invariably exaggerate the nature of the perceived Kremlin threat. Worse, they denounce atrocities such as the apartment block bombings in three Russian cities in September 1999; the murder of the journalist Anna Politkovskaya in Moscow in October 2006; the assassination of Sasha Litvinenko in London in November 2006, or the destruction of the Malaysian Airlines Flight 17 over the Ukraine in July

2014, as evidence of a pattern of criminal behaviour that could just as easily be seen as evidence of a dysfunctional command-and-control system that is more reminiscent of a medieval barons' court, jockeying for position and the king's favour, rather than proof of any Machiavellian masterplan, Moscow's reaction to these events has served to reinforce German Chancellor Helmut Kohl's famous characterisation in 1988 of the Soviet Union as 'Upper Volta with nuclear weapons' followed in 2013 by the condemnation 'Nigeria with snow'.

In the face of unchecked corruption, inconsistent governance, rigged elections and the absence of a dependable legal system, the regime has bet heavily on permanently high oil prices, and has adopted unbridled opportunism as a foreign policy in the Crimea, Georgia and Syria. On the basis that the best form of defence is attack, Vladimir Putin has either sponsored or tolerated various degrees of cyber-warfare, ranging from election interference to wholesale sabotage of target sectors, such as banking and utility companies.

With his own Line KR background, Putin understood better than most the scale of the betrayals perpetrated by Vladimir Mitrokhin, Sergei Tretyakov, Alexander Zaporozhsky, Gennadi Vasilenko, Alexander Poteyev and Alexander Shcherbakov. He would also have recognized the remarkable professionalism of the FBI over the ten years of the surveillance conducted against the Directorate S network in the United States.

Putin had been an eyewitness to the collapse of the GDR in November 1989 while serving in Dresden, the country's third largest city, in Line KR. The impact on all concerned is hard to exaggerate, and one of Putin's East German colleagues, Dresden's Stasi chief General Horst Boehm, committed suicide in February 1990 as the socialist state imploded. According to some reports, based on his authorised 1990 autobiography *First Person,*[9] on the night of 5 December 1989 Putin had stood at the gate of the walled compound and brandished his handgun at a small crowd of demonstrators outside the KGB building, across the street from the local Stasi headquarters located in a converted paper mill at Bauznerstrasse 112a in Dresden, to prevent the site from being occupied. The KGB building itself was a large, two-storey detached villa once owned, before the war, by the well-known Austrian conductor Karl Bóhm, at the heart of Loschwitz, a district that accommodated numerous Stasi offices and personnel. Allegedly Putin had telephoned the local Red Army garrison to request protection, but the duty officer had refused, saying, 'We cannot do anything without orders from Moscow ... and Moscow is silent.'

Putin had graduated in law from the St Petersburg State University and, aged thirty-three, after ten years in the KGB, and married to Lyudmila, with Maria, the first of two daughters, he had been posted to Dresden in August 1985 with the rank of major, to be based at a KGB sub-*rezidentura* at Angelikastrasse 4, a sub-office headed by Lazar Matveev, who was subordinate to the KGB *rezident* in Karlshorst, Aleksandr Prinzipalow. There Putin shared a *referentura* on the first floor with six other colleagues, adopted an operational cover name and, when necessary, posed as an interpreter for the German–Soviet Friendship Society. He shared an office with a Siberian, Vladimir Ussotsev, who was the same age and rank, and lived in a modest, three-room apartment at 101 Raderbergersrasse in a yellow-painted block reserved for Stasi families overlooking the forested Jagerpark. The conditions must have been cramped following the birth of his second daughter, Yekatarina, but they would have been infinitely better than anywhere he had lived in St Petersburg or, during training, in Moscow. Although he was poorly paid, at 1,800 Ostmarks ($150) a month, he had access to the subsidised store at the local Soviet military garrison, home of the 1st Guards Tank Division.

Within the FCD a posting to Dresden was regarded as a transfer to a backwater, relative to the 4th Department *rezidenturas* in Bonn, Hamburg or Vienna. The most prized positions were in the 1st (North American) or 3rd Department (Great Britain and Scandinavia), so the GDR was rather looked down upon as a slightly second-rate appointment usually filled by those who had been passed over for better, more challenging jobs on the intelligence front line.

As it turned out, Dresden would be something of the epicentre of the climactic events of 4 October 1989, when an estimated 20,000 would-be emigrants crowded into the city's railway station in a desperate attempt to catch a train to Czechoslovakia, where the authorities had declared an open frontier. Fearing an insurrection, the Stasi drafted in emergency reinforcements, of whom forty would suffer injuries in the disorder that ensued. These seismic events would herald dramatic changes, including the historic unification of the two Germanys, the dissolution of the Warsaw Pact and the collapse of the entire Soviet bloc.

Reportedly, as the regime began to crumble, and in the absence of any coherent direction from Moscow, where Mikhail Gorbachev had called for a change in the GDR's leadership, Putin devoted himself to the destruction of the sub-*referentura*'s records, which were burned in an incinerator. 'We burned so much stuff that the furnace burst.'[10] In February 1990 he was recalled to the Soviet Union, having been promoted to the rank of lieutenant-colonel.

The precise nature of Putin's duties during his nearly six years in Dresden has not been disclosed officially, but it is likely that he concerned himself with the recruitment of potential sources among the large number of foreign students at Dresden's University of Technology. Certainly such a group of vulnerable youths, often from third world countries, could not be ignored, either from a counter-intelligence perspective, in the likelihood that they would include some foreign agents, or from a recruitment viewpoint, as the student body might offer targets who would be destined for government posts upon their return home, and would therefore prove worthwhile investments. At least two of the four agents known to have been run from Angelikastrasse were German Volkspolizei intermediaries who routinely had direct contact with foreign students, and one in particular, named only as 'Rainer M', specialised in the recruitment of Latin Americans.

In addition, and in the absence of a permanent Line N officer in Dresden, for which there was probably no need, Line KR staff were often detached on temporary assignments, and were briefed accordingly, so it is very probable that Putin possessed rather more than a passing knowledge of, and interest in, KGB illegals travelling through his city. If Putin conformed to usual Line KR preoccupations, his job would have been partly operational, but mainly clerical, sifting through travel requests, reconciling records and checking files for matches. The 4th Department's overall objective was to monitor NATO readiness and maintain a watch on key installations, such as US Army bases in the Federal Republic, which could act as mobilisation indicators, and these goals was accomplished by interviewing visitors from the west and briefing East Germans with permission to travel outside the bloc.

During 1986, as relations between the GDR and the politburo in Moscow deteriorated, the KGB was directed to focus on local political developments and to detect unwelcome signs of closer ties between Bonn and East Berlin. This was a tricky task, especially as the KGB's own links with the Stasi became strained and the *rezidentura*'s members were no longer allowed unrestricted, unescorted visits to Stasi premises. Under instructions from Karlshorst, an operation code-named LUTSCH ('ray' or 'beam' of light in Russian) was initiated as a futile, last-ditch attempt to extend Soviet political leverage over influential figures within the regime. Having been at the heart of a fraternal bond between two allied services, Putin and his colleagues essentially had been ordered to subvert Erich Honecker.

In short, Putin was inculcated in the Chekist philosophy, and it is noticeable that during his rise to political power he came to rely increasingly on the *Siloviki*, an inner circle of his former KGB colleagues whom he appointed to key positions in his administrations, such as Igor Sechin, his long-serving chief of staff. Sechin had a GRU background in Mozambique before joining Putin's entourage in St Petersburg, and his son-in-law is currently a serving FSB officer. It was also noticeable that the status of the SVR and FSB would be elevated by the appointment of, for example, the former prime minister Mikhail Fradkov to head the SVR in 2007. Fradkov's successor, Sergei Naryshkin, appointed in December 2016, was also a former KGB officer, and sat on the Security Council.

The FSB chief, Nikolai Patrushev, had been a career KGB SCD officer in Leningrad. In May 2008 the new FSB director was another former KGB officer, General Alexander Bortnikov, who had joined SCD in 1975, and in June 2003 had been appointed head of the FSB in St Petersburg. Similarly, Putin's former chief of staff, Sergei Ivanov, had been a KGB FCD officer; and deputy prime minister Dmitry Kozak came from the GRU *Spetsnaz*. The *Siloviki* shared similar service backgrounds and often had strong connections to Putin when he was in St Petersburg.

The competition within the Kremlin is fuelled by a Soviet-era belief that the United States still represents 'the main adversary', as demonstrated by its participation in hostile operations, such as the entrapment by the FSB of the CIA case officer Ryan Fogle in a Moscow street in May 2013, when the incident was exploited for maximum propaganda value, both for domestic and international consumption. The twenty-six-year-old Fogle, wearing a blond wig and a baseball cap, had been lured to a rendezvous by what turned out to be an FSB 'dangle', and the hapless accredited member of the embassy's political section with the rank of third secretary was apprehended with his collection of espionage paraphernalia: two wigs; three pairs of sunglasses, a compass; a torch; penknife; Moscow street map; €100,000 in banknotes and a highly compromising letter:

Dear Friend

This is an advance from someone who is very impressed by your professionalism and who would greatly value working together with you in the future. For us, your safety is of the utmost importance, so we have chosen this route to make contact with you. And we will continue to take steps to secure your safety and keep our correspondence secret.

We are prepared to offer you $100,000 and discuss your experience, expertise and co-operation, and your payment might be far greater if you are prepared to answer some specific questions. Additionally, for long-term co-operation we offer up to $1,000,000 a year with the promise of additional bonuses for information that will help us.

To contact us again, please open a new Gmail account, which you will use only for communicating with us, in an internet café or a café with a WiFi connection. When signing up, do not use any personal information that could be used to identify you and the new account. So do not offer any real contact information, i.e. your telephone numbers or other email addresses.

If Gmail asks for your personal information, please, start the registration process again and try not to give them any information. After you register the new inbox, send an email to the address unbacggdA(at)gmail.com, and then check the inbox again exactly one week later to see if you have received our reply.

If you register the new email account in a café with a netbook or another device (for example, a tablet), then please do not use your own device with your own personal data on it. If possible, you should get a new device to connect with us, for cash. We will reimburse you for the purchase.

Thank you for reading this. We eagerly await the possibility of working with you in the near future.

Your friends.

Caught red-handed, the Colgate University graduate was declared *persona non grata* and expelled. This incident not only demonstrated the local

CIA station's willingness to engage in a mildly high-risk undertaking, but showed a level of aggression on the part of the FSB. Sometimes referred to by the *cognoscenti* as 'cage rattling', the business of establishing contact with a potential source is invariably fraught with danger, especially in a 'denied area' where an opponent can deploy a ubiquitous security apparatus. However, in a Moscow context, some risks are rewarded, as was demonstrated when an aeronautical engineer, Adolf Tolkachev, proved to be one of the CIA's greatest assets despite an initial reluctance to accept him at face value.[11]

Clearly, bilateral tensions were high, partly as a result of the imposition by the US Treasury and the European Union of economic sanctions on those associated with the leadership and the businesses linked to them also served to reinforce the siege mentality within the Kremlin. To underscore the point, the Russian media revealed the identity of Fogle's station chief, an almost unprecedented breach of protocol in the modern era.[12] Instead of restricting the discomfort to Russian state institutions, the sanctions were placed firmly on named individuals, their families, their companies, investments, bank accounts, credit cards, foreign homes, visas, mistresses and private jets. Their obvious purpose was to impose maximum inconvenience on those perceived to be Putin's cronies.

In terms of personal trust, Putin's knowledge of, or participation in, LUTSCH must have taken a toll in that he was being asked, through political expediency, to alter the nature of his friendships built up over recent years, and to some extent exploit them in the interests of socialist discipline.

Another Putin characteristic that may have its roots in his experience in Dresden is his dislike of the power exercised by street protestors, as manifested in Moscow and Kiev. He saw at first hand the destruction of Erich Honecker's distrusted regime as the GDR's unarmed population took to the streets and overwhelmed his security apparatus by sheer force of numbers in mainly non-violent demonstrations. He also had a ringside seat as the Stasi apparatus, the Ministry of State Security and its foreign intelligence branch, the HVA, was dissolved. He must also have been aware of the panicked efforts to shred the Normanienstrasse archive, and perhaps even of the corruption that led to the illicit sale by Alexander K. Prinzipelow and Alexander Sjubenko of the HVA's entire digitalised agent roster stored on disc. Code-named ROSEWOOD, the $2 million transaction would make the shredding operation largely redundant and open the HVA's secrets to the CIA. Despite the determination of two senior Stasi officers, Werner Grossmann and Rainer Hemmann, to protect the Stasi's crown jewels by passing the encrypted disks to the Karlshorst *rezidentura* for safe keeping, they ended up in the hands of the main adversary, and some 3,151 West Germans were identified as HVA spies in yet another humiliation.

Given Putin's background it is not hard to imagine that he would take the very closest professional interest in the performance of his country's intelligence agencies, and be anxious to avoid a repetition of past mishaps, and maybe even restore Russia to what he termed 'the first tier of nations'. However, the extent to which he directed, or even had advance knowledge of, the attack on Sergei Skripal remains moot. Among western Kremlin watchers, there are two views. One is that the state sponsorship of a series of incidents, dating back to the Litvinenko murder, is so obvious, almost to the point of advertising its complicity, that the pattern of behaviour cannot be explained by anything other than the adoption of a policy of extra-judicial killings that extended to émigrés, outspoken opponents of the regime, inquisitive journalists, anti-corruption campaigners, defectors, Chechen warlords and simply Kremlin critics. The list of potential victims includes an opposition parliamentarian, Vladimir Golovlyov, shot dead in a Moscow wood while walking his dog in August 2002; Sergei Yushenkov, one of the founders of the Liberal Russia Party, gunned down in a street in Moscow in April 2003. In July 2003 the Russian politician Yuri Shchekochikhin died of some toxin, probably a dioxin. In March 2004 the Islamist guerrilla leader Ibn al-Khattab died after he had been contaminated by a poisoned letter, and the St Petersburg businessman Roman Tsepov also died, possibly from radioactive poisoning. In April 2004 a Chechen guerrilla, Lecha Islamov, died in a Volgograd hospital while serving a nine-year prison sentence. In September 2004 the Ukrainian leader Viktor Yushchenko survived being poisoned. The journalist Anna Politkovskaya was shot dead in the lobby of her Moscow apartment building in October 2006.

There was also an attempt on the life of Boris Berezovsky at the London Hilton in June 2007 by a Chechen, Movladi Atlangeriev. The plot was foiled by Scotland Yard detectives, but when Atlangeriev was deported to Moscow he was abducted off the street, driven to a wood and shot dead. Perhaps most notoriously, the liberal politician Boris Nemtsov was shot in the back on the Bolshoi Moskvoretsky Bridge in February 2015, just yards away from the Kremlin, ostensibly by a single gunman who escaped the scene. A group of seven Chechens were later convicted of the crime, carried out for a promise of $250,000, but their paymaster was never identified.

The second explanation is that individual agencies, such as the FSB and GRU, have taken the initiative to exercise discipline, very possibly in support of their growing commercial interests, if not simply to deter other potential traitors. While such operations may not have been sanctioned in advance, those responsible would have been confident that they would be protected by one of the competing power groups close to the Kremlin leadership.

Some of the killings certainly bore the increasingly distinctive Russian government hallmark, and in July 2006 the Duma specifically authorised the extra-territorial execution of terrorists, a category that was drawn widely enough to include almost any political dissident. Indeed, the legislation included one definition of 'extremists' as 'those slandering the individual occupying the post of president of the Russian Federation'.

Even without this apparent legal immunity, the Kremlin had been emboldened, as had been demonstrated in February 2004 when the former Chechen president Zelimkhan Yandarbiyev was killed with his two body-guards by a bomb that detonated under his SUV in Doha as they drove home from a local mosque. Suspicion quickly focused on two men of Slavic appearance who had been seen carrying a plastic bag in the mosque car park and had rented a vehicle using forged documents. Six days later the Qatari police arrested three Russians: the first secretary of the Russian embassy, Aleksandr Fetisov; Anatoli V. Yablochkov, alias Belashkov; and thirty-two year-old Vasili A. Pugachyov, alias Bogachyov. The latter pair, both GRU officers, were charged with the murder, convicted on 30 June 2004, and sentenced to life imprisonment. In their confessions, which they alleged had been extracted under torture, they identified the Russian defence minister, Sergei Ivanov, as the person who had issued them with the orders to kill Yandarbiyev. Their lawyers disputed the legality of the arrests, which had taken place at a villa used to accommodate embassy staff. Six months later they were repatriated to Moscow to serve the remainder of their sentences, but instead received a hero's welcome at Vnukovo and were released. Fetisov, who had only taken up his appointment in January 2004, had been released on the basis of his diplomatic immunity and expelled on 24 March.

At the time of the arrests, two members of Qatar's wrestling team were detained in Russia and accused of possession of more than $7,000 in undeclared currency. They too were released after high-level diplomatic negotiations.

The Kremlin, which claimed that the two GRU officers had been sent to Qatar on a legitimate anti-terrorism liaison assignment to research links with a local al-Qaeda cell, hired some very high-priced lawyers to defend them, including the firm founded by Nikolai Tegorov, President Vladimir Putin's chief of staff; former US attorney-general Dick Thornburgh; and the former US ambassador to the UN Human Rights Commission, Jerome J. Shestack.

The Doha car bomb demonstrated undeniable Russian government complicity in that the two serving GRU officers found guilty of the crime not only confessed their role, but implicated the minister of defence. The circumstances of their arrest, at an official Russian villa, their release from prison after intense diplomatic pressure, and their repatriation to Moscow and instant freedom, also added to the weight of the case for the Kremlin's complicity. Given that Chechen guerrillas are regarded as legitimate targets, the only real question concerns the limits, if any, of the regime's determination to eliminate its perceived enemies.

Aspects of the murder of the former Second Chechen War military commander Zelimkhan Khangoshvili in Berlin's Kleiner Tiergarten on 23 August 2019 also appear to conform to the others, except that on this occasion the gunman, a forty-three year-old Russian with a passport identifying him as Vadim Sokolov, was arrested at the scene. Investigation of Sokolov, supposedly an engineer employed in St Petersburg, established that he was really fifty-four year-old Vadim N. Krasikov, a suspected contract killer previously linked to the assassination in April 2007 of Yuri Kozlov, an entrepreneur and prominent town councillor in Kostomuksha, Karelia. Kozlov's decomposed, bullet-riddled body would not be found for a further three months.

On that occasion two suspects, Vladimir Fornenko and Oleg Ivanov, both aged thirty-eight and decorated FSB *Spetsnaz* veterans, were charged in November 2014, but while Krasikov was questioned by the local police, he was never detained. Reportedly, two of the accomplices confessed that they had been contracted to kill Kozlov by a business rival over a dispute about the construction of a shopping mall. However, at a pre-trial hearing in Petrozavodsk both defendants were released on the basis of character references submitted by the FSB testifying to their distinguished military service. With all charges dropped, the pair later founded a security company in Crimea soon after the Russian annexation.

Krasikov was also a suspect in the murder of a prominent Kabardino-Balkarian businessman, Albert Nazranov, in Moscow in June 2013. As had happened in the Khangoshvili case, Nazranov had been shot twice at close range with a Glock semi-automatic by a gunman on a bicycle, having survived another assassination attempt eight months earlier while on an early morning jog in Nalchik park. An influential friend of the political leader Arsen Kanokov, Nazranov had acted as a controversial intermediary with Muslim insurgents in the North Caucasus, where he had gained considerable notoriety.

Krasikov had recently travelled from Warsaw, and earlier in the week had flown to Paris from Moscow. Analysis of his mobile phone use disclosed his home address in Moscow and his close association with FSB facilities training sites, suggesting a high degree of the official co-operation required to develop and sustain the authentic paperwork issued to him under alias. When the Russian authorities declined to assist the Federal German police enquiries, two diplomats were expelled from the Berlin embassy.

The implication of the three incidents, in which Krasikov had been a common denominator, was that FSB *Spetsnaz* veterans had made themselves available as hitmen. Further confirmation of the overlap between organised crime and the FSB emerged when another gun for hire, Oleg Smorodinov, an ethnic Russian, was arrested in the Ukraine, having undertaken a mission to kill Ivan Mamchur, a prison guard in Rivne in September 2016, the first of six assassinations he had been contracted to complete in Ukraine. Smorodinov had watched his prey over several weeks and then, having reported his progress in coded calls to Moscow, pumped eight bullets into him. Turned in to the Kiev authorities by his girlfriend, Smorodinov agreed in March 2018 to pretend to kill his next target, the dissident Russian war correspondent Arkadi Babchenko, whose death was announced at the end of May in an elaborate charade designed to entrap the gunman's FSB handlers, known only as 'Maksim' and 'Fillip', whom he had met at the Café Vienna, close to the FSB headquarters in Moscow. Having announced Babchenko's death from three bullet wounds, and distributed lurid photos of the crime scene, the Ukrainian Security Service's (SBU) director, Vasili Gritak, called a press conference to produce the supposed victim, who apparently had been shot at his home and ambulanced to the morgue in an effort to enhance the scheme's authenticity, and to denounce the FSB. The staged assassination, complete with pools of pig's blood, had taken the SBU two months to plan and not even Babchenko's distraught family had been let in on the secret.

At his trial in October 2019 Smorodinov, the former policeman who had undertaken his military service in the Soviet Red Banner Fleet, received a reduced prison sentence for Mamchur's murder, having been credited with his co-operation with the SBU on his next shooting, for which he had received $15,000 from Boris Herman, another suspect charged with complicity in the murder plot. A fifty-year-old co-owner of a firearms factory, Herman had been entrapped the day after the assassination as he paid for the crime, and was sentenced to four and a half years' imprisonment, having incriminated a third conspirator, Vyacheslav Pivovarnik, a well-connected young Ukrainian businessman who had already fled to St Petersburg. Accordingly, in May 2018 the SBU recommended his prosecution *in absentia*.

The SBU's investigation of Herman also implicated another co-conspirator, Taras Telmanshenko, who was arrested in June 2018 but only convicted of the illegal possession of weapons.

Taken together these incidents provide a compelling view of a lawless Russian Federation in which the FSB and GRU have been implicated in numerous gangland murders and in some other politically motivated killings. Yet, in spite of these obvious flaws in the Russian system, there remained post-Cold War a willingness on the part of many individuals who saw themselves as patriots to serve the state, whatever the legality or morality of its demands. This is the essential grip of the motherland tradition.

Chapter X

Consequences

Aldrich Ames is serving a life sentence without parole at Terre Haute, Indiana.

Ames, Rosario. Upon her early release from a five-year prison sentence served at Danbury, Connecticut, Maria Rosario Casas Dupuy returned to Bogota with her son Paul and received $2 million from the SVR of her husband's savings accumulated in an escrow account. She is now professor of literature at the Pontificia Universidad Javeriana.

Felix Bloch drives a bus in Chapel Hill, North Carolina.

Jack Barsky has acquired American citizenship legitimately and lives in Atlanta, Georgia with his third wife.

Alex Chapman died of a drug overdose in 2016, aged thirty-six.

Anna Chapman is pursuing a television career in Moscow.

Viktor Cherkashin published his unauthorised memoirs *Spy Handler* in Moscow in 2005, since when he has been banned from travelling abroad.

Rick DesLauriers was promoted Special Agent in Charge of the Boston Division in July 2010 and retired from the FBI in July 2013. He then joined the Penske Corporation in Michigan.

Robert Hanssen has gone insane while serving a life sentence without parole in isolation at SuperMax in Florence, Colorado, where he has been the subject of Special Administrative Measures to isolate him from prisoners and staff.

Alan Kohler was transferred to the Legal Attaché's office in London, and in September 2019 was promoted Special Agent in Charge of the FBI's Counterintelligence Division at the Washington Field Office.

Juan Lazaro renewed his Peruvian passport and returned to Lima.

Vicky Pelaez has returned to Peru with her husband.

Earl Pitts was released from prison in December 2019.

Jack Platt died in February 2017, aged eighty.

Alexander Poteyev lives in the United States under CIA protection.

Joe Reilly is retired in Pennsylvania.

Maria Ricci participated in the FBI's investigation of Carter Page in March 2017.

Mike Rochford received the National Intelligence Medal of Achievement Medal from the CIA and retired from the FBI in August 2004 as chief of the Russian Espionage Section.

Alexander Shcherbakov remains in the United States under CIA protection.

Sergei and **Yulia Skripal** remain under MI6's protection.

Mike Sulick resigned from the CIA in July 2010 as head of the National Clandestine Service and retired to North Carolina.

Oleg Sutyagin lives openly in London, working as a strategic issues analyst.

Gennadi Vasilenko lives in northern Virginia under CIA protection.

Elena Vavilova is in Moscow and has published a novel based on her experiences.

Vitali Yurchenko retired from the KGB and worked as a bank guard.

Boris Yuzhin was amnestied and released from a fifteen-year prison sentence in February 1992, emigrated in 1994, and now lives with his wife and daughter in Rohnet Park, Santa Rosa, in northern California.

Alexander Zaporozhsky lives in the United States under CIA protection.

Michael Zottoli was appointed deputy head of planning for international economic activity at Gazprom in 2012.

Appendix 1

Organizational Chart of Directorate S
Operations in the US

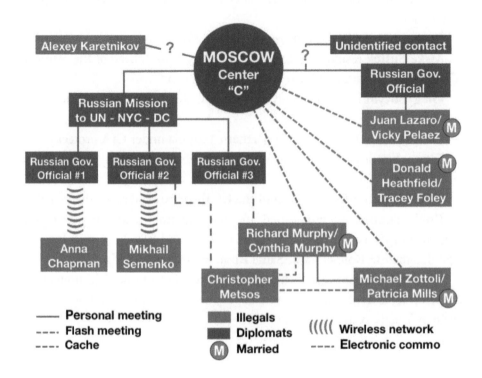

Appendix 2

Chronology

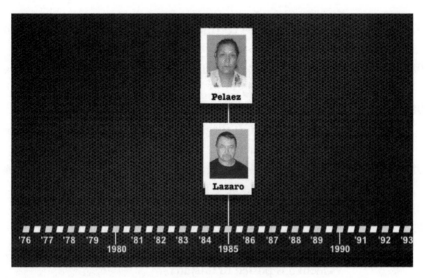

GHOST STORIES commences in January 2000.

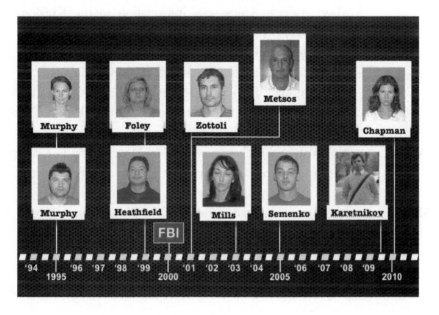

Appendix 3

Timeline of Events

1979	**March:** Jack Platt recruits Gennadi Vasilenko in Washington, DC.
1980	**January:** Ron Pelton sells information to the Soviet embassy in Washington, DC.
1981	**June:** Vasilenko returns to Moscow from Washington, DC. **September:** KGB illegals Karl and Katarina Krumisch are arrested in Zurich.
1982	**June:** Vladimir Kuzichkin defects in Tehran. Oleg Gordievsky is posted to London.
1983	**June:** Edward Howard is dismissed from the CIA.
1984	**April:** RCMP mole Gilles Brunet dies in Montreal. Soviet bugs are discovered in the US embassy in Moscow. Vasilenko is posted to Guyana.
1985	**April:** Aldrich Ames contacts the KGB in Washington. **May:** Aldrich Ames sells information to the KGB. Oleg Gordievsky is recalled to Moscow from London. **July:** Oleg Gordievsky is exfiltrated from Moscow. **August:** Vitali Yurchenko defects to the CIA in Rome. **September:** Ed Howard escapes from Santa Fe to Helsinki. **October.** Robert Hanssen contacts the KGB's Viktor Cherkashin in Washington. **November:** Yurchenko returns to Moscow and is accompanied by Motorin and Martynov. Lazaro and Pelaez arrive in the United States.
1986	**January:** Vasilenko is detained in Havana and shipped to Odessa. **February:** Viktor Gundarev defects in Athens. **March:** Hanssen suspends contact with the KGB. **July:** Robert Hanssen re-establishes contact with the KGB.

	December: Sargeant Clayton Lonetree confesses to having given the KGB access to the CIA station in Moscow.
1987	Alexander Zaporozhsky offers information to the CIA in Addis Ababa.
1988	**October:** David Boone walks into the Soviet embassy in Washington.
1989	**April:** FBI begins investigation of Felix Bloch.
	May: KGB illegal Stephen Ratkai sentenced to nine years' imprisonment.
	November: Defection of ex-KGB officer Sergei Papushin.
1990	**February:** Papushin dies in Maryland.
	December: Felix Bloch is fired from the US State Department.
1991	**August:** Aleksandr Shcherbakov steals file from Yasenevo.
	December: The SVR is formed from the KGB.
1992	**March:** GRU Colonel Stanislav Lunev defects in Washington. Vasili Mitrokhin approaches MI6 in Riga. Vladimir Konoplev defects in Brussels.
	September: ASIO identifies mole code-named JABAROO.
	October: KGB retiree Vasili Mitrokhin defects to MI6 via Riga.
1993	**May:** Robert Lipka is entrapped by the FBI.
	June: George Sadil is arrested in Australia.
	October: Sergei Skripal is posted to Madrid.
	December: Zaporozhsky provides clue to identity of mole in the CIA.
	KGB General Oleg Kalugin refers to Gilles Brunet, Robert Lipka and an Australian mole.
1994	**February:** Arrest of Aldrich Ames.
	March: Espionage charges against George Sadil are dropped.
	December: Sadil sentenced to three months' imprisonment. Albrecht Dittrich put under FBI surveillance in Queens, New York.
1995	Aleksandr Poteyev is posted to New York.
	Aleksandr Shcherbakov retires from the SVR.
1996	**February:** Robert Lipka is arrested.

	May: SVR illegals Ian and Laurie Lambert are arrested in Canada.

May: SVR illegals Ian and Laurie Lambert are arrested in Canada.

July: Sergei Skripal is recruited in Madrid by MI6 as FORTHWITH.

December: Earl Pitts is arrested.

1997   **May:** Albrecht Dittrich is detained by the FBI in Pennsylvania.

October: Zaporovhsky retires from the SVR and settles in Maryland.

1998   **February:** Igor Sutyagin attends conference at Birmingham University,

October: David Boone is arrested.

1999   **February:** Daniel Boone is imprisoned for twenty-four years.

August: Donald Heathfield and Tracey Foley arrive in the US.

September: Publication of Vasili Mitrokhin's memoirs, Skripal retires from the GRU.

October: Igor Sutyagin is arrested at home in Obninsk.

2000   **January:** Pelaez under surveillance in Peru.

March: FSB's Valeri Ojamae is arrested and charged with espionage for MI6.

July. Mike Rochford recruits Aleksandr Shcherbakov.

October: Sergei Tretyakov defects in New York with his wife and daughter.

November: Shcherbakov hands over the RAMON file to the CIA in Moscow. Hanssen makes his largest drop and compromises Zaporovhsky.

Aleksandr Poteyev is recruited in New York.

2001   Anya Kushchenko visits London.

Michael Zottoli arrives in the United States.

January: The FBI searches Heathfield's bank deposit box.

February: Robert Hanssen is arrested. Metsos meets Richard Murphy at a restaurant in Sunnyside, New York.

June: The FBI searches Heathfield's bank deposit box.

July: Hanssen reaches a plea bargain with the prosecution.

November: Zaporozhsky is lured back to Moscow and arrested.

	December: Roberto Flóres betrays Skripal to the SVR's Petr Melnikov in Madrid for $275,000.
2002	**February:** Pelaez returns from Peru with money.
	March: Anya Kushchenko marries Alex Chapman in London.
	November: Alexander Sypachev sentenced to eight years' imprisonment having been convicted of spying for the CIA.
2003	**June:** Zaporozhsky is sentenced to eighteen years' imprisonment.
	Patricia Mills arrives in the United States.
	January: Lazaro recorded by the FBI in conversation with Pelaez.
	February: The FBI record Lazaro and Pelaez counting money.
	May: Lazaro recorded by the FBI telling Pelaez he was receiving radio transmissions.
2004	**January:** The Murphy home in New Jersey is searched and a shoebox found containing espionage paraphernalia. Igor Sutyagin sentenced to 15 years' imprisonment.
	February: Roberto Flóres leaves CNI.
	May: Metsos caches money at a dead drop in Wurtsboro, NY.
	December: Sergei Skripal is arrested in Krylatskoye.
2005	**April:** Metsos meets Richard Murphy in Sunnyside, NY.
	June: Zottoli and Mills marry in Seattle.
	July: The Murphy home in New Jersey is searched and a twenty-seven-character password copied. Roberto Flóres is placed under surveillance in Spain.
	August: Gennadi Vasilenko is arrested in Moscow.
	September: Mikhail Semenko enters the United States as a student.
2006	**June:** Zottoli and Mills empty a dead drop in Wurtsboro, NY.
	July: The Heathfield home is searched and diskettes containing deleted messages are copied.
	August: Sergei Skripal is sentenced to thirteen years' imprisonment in Moscow.

	November: Paul Hampel is arrested in Montreal. Sasha Litvinenko is murdered in London.
2007	**June:** Vyeschslav Zharko confesses to espionage on behalf of MI6.
	Lieutenant Jeffrey Delisile walks into the Russian embassy in Ottawa.
	July: Roberto Flóres is arrested in Tenerife.
2008	**September:** Herman Simm is arrested in Tallinn.
	Robert Rakhardzho exfilrated from Prague to Russia.
2009	Semenko moves from New York to Washington.
	February: Herman Simm is sentenced to twelve years' imprisonment.
	Tadeusz Juchniewicz is arrested in Poland.
	September: Richard Murphy gives Zottoli $150,000 in Brooklyn.
	October: Zottoli and Mills move from Seattle to Arlington.
2010	**January:** Anna Chapman holds electronic rendezvous in New York.
	Roberto Flóres is sentenced to twelve years' imprisonment in Madrid.
	March: Zottoli meets Murphy in Brookyn café and receives $9,000.
	June: Exfiltration of Poteyev to Frankfurt via Minsk.
	Exfiltration of Shcherbakov to the United States.
	Arrest of ten SVR illegals in the US. Arrest of Metsos in Larnaca.
	Offer made to Sergei Cherepanov in Madrid.
	July: Ten illegals swapped in Vienna for Sergei Skripal, Igor Sutyagin, Alexander Zaporozhsky, Gennadi Vasilenko.
	July: Death of Sergei Tretyakov at home in Jacksonville.
2011	**June:** Poteyev is convicted of treason and desertion *in absentia*.
	October: Andreas and Heidrun Anschlag are arrested in Germany.
2012	**January:** Lieutenant Jeffrey Delisile arrested in Bedford, Canada.
	February: A Russian rocket scientist is sentenced to thirteen years.

Alekxsei and Viktoria Dressen are arrested in Tallinn.

March: Raymond Poeteray is arrested in Amsterdam.

The FBI places Evgeni Buryakov under surveillance.

May: Russian army colonel sentenced to twelve years' imprisonment.

June: Colonel Valeri Mikhailov is gaoled in Moscow.

2013   **May:** The FSB entraps the CIA's Ryan Fogle in Moscow.

August: Vladimir Veitman is arrested in Estonia.

2014   **June:** Eduard Shishmakov is expelled from Warsaw.

September: Eston Kohver is abducted on the Estonian border.

November: Heidrun Anschlag is deported to Moscow.

2015   **January:** Buryakov is arrested in New York.

June: Andreas Anschlag is deported to Moscow.

September: Eston Kohver is exchanged for the Dressens.

2016   **January:** The Litvinenko Inquiry Report is published.

May: Colonel Zbigniew J. is imprisoned for six years in Warsaw.

October: Two GRU officers are implicated in the Montenegro coup plot.

2017   **April:** Emilian Gebrev survives murder attempt in Sofia.

2018   **March:** Sergei Skripal and his daughter are attacked in Salisbury.

Arkadi Babchenko participates in a trap for the FSB in Kiev.

April: Four GRU officers are arrested in The Hague.

October: Poteyev's mobile phone is traced in Florida.

2019   **October:** Oleg Smorodinov is imprisoned for the murder of Ivan Mamchur.

Appendix 4

Kalaris and McCoy Monograph

Counterintelligence for the 1990s by George Kalaris and Leonard McCoy, March 1989.

Background

As we contemplate the counterintelligence (CI) challenge of the 1990s and seek a CI structure and posture appropriate to that challenge, our outlook is inevitably conditioned by the discovery in the past several years of a devastating series of CI setbacks. Our most sensitive intelligence agencies have been penetrated. We have suffered damage in the strategic national defense area. Costs of these compromises are estimated in the billions of dollars. Certainly there is a basis in these recent cases for forming a perception that our national CI program has failed to carry out its mission in the 1980s. Even with improved performance by the US Government components charged with CI responsibilities over the past decade, hostile intelligence services have inflicted severe damage on our national interests. The CI system has proved to be inferior to the excellence of its component parts. We can expect hostile intelligence services to intensify their activities against us in the 1990s. We can also expect that the present structure of the CI community, having been inadequate to meet the threat in the 1970s and 1980s, will be overwhelmed in the 1990s unless we improve it.

Thinking in the late 1970s and early 1980s about the needs, direction, and requirements appropriate to ·the US CI effort in the 1980s was for all practical purposes a straightline projection of what was then in hand. All that was advocated was more of the same. Even before the mid-1980s, that thinking had proved to be totally inadequate to the challenge faced. Therefore, this paper proposes a radical revision in the structure of the US CI community. The purpose: to effect changes in our CI posture which will dramatically improve our CI capacity for the 1990s.

The Challenge

US counterintelligence concentrates primarily, and appropriately, on the Soviet services as the major adversaries. As we have seen in the 1980s, we also have had to place increased emphasis on countering the East European intelligence services acting on behalf of the Soviets or in the interests of their own countries. Several of these services have scored major successes against us.

In the 1990s we can expect to see even more such operations against us and our closest allies, spurred on by our opponents' success to date and by Soviet pressure for increased effort, especially in technical areas. Beyond the numerous intelligence services of the USSR and Warsaw Pact countries, we also project increased intelligence collection efforts against us on the part of Asian communist countries and Cuba. In both of these areas, the US has suffered grave injury at the hands of hostile services in the 1980s.

In addition to the increasing threat from communist countries, the US must expect to have to counter intelligence operations by a growing number of underdeveloped countries, as well as operations conducted by friendly countries which are not satisfied with particular aspects of US policy or believe that the most direct way to information satisfying their own intelligence requirements is to penetrate US intelligence agencies. Operations in these areas have been discovered in the 1980s and should be looked upon as examples of what to expect in the 1990s. Most such activities will be in the classical human source recruitment category, but some of the countries most likely to be involved also have substantial technical intelligence collection capabilities. In several cases, we will find ourselves co-operating in intelligence and counterintelligence matters with these countries at the same time they are operating against us (and we against them).

A greatly increased unilateral counterintelligence capability overseas will be among our most crucial needs of the 1990s, along with the need to increase our ability to detect and counter technical intelligence collection advances by opposition services. We anticipate that increased FBI capabilities and enhanced public awareness of espionage will cause the Soviets to concentrate their recruitment activities against the American target outside the US. An increasing burden, therefore, will descend on those American intelligence organizations charged with espionage and counterespionage responsibilities abroad.

Definition

The definition of counterintelligence crafted in the mid-1950s had outlived its relevance to the realities confronting the intelligence community by the early 1970s. By the late 1970s it had literally fenced in the efforts that had to be made to counter the multi-faceted threat directed against our national security interests. It had reduced counterintelligence to a passive discipline concerned primarily with 'locking up the barn door after the horses had been stolen'. In the late 1970s we finally took official cognizance that the threat to our security was not limited exclusively to the human element. It became clear that collection against us by Soviet agencies using technical means was substantially greater and more significant than we had generally believed.

Therefore, in the 1980s some American intelligence organizations revised their CI components to analyze and contend with this multi-faceted threat.

Fundamentally, CI for the 1990s should be defined as that discipline of the intelligence sphere that is concerned with the actions of foreign intelligence services and organizations, friendly or not, against us, employing human and technical means, which impact adversely on our national interests and goals. It naturally includes those actions which we, the CI agencies of the US, take to negate such inimical activities. Thus, CI includes, as component disciplines, counterespionage, counter-sigint, and counter-imagery. The instrumentality used by the foreign entity against us is what determines our actions to counter the effort.

The substance of CI does not change with time, but its emphasis must inevitably shift to meet the nature of the attack on our national security. Before we reach the 1990s, it is imperative that the American CI community accept the concept of a multi-disciplinary threat and the need for a multi-disciplinary response. If counterintelligence remains limited in the 1990s to what is in effect only counterespionage, we will be dealing with only one aspect. In the 1990s we must redefine the threat as the composite human and technical threat it is, and we must develop appropriate cross-disciplinary countermeasures to overcome the threat.

Not that technology transfer or state-sponsored terrorism are likely to abate, but to the extent that these threats are susceptible to countermeasures, the foreign policy, security, and police mechanisms of the government will contribute the lion's share of countermeasures and defensive operations.

Actions taken to identify, monitor, control, and neutralize foreign intelligence operatives will continue to constitute the major counterintelligence contribution to frustrating these threats to our national security by hostile services. As in counterespionage, one of the most significant sources of information on such hostile activities will continue to be the penetration of the hostile service.

Under our definition, personnel security of those elements of the US Government and its contractual components whose activities have an impact on our national security interests also falls within the purview of counterespionage as a discipline. The vetting of new employees, as well as those in more advanced stages of their careers in national security related work, including contractor personnel, is a counterespionage responsibility. Our definition would also include the manufacturer abroad, under licensing, of classified American defense equipment.

The Status Quo

The present counterintelligence response to the generally recognized multi-faceted threat is fragmented, with each counterintelligence component (other than the FBI) focusing primarily on the threat to its own parent organization component or program. We are not suggesting that this is in itself improper, only that fragmentation and departmentally oriented efforts do not constitute in their sum an effective national counterintelligence program.

Rather, this approach impedes considerably the formulation and execution of a national program, the development of universal guidelines, and the establishment of homogeneous national CI objectives. A more integrated approach is imperative for the 1990s.

The FBI CI program continues to expand and improve, and needs only to re-evaluate its capabilities under the increased multi-disciplinary concept in its CI program for the 1990s. Its involvement in Defense Department CI/industrial security operations and programs is the most important step necessary to the over-all enhancement of the domestic CI program. With primary responsibility for CI overseas, CIA has a tremendous challenge for the 1990s. Pressure for enhanced CIA capabilities overseas has now reached irresistible proportions in the wake of revelations of repeated agent meetings overseas in all of the extremely damaging cases of 'the year (plus) of the spy'. This effort will be crippled without full integration of FBI, DoD, and CIA efforts. It will not suffice for CIA to monitor the Soviets overseas, or for the FBI to do so in the US, without extensive knowledge of the Soviet primary target: the US defense complex-and without CIA and FBI participation in DoD CI and security programs set up to ·identify, neutralize, and exploit opposition penetration efforts directed against that target.

The greatest damage to national security has been in areas for which the DoD is responsible national defense as that is the target area of our major opposition. All CI resources must be brought to bear in this area. The departmental and geographical CI boundaries which we have established are not honored by the primary opposition services, which use them to defeat us.

They recruit in one area and run the case in another, moving agent and operations officers about the map at will, and engendering among US CI agencies a cumbersome, lumbering co-ordination process which seldom catches up with opposition actions. This bureaucratic weakness was cited in a recent legislative review as having caused a crippling delay in introduction of the FBI into a major espionage case. We must eliminate the opposition advantage in this area by bringing our three primary CI bodies together at the sources of our vulnerability.

New Look Overseas

In overseas installations, we must develop new personnel configurations which take into account the shift in emphasis which the Soviets will place on their activities against us. Not only should the recruitment of Soviet intelligence officers remain high on our priority list at each foreign-based American intelligence installation; we also must substantially increase our ability to monitor the activities of Soviet intelligence officers, whether they represent a recruitment target or not.

Tokyo, Vienna, Paris, and Mexico City are today, and are likely to remain in the 1990s, the favorite agent-meeting and walk-in locales of the Soviet intelligence services. Accordingly, we must expand our coverage of Soviet activities in those cities, and others which may well be added as the opposition detects our efforts.

Technical Licensing

Extensive licensing by DoD of foreign companies to manufacture US weapons systems and technology has added another dimension to the CI problem overseas. Not only must our unilateral CI capability overseas be prepared to counter hostile collection action against these exposed targets, but we must also develop effective local liaison relationships which will assist in protecting these weapons systems and technology from hostile intelligence collection.

Personnel Staffing

A separate career track for counterintelligence analysts must be established for the 1990s as the core of the new CI component. Entry into the track must be competitive, requiring at a minimum four years actual and successful operational experience in the recruitment and handling of agents. To ask a counterintelligence analyst with no direct operational experience to analyze and judge developments in any agent case is tantamount to asking a pre-med student to diagnose gastrointestinal anomalies. Unless the analyst has experience in handling agents, he/she really has no sound basis for evaluating behaviour and spotting discrepancies. Sophisticated countermeasures will have to be developed, springing in large part from our own development of technical collection systems. This threat will dictate recruitment into counterintelligence of technically qualified officers who can keep CI abreast of technical developments and conceive defensive and counter operations against such capabilities.

The counterintelligence component of any intelligence organization cannot be the depository for has-beens. The component must command respect not only because of where it is placed on the organizational chart, but because of the quality of its officers and their individual records of achievement in the more traditional facets of the intelligence business.

Training Approach

Regardless of whatever other training is given prospective operations officers, in preparation for the 1990s the curriculum must include heavy exposure to counterintelligence information. We recommend a minimum of 50 hours of appropriate training. No intelligence officer should be allowed to venture into operations at home or abroad without a solid understanding and appreciation of the capabilities of our principal adversaries. To do otherwise is the equivalent of casting a lamb into a wolf-infested forest.

The ultimate objective in exposing all prospective operations officers to intensive counterintelligence training is not to produce 50-hour counterintelligence wonders, but rather to ensure that all operations officers of the 1990s will be acutely aware of the lessons learned in the past 65 years of our encounters with hostile intelligence agencies. Unless the first echelon of defense, the operations officer, is aware of the possibility for fabrication, deception, and misinformation, the early warning signs of a bad case may be completely overlooked, not understood, and not reported.

The Ultimate Need

Responsibility for the establishment of a national counterintelligence policy, the allocation of tasks to the various counterintelligence organizations, monitoring of progress, and resolution of inter-agency conflicts must be lodged in some entity or person. Continuation of the piecemeal and parochial approach to counterintelligence can only perpetuate damage to the national security.

Existing interagency co-ordination procedures, NSC interagency committees, and excellent personal relationships between the heads of counterintelligence components have not and cannot produce and implement a national policy with teeth in it, nor insure that maximum effort will be applied to a particular national counterintelligence objective.

The present structure of US counterintelligence is inadequate to fulfill the tasks posed by the CI challenge of the 1990s. A centralized authority is required which will be capable of, and responsible for, mobilizing all US CI agencies and capabilities against the common foreign intelligence and security threats:

Wherever this authority is placed, a very great role in its day-to-day functioning must be played by a newly constituted DoD CI office which is directly and vigorously involved in national counterintelligence management of service CI/Security agencies.

Within the CIA, CI must be raised out of the Operations Directorate to a level of authority within the Agency which gives it command and operational responsibility across the entire intelligence community as well as throughout the Agency itself. The level of Deputy Director may well be too low for it to have such authority. While such a step might be taken to temporize, until staffing and organizational complications are resolved, it will eventually be necessary for the CI responsibility to be placed in a DDCI for Counterintelligence. Only then will the full integration of all interagency CI capabilities become feasible.

A number of the functions of other CIA components will have to be assigned to the 'DDCI/CI', namely those elements of security concerned with personnel security, communications security personnel, DI elements working on strategic deception, and elements responsible for defensive measures against hostile technological attack. The 'DDCI/CI' would have to be placed in the chain of command for oversight of all operational matters concerned with CI, and have responsibility for a portion of the performance evaluation and reassignment of all senior CIA officers.

One of the first tasks of any such new counterintelligence leadership of the 1990s should be to define its area of responsibility – specifically the elements of counterintelligence which are to be the focus of the counterintelligence community. This task is not the domain of lawyers, academicians, or dilettantes.

It is the prime responsibility of those who have practiced the craft. On 29 March 1988 the Chairman and Vice Chairman of the Senate Select Committee on Intelligence informed the press that the Director of Central Intelligence told the committee, in closed session, that he has 'reorganised the counterintelligence function within the CIA and appointed a senior official to head it.'

Notes

Introduction

1. Angleton wrote thirty-six contact reports of his meetings with Philby, but later destroyed them.

Chapter I: Recruitment

1   *Spy in the Sun* by Barbara Carr (Howard Timmins, Cape Town, 1969) was based on the CIA interrogation. Loginov survived the experience and was eventually released from prison.

2   Enger and Chernyaev were exchanged in 1979 for five Soviet prisoners.

3   Edwin Moore retired from the CIA in 1973, taking ten boxes of classified material with him, which he stored at his home and attempted to sell to the Soviets for $200,000.

4   See Philip Agee's *Inside the Company: CIA Diary* (Farrar, Straus & Giraux, New York, 1975).

5   See Victor Cherkashin's *Spy Handler: Memoir of a KGB Officer* (New York: Basic Books, 2005).

6   See Oleg Kalugin's *Spymaster* (London: Smith Gryphon, 1994) p. 202.

7   Ibid., p. 137.

8   Ibid., p. 153.

9   As a live investigation the ASIO mole was not mentioned in Vasili Mitrokhin's *The Sword and the Shield* (New York: Basic Books, 1999).

10 See *The Spy in Moscow Station* by Eric Haseltine (New York: Thomas Dunne, 2019).

11 See the FBI Complaint Affidavit dated February 2001, para. 79.

12 See *Circle of Treason* by Sandy Grimes & Jean Vertefeuille (Annapolis: Naval Institute Press, 2012.

13 Ibid., p. 144.

Chapter II: KARAT

1   *Falsely Accused*, Brian Kelley's unpublished memoirs.

2   Ibid.

3   Colonel Trofimoff was the most senior US Army officer to be convicted of betraying his country. He was sentenced to life imprisonment in September 2001. He died in September 2014 in the federal penitentiary at Victorville, California.

4   See Kalugin, p. 83.

5   See *Deep Undercover* (New York: Tyndale House, 2017).

6   See Mitrokhin's *The Sword and the Shield*, p. 195.

7   Ibid. p. 202.

8   The KGB never identified RAMON as Hanssen and deliberately passed up the opportunity to do so, to avoid angering him.

9   For other versions of Rochford's pitch, see Ronald Kessler's *The Secrets of the FBI* (New York: Crown, 2011); David Wise's *The Seven Million Dollar Spy* (New York: Audible, 2018); *Best of Enemies* by Gus Russo and Eric Dezenhall (New York: Twelve, 2018); C-SPAN video of the International Spy Museum, 1 October 2003; Jerri Williams podcast 031. Also, Devlin Barret named Shcherbakov in the *Wall Street Journal*, 26 July 2012.

10   FBI arrest affidavit, February 2001.

11   Ibid.

12   Ibid.

13   *Falsely Accused.*

14   Ibid.

Chapter III: *Konspiratsia:* The Soviet Legacy

1   Krivitsky's MI5 file at Kew is at KV2/802.

2   Wilhelm Fliske's MI5 file is at W 40/195.

3   Horst Kopkow's MI5 file is at KV2/1500.

4   *War Secrets in the Ether*: NSA Archive 1953, Ref: A59332.

5   Foote's *Handbook for Spies* was ghosted by a currently serving MI5 officer, Courtenay Young, and published by Robert Hale, where his editor was a former wartime MI5 officer, Desmond Vesey.

6   The MI5 file on the ROTE KAPELLE is at KV3/350.

7   Kopkow. *Ibid.*

8   Ernest Weiss's MI5 file is at KV2/2230.

9   Robert Switz's MI5 file is at KV2/1587.

10   Lydia Stahl's MI5 file is at KV2/1590.

11   Wilfred Vernon's MI5 file is at KV2/992.

12   Wilfred Meredith's MI5 file is at KV2/2201.

13   *Cassidy's Run* by David Wise (New York: Random House, 2000).

Chapter IV: GHOST STORIES

1   Maria Ricci complaint affidavit, dated 25 June 2010.

2   *Comrade J* by Pete Earley (New York: Berkeley Publishing, 2009).

3   Ricci affidavit. p. 11.

4   Ibid., p. 35.

5   Ibid., p. 35.

6   Ibid., p. 36.

7   Ibid., p. 34.

8   Ibid., p. 34.

9   Ibid., p. 24.

10 Ibid., p. 25.

11 Ibid., p. 25.

12 Ibid., p. 5.

13 Ibid., p. 27.

14 Ibid., p. 27.

15 Ibid., p. 37.

16 Ibid., p. 13.

17 Ibid., p. 30.

18 Ibid., p. 32.

19 Ibid., p. 32.

20 Ibid., p. 20.

21 Ibid., p. 12.

22 In August 2019 Elena released a fictionalised co-authored account of her espionage mission, *The Woman Who Can Keep Secrets*, and launched her own website, www. ElenaVavilov.ru. Like the other arrestees, she had signed an agreement with the US Department of Justice that she would not profit financially from her crime.

23 Ibid.

24 Interview with Tim by Shaun Walker, *Guardian*, 7 May 2016.

Chapter V: Take-Down

1   Maria Ricci complaint affidavit, dated 25 June 2010.

2   A Russian version of Poteyev's exfiltration alleges that he borrowed his brother's passport to make the journey.

3   See Chapter VI for details of the Flores mole hunt.

Chapter VI: Negotiations
1   Chapman's British citizenship was revoked on 13 July 2010.
2   CNN *Declassifed*, Season 2, Episode 1, *The Spies Next Door*, 2 April 2012.

Chapter VII: Aftermath
1   Loginov was almost traced by the KGB. See p. 138.
2   Litvinenko Report, Sir Robert Owen, January 2016.

Chapter VIII: Salisbury
1   Bellingcat Parliamentary briefing, October 2018.
2   Michael Schwatz, *New York Times*, 8 October 2019.
3   In October 2018 Serebriakov, Morenets and Minin were among seven GRU officers indicted on charges of conspiracy to commit computer fraud by a grand jury in Pennsylvania.
4   *Daily Telegraph*, 9 August 2017.

Chapter IX: Directorate S
1   See *Book of Honor* by Ted Gup (New York: Anchor Books, 2001).
2   Gordon Lonsdale's MI5 file is at KV2/4447.
3   Among the items recovered from the search of Fisher's Brooklyn studio was a packet of US dollars containing passsport photographs of the Cohens. It was later established that Fisher had been in contact with Lona Cohen in Manhattan in 1950. The true identity of the Krogers was not established by the FBI from their fingerprints until a fortnight after their arrest in January 1961.
4   See *Fair Game* by Valerie Plaime (New York: Simon & Schuster, 2010).
5   See *Crosby's Luck* by Ken Crosby (Amazon, 2020).
6   FBI complaint against Podobny.
7   Ibid.
8   *First Person* by Vladimir Putin (New York: Public Affairs, 2000).
9   Ibid.
10   Adolf Tolkachev was recruited in March 1978 and remained in contact with the CIA until January 1985, when he was betrayed by Edward Howard. Tolkachev was executed in September 1986. In his autobiography *Safe House*, (New York: National Press, 1995) Howard denied he had been responsible for his compromise.
11   On 17 May 2013 the FSB identified Steve Holmes was the CIA station chief, operating under counsellor cover at the US embassy.

Index

1st Guards Tank Division, 158
15th International Brigade, 58
40 School, Skhodnya, 61
101st Airborne Division, 147
161st Specialist Training Centre, 142

Abel, Rudolf (alias of Willie Fisher), 150
Abramson, Alexander (ISAAK), 60
ABSORB, 10–11
ABW, see Polish Security Service
Abwehr, 60, 62, 64, 66
Adrianov, Vladimir, 37
AE/PROLOGUE, see Aleksandr Zhomov
AE/SPHERE, see Adolf Tolkachev
Agee, Philip, 5
AH, see Polish Security Service
AIVD, see Dutch Security Service
Akademik Boris Petrov, 74
Alarcon–Correas, Luis Miguel (alias of Pavel Kapustin), 120
ALFRED, 59
al–Khattab, Ibn, 163
Alternative Futures, 124
Altorelli, John J., 104, 113
Alvares de Idalgo, Antonio, 120
AM/LACE (CIA/FBI Task Force), 22, 24–5, 28, 30
American Foreign Policy Council, 98
Ames, Aldrich ix, 7–11, 21, 24–5, 28, 30–1, 35, 46, 129, 168, 172–3
Ames, Rosario, 46, 168
Amt IV, 66
Amtorg, 69
Andropov Institute, 5
Angleton, James J., 1–3
Anschlag, Andreas, ix, 134–6, 176
Anschlag, Heidrun, ix, 134–6, 176
Antonio, Diego Cadenilla Jose (alias of Pavel Kapustin), 120
Arma Engineering Corporation, 68
Arnould, Rita, 63
Ashcroft, John, 42
ASIO, see Australian Security Intelligence Organisation
Atlangeriev, Movladi, 163
Australian Joint Intelligence Organisation, 17
Australian National Assessments Staff, 16

Australian Security Intelligence Organisation (ASIO), 12–15, 173
AVENGER, see Alexander Zaporozhsky
Averyanov, Andrei, 142

Babchenko, Arkadi, 166, 177
BACK ROOM, 80
Bagley, Pete, xi, 1
Barcelona Olympics, 128
Barcza, Margarete, 66
Baré, Charles, 12
Baré, Charles F., ix
Barnett, David, 4, 31
Barsky, Jack, ix, 168
Barsky, Penny, 34
Basford, Trenwith, 79
Basque separatist organization (ETA), 127
Battle of the Bulge, 147
Becker, Annie, 61
Bekhterov, Gennadi, 3
Berezovsky, Boris, 163
Berlin Base (CIA), 2
Berliner Tagebltat, 64, 68
Berzin, Gen. Jan, 52, 55
Bezrikov, Andrey,   ix, 99
BfV, see German Federal Security Service
BIS, see Czech intelligence service
Bittan, Michel, 104
Blackbird, 2
Blake, George, 151
Bloch, Felix, ix, 25–9, 43, 45, 168, 173
BND, see Bundesnachrichtendienst
Boehm, Horst, 157
Bogadyr, Peter, 9
Bóhm, Karl, 157
Bokhan, Sergei (GT/BLIZZARD), 18
Bolli, Marguerite, 58
Boone, David, ix, 24, 173–4
Bortnikov, Alexander, 160
Boshirov, Rusian, ix, 140
Bracey, Corp. Arnold, 8, 23
British Secret Intelligence Service (MI6), 112, 120, 129, 137, 140, 147, 151, 153
Chief of, see John Sawers; John Scarlett
British Security Service (MI5), 120, 138, 144
Director–General of, see Ken McCullum
Brodie, Ian, ix, 74–75

Brodie, Laurie (alias of Yelena Olshevskaya), ix, 74
Brooke, Gerald, 152
Brunet, Gilles, ix, 14, 172,–3
Bryant, Robert, 28
Building a Comprehensive Strategic Future Management System: A Future Map Approach, 99
Bulatov, Aleksandr, 153
Bulgarian military intelligence (RUMNO), 4
Bundesnachrichtendienst (BND), 4, 36
Bundespolizei, 58
Bureau of Intelligence and Research (INR), 96
Bureau of State Security, 3
Burlatov, Yuri, ix, 126–7
Burrows, Christopher, 126
Buryakov, Evgeni, 153, 156, 177
Buryakova, Marina, 153
Bush, George H, 98
BYPLAY, 9–10
Bystrolyotov, Dmitri, 48

CAESAR cipher system, 62
Camilerri, Nicholas, 103
Canadian Security Intelligence Service (CSIS), 74, 101
Carlson, Rod, 5
Carnegie Endowment for International Peace, 98
Caruso, Tim, 42
CASCADE, 80
Cassidy, Joe, ix, 78
Castellanos, Alicia, 79
Castro, Fidel, 81
CAT, 96
Central Intelligence Agency (CIA) 61, 112, 123, 147, 151–2, 173, 175, 178–85
Directors of, *see* Bill Colby; Leon Panetta, James Schlesinger; George Tenet; Stansfield Turner
KGB penetration, *see* Aldrich Ames; David Barnett; Edward Howard; Edwin Moore
See also, Clandestine Service; Internal Operations Course; Office of External Development; Soviet/Eastern Europe Division;
Soviet Bloc Division.
Centro Nacional de Inteligencia (CNI), 121, 125, 128, 138, 175

Chief of, *see* Alberto Saiz Cortes; Felix Sanz Roldin
Centro Superior de Información de la Defensa (CESID), 127–8
CESID, *see* Centro Superior de Información de la Defensa
Channing Real Estate, 200
Chapman, Alex, 102, 168
Chapman, Anna (Nee Kushchenko), ix, 95, 102, 112–16, 121, 130–3, 168, 170–1, 175
Chavez, Hugo, 81
Chebrikov, Viktor, 23
Chepiga, Anatoli (alias Rusian Boshirov), 140–3
Chepil, Aleksandr M., 11
Cherepanov, Andrei, 120
Cherepanov, Olga, 120
Cherepanov, Sergei (alias Henry Firth), ix, 120–1, 176
Cherkashin, Alyona, 120
Cherkashin, Elena, 21
Cherkashin, Viktor, ix, 4, 21, 31, 39, 168, 172
Chernayev, Rudolf, ix, 5
CI–4 Squad (FBI), 4, 5, 31
CIA, *see* Central Intelligence Agency
Circle of Treason (Grimes & Vertefeuille), 34
Clandestine Service (CIA Directorate of Operations), 1, 9, 124, 169
Deputy Director for, *see* Steve Kappes; John Stein; Mike Sulick
Clemons, Steve, 98
Clinton, Bill, 85
Clinton, Hillary Rodham, 85, 131
Clucksmann, Rubin, 54
CNI, *see* Centro Nacional de Inteligencia
Cohen, Lona (alias Helen Kroger), ix, 151
Cohen, Morris (KILLJOY, alias Peter Kroger), ix, 151
COINS–II, 21
Colby, Bill, 1
Coll Real, Juan, 127
Comintern, 55
Communist Party of Great Britain (CPGB), 55, 58, 71
Communist Youth International, 66
Comrade J (Earkey), 84
Conflict Resolution Centre, 128
Control Commission Intelligence Division, 57
Cook, Michael, 15
Coordination Unit (KGB), 30
Corbin, Alexander, 11

Counterintelligence Center (CIC), 27–8
Counterintelligence for the 1990s (Kalaris & McCoy), 178–85
Counterintelligence: Identifying Foreign Agents, 44
Counter–Terrorism Command, Scotland Yard, 142
COURTSHIP, 1, 3
Cox, Graham Douglas, (alias of Pavel Kapustin), 20
CPGB, *see* Communist Party of Great Britain
Crundall, Tarryn, 103
CSIS, *see* Canadian Security Intelligence Service
Czech intelligence service (BIS), 111, 138

Danilin, Mikhail, ix, 78
Danilov, Anton, 62
DDO, *see* Deputy Director for Operations
DECANTER, 22
Defectors,
   CIA to KGB, *see* Edward Lee Howard
   GRU to MI6, *see* Allan Foote; Vladimir Rezun
   GRU to RCMP, *see* Igor Gouzenko
   MI6 to KGB, *see* George Blake; Kim Philby
   KGB to MI5, *see* Oleg Lyalin
   KGB to MI6, *see* Oleg Gordievsky; Vladimir Kuzichkin; Vasili Mitrokhin; Viktor Oshchenko
   KGB to CIA, *see* Anatoli Golitsyn; Viktor Gundarev; Reino Hayhanen; Nikolai Khokhlov; Vladimir Konoplev; Stanislas Levchenko; Yuri Nosenko; Victor Sheymov; Boris Yezhin; Vitali Yurchenko
   MFA to CIA, *see* Arkadi Shevchenko
   SVR to CIA, *see* Stanislav Lunev; Sergei Papushin; Alexander Poyeyev; Aleksandr Shcherbakov; Sergei Tretyakov; Alexander Zaporozhsky
Defense Intelligence Agency (DIA), 124
Degtyar, Viktor, 39
Delisle, Jeffrey, ix, 136, 176
Delisle, Jennifer, 136
Department of Homeland Security, 93
Demetz, Hans, 68
Deputy Director of Operations (DDO), *see* Steve Kappes; John Stein; Mike Sulick
DesLauriers, Richard, ix, 80, 168
Deutsch, Arnold, 48
Deuxieme Bureau, 70
Dewey & LeBoeuf, 104

DGI, *see* Dirrection General de Inteligenia
Dibb, Paul, 16
Direction de la Surveillance du Territoire (DST), 26
Director of Central Intelligence (DCI), *see* Bill Casey; Leon Panetta; James Schlesinger; George Tenet; Stansfield Turner
Directorate K (KGB), 13, 24, 30
   Deputy Director of, *see* Oleg Kalugin
Directorate S (KGB), 3, 37, 73–7, 80, 84, 99, 102, 105–106, 112, 114, 131, 133, 135, 147, 149, 151–4
   4th Department, 121
   Deputy Director of, *see* Vladimir Adriano
Directorate of Operations, *see* Clandestine Service
Direction General de Inteligenia (DGI), 6
Disch, William, 68–9
Dittrich, Albrecht (alias Jack Barsky), 33–4, 36, 173–4
Djukanovic, Milo, 145
Doherty, Eunan Gerard, 91
Dominratsky, Vitali, 84
DORA, *see* Sandor Rado
DOVKA (Gennadi Vassilenko), xii
Dressen, Aleksei, 108–10, 177
Dressen, Daniel, 109
Dressen, Viktoria, 108–109, 177
Droulimsky, Dmitri, ix, 75
Drozdov, Yuri, 77
Dúbendorfer, Rachel (SISSY), 59
DUMB LUCK (Alexander Poteyev), 80
Dupuy, Maria Rosario Casas, *see* Rosario Ames
Dutch Defence Intelligence Service (MIVD), 143
Dutch Security Service (AIVD), 135
Dyson, William (alias of Jack Barsky), 35

Earley, Pete, 84, 188
East German Foreign Intelligence Service (HVA), 162
Economist, 68
EDELSWEISS, 58
EDUARD, 59
Effremov, Konstantin, 64
Ehrenlieb, Aaron, 52–3
Ehrenlieb, Abraham, 52–3
Eisenberg, 54
El Diario La Prensa, 81
Elliott, John C. (BOOKBINDER), ix, 12
Elwell, Charles (alais Charles Elton), xi, ix, 150

Emerging Markets Research & Consultancy Ltd., 75
Enger, Valdek, ix, 5
Erdberg, Alexander (alias of Sergei Kudriatsev), 61
Espinosa, Maria Jose, 178
Estonian Security Service (KaPo), 106–109, 125
ETA, *see* Basque separatist organization
EUCLID, 148
Europa Press, 128
EVI, *see* Katarina Nummerk
Executive Committee of the Communist Party of Great Britain, 55
Exfiltration 4, 12, 35, 76, 110, 112, 119, 130, 151, 172, 176
  See also Oleg Gordievsky to Finland (PIMLICO); Vladimir Kuzichkin to Turkey; Vasili Mitrokhin to Latvia; Viktor Oshchenko to England; Alexander Poteyev to Kiev; Aleksandr Shcherbakov and son to the U.S. Victor Sheymov to Finland
Ezhov, Nikolai (alias Nikolai Kononnykhin), 144

Fair Game (Plaime), 153
Far Eastern Fur Trading Co., 53
Far Eastern Trading Co., 53
FARBSTIFT, 34
Farcia, Alan, 127
FARMER, 96
Farrell, Victor, 60
FBI, *see* Federal Bureau of Investigation
FCD, *see* First Chief Directorate
Federal Bureau of Investigation (FBI), 61, 72, 78–81, 84–90, 104, 112–14, 130, 149, 153–5, 177, 179, 181
  Director of, *see* Louis Freeh
  KGB penetration, *see* Robert Hanssen; earl Pitts
  See also, New York Field Office; MC–43; Philadelphia Field Office; Special Surveillance Group; Washington Field Office
Fedorenko, Sergei (GT/PHYRRIC), 9–10
Fedotov, Sergei, 144
Fefelov, Aleksandr, 40–42
FERNAND, 59
Fetisov, Aleksandr, 164
Feurth, Prof. Leon, 96
Figliuzzi, Frank, 131, 137

First Chief Directorate (FCD), 12, 19, 84, 30–2, 37, 84, 158, 160
  Chief of, *see* Vadim Kirpichenko; Vladimir Kryuchkov
  1st Department, 22, 46, 80
  4th Department, 158–59
FISA, *see* Foreign Intelligence Surveillance Act
Fisher, Willie (alias Rudolf Abel), 73, 149
Flicke, Wilhelm, 59, 61
Flóres Garcia, Roberto (alias Rafael Vera), ix, 121, 127, 175–6
Fogle, Ryan, 160
Foley, Tracey (alias of Elena Vavilova), ix, 99, 170–1, 174
Foote, Allan (SNEAK), 57–61, 73
Foreign Intelligence Surveillance Act (FISA), 34, 115
Foreign Liaison Department (OMS), 55
Fornenko, Vladimir, 165
Fort Meade, 43
Fort Monckton, 15, 137–8
FORTHWITH (Sergei Skripal), xi, 174
Fourth Department of the Red Army General Staff (GRU), 49–57
Fradkov, Mikhail, ix, 123, 129, 160
Franklin, Peter Michael Franklin, (alias of Pavel Kapustin), 120
Frecuencia Latina, 81
Freeh, Louis, 38, 42
Freud, Heidrun, 134
Frick Collection, 38
Frith, Henry (alias of Sergei Cherepanov), x, 120
Frolov, Konstantin, 4
From Where the Motherland Begins, 133
FSB, *see* Russian Federation Security Service
Funkabwehr, 62
Future Map Strategic Advisory Services, 99

Gallacher, Willie, 55
Garcia–Estrada, Dr Luis Espinosa, 128
Gaynor, Michael, 98
Gazprom, 153, 155
GDR, *see* German Democratic Republic
Gebrev, Christo, 144–5
Gebrev, Emilian, 144, 177
Gee, Ethel (TRELLIS), x, 151
Geiger, Donna, x, 74
Gergely, Tibor, 61
German Democratic Republic (GDR), 158, 162

German Federal Security Service (BfV),
134–5
German High Command (OKW,) 64
Geschwinnt, Michel, alias of Karl Kru-
minsch, 76
Geschwinnt, Ursula, alias of Katarina
Nummerk, 76
Gestapo, 59, 61
GHOST STORIES, 80, 84, 94, 112, 137,
147, 154, 171
Giering, Karl, 62
Gikman, Reino, 26
GLAZING (Gennadi Vassilenko), xii
Global-Car, 76
Global Energy Capital, 153
Global Partners Inc, 99
Goldfus, Emil (alias of Willie Fisher), 149
Golitsyn, Anatoli, 1
Gollnow, Herbert, 64
Golovanov, Vladimir, 77, 163
Gorbachev, Mikhail, 10, 21, 37
Gordienko, Egor (alias Georgi A. Gorshkov),
144
Gordievsky, Anna, 138
Gordievsky, Leila, 138
Gordievsky, Maria, 138
Gordievsky, Oleg (NOCTON), vi, x, 12–15,
19, 137–8, 172
Gore, Al, 96
Gorriti, Gustavo, 127
GORT, *see* Wolfhard Thiel
Gouzenko, Igor, 59
GRAY DAY (Robert Hanssen), 42
GRAY DECEIVER (Brian Kelley), 27
GRAY SUIT, 27, 29, 36
Gregory, Doug, 43
Gregory, Susan, 35
Grimes, Sandy, 24
Gritak, Vasili, 166
Grossmann, Werner, 163
GROUP NORTH, 30, 37
GRU, *see* Soviet Military Intelligence Service
Grueter, Mark, 98
GT FITNESS, *see* Gennadi Varenik
GT/ACCCORD, *see* Vladimir Vasiliev
GT/BLIZZARD, *see* Sergei Bokhan
GT/COWL, *see* Sergei Vorontsov
GT/FITNESS, *see* Gennadi Varentsov
GT/MEDIAN, *see* Vladimir Potashov
GT/MILLION, *see* Gennadi Smetanin
GT/PHYRRIC, *see* Sergei Fedorenko
GT/PROLOGUE, *see* Aleksandr Zhomov
GT/TWINE, *see* Boris Yuzhin

GT/WEIGH, *see* Leonid Poleschuk
Guilsher, John, 10
Gukov, Pavel (alias of Pavel Kapustin), 120
Gundarev, Viktor, x, 39, 172
GUNMAN, 22
GUNNER, 32
Guryev, Lydia, x, 85
Guryev, Vladimir, x, 85
Guryevitch, Viktor (KENT), 62–3, 65–6
Gutiérrez, Juan, 127
Gwyer, John, 67

Haenseler, Hermann, 60
Halloween Massacre (1977), 9
Hambleton, Hugh, 73
Hamel, Edmund, 58
Hamel, Olga, 58
Hampel, Paul William, x, 75, 176
Handbook for Spies (Foote), 61
Hansen, Georg, 50
Hanssen, Robert (KARAT), x, 21, 28–30, 37,
39–40, 42–6, 83, 129, 168, 172, 174
Hanssen, Bonnie, 44
Harnack, Arvid von, 64
HARRY, I, 68
HARRY II, 68, 70
Hathaway, Gus, 9
Havemann, Wolfgang, 64
Hayden, Tom, vi
Hayhanen, Reino, 73, 149
Heathfield, Alex, 100
Heathfield, Donald (alias of Andrey Bez-
rikov), 9, 98–101, 131, 133, 170–1, 174–5
Heathfield, Howard William, 100–101
Heathfield, Tim, 100–101
Heijden, Kees van der, 99
Heilman, Horst, 64
Helbein, William, 61
Hemblys–Scales, Bob, 57
Hemmann, Rainer, 163
Henningsen & Co., 147
Herman, Boris, 167
Hermann, Rudi (AT LAST), 73
Herrnstadt, Rudolf, 64
Hidson Institute, 136
Hiller, David (alias of Richard Murphy), 92
Hobart, Helga, 27
Hochstedt, Samuel, 54
Hoffman, Daniel M., x, 124
Holt, Jimmy, 5, 28
Honecker, Erich, 162
Hood, Bill, 162
Hope, Judge Robert, 16

Houghton, Harry (REVERBERATE), x
Howard, Edward Lee, x, 8, 10–11, 17, 172
Howard, Mary, 11
Hrabal, Frantisek, 110
Hungarian Constitutional Protection Office (AH), 111
Hutchison, Charlie, 102
HVA, *see* East German foreign intelligence service

IK–11, 47
Illegals Directorate, *see* Directorate S
ILO, *see* International Labour Organisation
IMPULSE, 72
Inside the Company: A CIA Diary (Agee), 5
Intelligence Identities Protection Act, 152
Internal Operations Course (IOC), 11
International Labour Organisation (ILO), 60
Intourist, 11
IOC, *see* Internal Operations Course
Islamov, LechaIvan, 163
Ivanov, Oleg, 165
Ivanov, Sergei, 184
IVY BELLS, 20

J, Col. Zbigniew, 145, 177
JABAROO, 12, 15, 17, 173
Jaure, George, 152
JESSANT (Vasili Mitrokhin), 32
JIM, *see* Allan Foote
Jirousek, Tina 26
JOGGER, *see* Boris Piguzov
John F Kennedy School of Government, 99
John Paul II, 4
Juchniewicz, Tadeusz x, 109–110, 176

Kalaris, George, 1, 178
Kalinin, Alexei (alias Alexei Nikitin), 144
Kalugin, Oleg, xi, x, 8, 12–15, 33, 173
Kamenski, 4
Kanokov, Arsen, 166
Kantor, Solomon, 69
KaPo, *see* Estonian Security Service
Kappes, Steve, x, 46
Kapralov, Danil (alias Danil Stepanov), 145
Kapustin, Pavel,(alias Christopher Metsos), x, 120
KARAT, *see* Robert Hanssen
Karetkin, Vitali, 25
Karetnikov, Alexei V., x, 102, 112, 131, 170–1
Karpov, Aleksandr V., 44–5
Karry, Frema, 69
Katz, Leo, 52, 54

Kelleher, Gerard, (alias of Pavel Kapustin), 120
Kelley, Brian, vi, x, 27–30, 42–5
KENT, *see* Viktor Gutyrvich
KGB Line KR, 4, 133
KGB, *see* Soviet intelligence service
Khangostvili, Zelimkhan, 165
Khokhlov, Nikolai, 35
Kidd, Sean, 124
KILLJOY, Mrs, *see* Helen Kroger
KILLJOY, *see* Peter Kroger
Kimmel, Tom, 44–5
King, Bob, 29, 42–3
King, John, 48–9
Kirkland, Mark, 79
Kirpichenko, Vadim, 30
Klages, 54
Knecht, Charles, 60
Kohl, Helmut, 157
Kohler, Alan, vi, x, 80, 130, 168
Kohver, Eston, 108, 177
Konoplev, Vladimir, 33, 173
KONRAD, *see* Karl Kruminsch
Kopazky, Igor (SASHA), 2
Kopkow, Horst, 59, 66–7
Korabelnikov, Valentin, 110
Koshlyakov, Lev, 15–16
Kotloby, Anatole, 13
Kovacs, Bela, 111
Koval, Valeri, 84
Kovich, Richard, 3
Kovtun, Dmitri, 137
Kozak, Dmitry, 160
Kozlov, Yuri, 165
Krasikov, Vadim N., 165–6
Krivitsky, Walter, 48–50, 68
Mealticket of, *see* John King
Kroger, Helen (Mrs KILLJOY; alias of Lona Cohen), x
Kroger, Peter (KILLJOY; alias of Morris Cohen), x
Kruminsch, Karl (KONRAD,) x, 76–7, 172
Kruminsch, Katerina (EVA), x, 76–7, 172
Kryuchkov, Vladimir, 19, 23, 30, 37
Kuckhoff, Adam, 64
Kuczynsky, Ursula (SONIA), 58
Kudriavtsev, Sergei (alias Alexander Erd-berg), 61
Kushchenko, Vasili, x, 102–103
Kutafin, Sergei, 84
Kutzik, Mikhail (alias of Michael Zottoli), x, 93
Kuzichkin Vladimir (REDWOOD), vi, x, 76–7, 137, 172

La Republica, 127
Lambert, Ian, 174
Lambert, Laurie, 174
Larkin, Mary, 137
LAST ACT (Konon Molody), 151
Lazaro, Juan (alias of Mikhail Vasenkov), x,
    81–3, 95, 129, 168, 170–2, 175
Lazovik, Geronty, 15
LEMONADE, 5
Lenin, Vladimir, 48
LEONID, 135
Levchenko, Stanislas, 13
Leven, Charles, 8
Levine, Isaac Don, 48
Liberal Russia Party, 163
Lindberg, Arthur, vi
Line KR, 4, 6, 16, 37, 39, 133, 157, 159
Line N, 18, 27, 73, 76–7, 84, 88, 97, 105, 113,
    118, 121, 159
Lipka, Robert, x, 33, 75, 173
Litvinenko, Alexander, 138, 156, 163, 176–7
LIVWE, 17
Lo Shih–hsiang, 148
Locke, Nadia, 124
    Loginov, Yuri, 3
Loginova, Nita, 3
Lonetree, Sgt. Clayton, 8, 22–3, 173
Lonsdale, Gordon A. (alias of Konon
    Molody), x, 73, 151
Lothian, Lord, 48
LOUIS, 61
LUCY, *see* Rudolf Rössler
Lugovoi, Andrrei, 138
LUIZA, 36
Lunev, Stanislav, vi, 33, 173
LUTSCH, 159, 162
Lyalin, Oleg, 137
Lyudin, Yuri (alias of Yuri Modin), 4
Lyutenko, Sergei, 144

Macartney, Wilfred, 50
Magruder, John, 148
Makarov, Mikhail, 62
Malaysian Airlines Flight, 17, 156
Maly, Theodore, 48
Mamchur, Ivan, 166, 177
Mao Zedong, 152
Marek & Vyse, 68
Marek, Roman, 68
MARS, 66
Martin, Arthur, vi
Martin, Christopher, 125

Martynov, Valeri (PIMENTA), 5, 7, 29, 43,
    172
Masical, Waldo, 83
Mathieu, Charles, 65
Matlock, Ray, 28
Matveev, Lazar, 158
MAUD, 59
Maurer, 59
MC–43 Squad (FBI), 30
McCallum, Ken, 142
McCoy, Leonard, 1, 178
McCredie, Ian, 76
Mealticket, 29
Medvedev, Dmitri, 117
MEGAS, 7
Melnikov, Petr Y., 127, 175
Melton, Keith, vi
Meredith, William, 70–1
Merrill Lynch, 153
Metsos, Christopher (alias of Pavel
    Kapustin), x, 85, 93–4, 97–8, 119–20,
    170–1, 175–6
MFA, *see* Ministry of Foreign Affairs
MGIMO University, 133
MI5, *see* British Security Service
MI6, *see* British Secret Intelligence Service
Microsoft, 102
MIKE, 88
Mikhailov, Valeri, 135, 177
Milborn, Jim, 42
Miler, Scotty, 1
Miller, Pablo, x, 125–6
Mills, Kenny, 93
Mills, Patricia (alias of Natalia Pereverzeva),
    x, 93, 170–1, 135
Minin, Alexei, 143, 189
Ministry of Foreign Affairs (MFA), 4
Ministry of State Security (Stasi), 4, 37, 158,
    162
Mishkin, Alexander (alias Rusian Boshirov),
    140, 142–3
Mitrokhin, Vasili, x, 12–15, 31–3, 36, 75, 157,
    173–4
    Mealticket of, *see* JABAROO; Jack
    Barsky; Robert Lipka; Wolfhard Theil;
    George Trofimov
MIVD, *see* Dutch Defence Intelligence
    Service
    Modin, Yuri (alias Yuri Lyudin), 4
Moffat, Jim, 136
Moi*seev*, Vladimir (alias Vladimir Popov),
    144–5

Molehunt, *see* AM/LACE; GRAY SUIT;
   NIGHTMOVER
Molody, Galya, 150
Molody, Konon (LAST ACT; alias Gordon
   Lonsdale), xi, 149–50, 152
Molody, Lisa, 150
Molody, Trofim, 150
Molody, Yekatarina, 152
Monaghan, Gregory, 156
MONOLIGHT (Gennadi Vasilenko), 21
Moore, Edwin G., 4
Morales, Evo, 128
Moran, Sheila, 42
Morea Financial Services, 85
Morenets, Aleksei, 143, 189
Moreno, Carlos, 120
MORLOP, 140
Morton, David, 4
Moscow News, 130
   MOTORBOAT, 4
Motorin, Sergei (MEGAS), 5, 7, 29, 172
MRTA, *see* Tupac Amaru Revolutionary
   Movement
Mueller, Richard, 9
Mueller, Robert, 42, 131
Muller, Albert (alias of Allan Foote), 60
Mulvenna, Daniel, vi
Murphy, Cynthia (alias of Lydia Guryev), xi,
   85–90, 104, 170–1
Murphy, Katie, 85
Murphy, Lisa, 85
Murphy, Richard (alias of Vladimir Guryev),
   xi, 85, 94, 97, 170–1, 175
My Beautiful Balkans (Hampel), 75

Naryshkin, Sergei, 160
National Labor Relations Board, 2
National Security Agency (NSA), 20, 22, 24
   KGB penetration,, *see* David Boone;
   Robert Lipka; Ron Pelton
NATO, 18, 73, 105–107, 109–110, 133, 135,
   145, 159
Naval Investigative Service (NIS), 11, 23, 74
Nayanov, Gennadi P., 16
Nazranov, Albert, 165–6
Nemtsov, Boris, 163
NeoBIT, 102
New America Foundation, 98
New York Department of Investigation, 86
New York Field Office (NYFO), 112, 116,
   153
New York Times, 148
Nicole, Leon, 59

Nicole, Pierre, 59
NIGHTMOVER, 25–6
Nilov, Alexei, 9
NIS, *see* Naval Investigative Service
Nixon, Richard, 152
NOC, *see* Non–Official Cover
NOCTON (Oleg Gordievsky), 19
Nolan, James, 1, 20
Non–Official Cover (NOC), 152
Nosenko, Yuri, 1, 5
Novak, Bob, 152
Novikov, Col., 60
NSA, *see* National Security Agency
Nummerk, Katarina (EVI), 76–7
NYFO, *see* New York Field Office

O'Donnell, Pete, 44
O'Neill, Eric, 43
Obama, Barack, 87–8
Odehnalova, Vladimira, 110
Office of External Development, 147
Office of Research and Reports, 5
Office of Strategic Services (OSS), 148
Official Secrets Act, 71
Oflag IV-c, Colditz Castle, 150
Ogorodnik, Aleksandr, 9
OGPU, *see* Soviet intelligence service
Ojamae, Valeri, xi, 108, 126, 174
Okhota, 18, 48
OKW, *see* German High Command
Oldham, Ernest, 49
OLGA, 58
Olive, Ron, vi, 11
Olshevskaya, Yelena B (alias Laurie Brodie),
   75
Olshevsky, Dmitri V. (alias Ian Brodie), 75
Olson, Jim, 22
OMS (*Otdyel Mezhdunarodnoi Svyazi*), 55
OPCW, *see* Organisation for the Prohibition
   of Chemical Weapons
Oppenheimer, Herbert, 54
Orbis Business Intelligence, 126
Organisation for the Prohibition of Chemical
   Weapons (OPCW), 143
Orlov, Andrei, 137
Orlov, Igor, 2
Osman, Robert, 69–70
OSS, *see* Office of Strategic Services
Oshchenko, Viktor, 33

Paasche, Insp., 58
Page, Carter, xi, 153, 155–6
PAKBO, 59

Palacios, Alberto, 148
Palethorpe, T. Hardy, 15
PALMETTO, 78–9
Panetta, Leon, xi, 123, 129
Papushin, Sergei (DECANTER), 22, 173
PARROT, 96
Pasavant Werke, 76
Patricof, Alan, 85–6
Patrushev, Nikolai, 160
Pavlov, Sergei V, 144
    Pavlov, Vitali (alias Nikolai Kedrov), **4**
Pelaez, Juan, 81
Pelaez, Vicky, xi, 81–3, 130, 168, 170–3, 175
Pelton, Ronald, xi, 11, 20–1, 172
PENNYWISE, 28, 37
People, 114
Pereverzeva, Natalia (alias Patricia Mills),
    xi, 94
Peru Posible, 127
Peterson, Marti, vi, 9
Petrov, Alexander, xi
Pettit, Valerie, xi, 19
Philadelphia Field Office (FBI), 34
Philby, Kim, 2, 13–14
Piankova, Tatiana, 151
Piatnitsky, Osip, 55
Pickard, Tom, 42
Pieper, Derek, 86
Piguzov, Boris (JOGGER), 4, 10
PIMLICO, 19
Pioneer Corps, 68
PIPELINER, 11
PIT, 135
Pitts, J. Earl, xi, 44, 168, 174
Pitts, Mary, 44
Pivovarnik, Vyacheslav, 166–7
Plaime, Valerie, 152
Platt, Jack (alias Chris Llorenz), vi, 5, 11, 20,
    22, 30, 37–8, 47, 168, 172
Pluta, Stephan, 43
Podobny, Viktor, xi, 154–5
Poeteray, Raymond, xi, 135–6, 177
Poleshuk, Leonid (GT/WEIGH), 18
Poliakova, Vera, 60
Polikarpov, Boris, xi, 78
Polish Security Service (ABW), 109
    Politkovskaya, Anna, 156, 163
Pollit, Harry, 55
Polonik, Mikhail, 4
Polyakov, Dmitri, xi, 17–18, 24, 78
Pontificia Universidad Javeriana, 168
Posledov, Alexei, 108
Posnanska, Sofi, 63

Potashov, Vlladimir (GT/MEDIAN), 10, 18
Poteyev, Aleksandr (DUMB LUCK), xi,
    80–1, 105, 107, 110–13, 118–21, 129,
    131, 157, 173–4, 176
Poteyev, Margarita, 119, 131
Poteyev, Marina, 119, 132
Poteyev, Vladimir, 119, 132, 168
Powers, F. Gary, 73, 149
Premier Global Services, 93
Prietlov, Vladislav, 108
Prinzipalow, Aleksandr, 158, 162
Pritt, D.N., 71
Proinnsias, Sean (alias of Pavel Kapustin),
    120
Proks, Josef, 110
PropertyFinders Inc., 103
Pugachyov, Vasili A. (alias Bogachyov), 164
Púnter, Otto, 59
Purpis, Adam, 53
Putin, Lyudmila, 158
Putin, Maria, 158
Putin, Vladimir, 123, 133, 137, 141, 156,–60,
    162–3, 165
Putin, Yekatarina, 158
Puusepp, Uno, 107

Rabinowicz, Hermina, 61
Raborg, Percy, 81
Radio Moscow, 12
Rado, Lena, 58
Rado, Sandor (DORA), 58–60
Rakhardzho, Robert, 176
RAMON (Robert Hanssen), 21, 37, 174
Ratkai, Stephen (Istvan), xi, 74, 173
Razhardzho, Robert, 110
Razvedupr, 55
RCMP, *see* Royal Canadian Mounted Police
Redefector, *see* Vitali Yurchenko
Redfin Real Estate, 100
Redmond, Lydia, 147
Redmond, Paul (alias Jerome Strother),
    147–8, 152
Redmond, Ruth, 148
REDWOOD, *see* Vladimir Kuzichkin
Referat IIA3, 59–60
Reich Foreign Ministry, 64
Reilly, Joe, vi, 34–5, 169
Remembering Guernica, 127
Repkin, Aleksandr, 108
Reshetnikov, Leonid P., 145
REVERBERATE (Harry Houghton), 151
Rezun, Vladimir, vi, 137
Ricci, Maria L., 86–7, 91, 121, 169

Riccio, Joe, 11
Rivas y Lopez, Gilberto, xi, 78–9
Robbins, James S., 98
Robinson, Henri, 59, 66, 68
Rocca, Ray, 1
Rochford, Mike, xi, 30–1, 33, 37–8, 46, 169, 174
Rodriguez Galindo, Enrique, 127
Roldin, Felix Sanz, 121
ROSEWOOD, 162
Rosoboronexport, 119
Róssler, Rudolf (LUCY), 59–60
ROTE DREI, 58, 67
    Members of, *see* Alan Foote; Edmund Hamel; Sandor Rado
Rote Kapelle, 63, 71
Rothstein, Andrew, 50
Rothstein, Theodore, 50
Rowley, Charlie, 143
Royal Canadian Mounted Police (RCMP), 14, 136–7
Royal Commission, *see* Robert Hope
Rozen, Laura, 153
    RUMNO, *see* Bulgarian military intelligence
Russian Federal Drug Control Service (FSKN), 119
Russian Federal Security Service (FSB), 108–109, 125, 137, 160, 162, 164–5
    Director of, *see* Vladimir Putin
Russian Foreign Intelligence Service (SVR), 72–3, 84, 91, 98, 104–106, 109, 112, 120, 129, 133, 135, 145, 154, 160, 173–4
    Director of, *see* Mikhail Fradkov; Sergei Naryshkin
Russian Strategic Nuclear Forces, 124

SA–2 anti–aircraft missile, 1
SACKETT LAND, 11
Sadil, George, 17, 173
Sadil, Jenny, 17
Saiz Cortes, Alberto, 121
Samoshkin, Aleksandr N., xi, 121
SASHA (Igor Kopazky,) 2
Savitskaya, Elena, 103
Sawers, Sir John, 124
SB, *see* Soviet Bloc Division
SBU, *see* Ukrainian security service
SCD, *see* Second Chief Directorate
Scenarios for Success: Turning Insights into Action (Sharpe), 99
Scheffer, Philip, 68
Scheliha, Rudolf von, 64, 68

Schlesinger, James, 23
Schulze–Boysen, Harro, 64, 66
Schulze–Boysen, Libertas, 64
Scythia, SS, 149
SD, *see* Sicherheitsdienst
SE, *see* Soviet/Eastern Europe Division
    Sechin, Igor, 160
Second Chief Directorate (SCD), 6, 9, 18, 22, 31
Secret Intelligence Service (MI6), *see* British Secret Intelligence Service
Securitar, 37
Sedlak, Josef, 110
Seina, Violette, 23
Sellers, Michael, 18
Semenko, Mikhail, xi, 95, 97–8, 112–13, 118, 121, 170–1, 175
Serebriakov, Evgenni, 143, 189
Sereyev, Tatyana, 141
Sergeyev, Denis (alias Sergei Fedotov), 140–1, 143
Serkov, Vyacheslav, 102
Serpell, Michael, 57, 67
SHAROV, 77
Sharpe, Bill, 99
Shchekochikhin, Yuri, 163
Shcherbakov, Aleksandr, xi, 37–8, 43, 46, 110, 118, 129, 131, 157, 169, 173–4, 176
Shebarshin, Leonid, 76
Shestack, Jerome J., 165
Shevchenko, Arkadi, 10
Shishmakov, Edouard (alias Eduard V. Shirokov), 145
Shlyakthurov, Alexander, 110
SHOCKER, 78
Shokolov, Sergei, 137
Sicherheitsdienst (SD), 59, 62
Simbirsky, Anton O, xi, 121
Simexco, 66
Simm, Herman, 105, 110, 176
SIS, *see* British Secret Intelligence Service
Sissmore, Jane, 49
SISSY (Rachel Dubendorfer), 59
Sites, Erik, 9
Sjubenko, Alexander, 162
Skripal, Ludmilla, 126, 140
Skripal, Sasha, 140
Skripal, Sergei (FORTHWITH), xi, 125–36, 137–40, 169, 173–5
Skripal, Valeri, 138
Skripal, Yelena, 138
Skripal, Yulia, 126, 138, 140–1, 169
Smetanin, Gennadi (GT/MILLION), 19

Smetanin, Svetlana, 19
Smith, Geoffrey R, xi, 12, 15
Smorodinov, Vladimir, 166–7, 177
SNEAK, *see* Allan Foote
Sobell, Helen, 149
Sobell, Morton, 149
Sokolov, Vadim, 165
Solomatin, Boris, 13
Sonderkommando Rote Kapelle, 62
SOSUS, 74
Sotnikov, Oleg, 143
Soviet Bloc Division (SB,) 2
Soviet/Eastern Europe Division (SE), 9,
    24, 32
Soviet intelligence service (OGPU. NKVD.
    KGB), 55, 62, 72–3, 151
    Chairman of, *see* Mikhail Fradkov
See also, Coordination Unit; Directorate K;
    Directorate S; First Chief Directorate;
    GROUP NORTH; Second Chief
    Directorate
Soviet Military Intelligence service (GRU),
    58, 64, 70, 109, 135, 138, 140–4, 164–5,
    174, 177
Chief of, *see* Valentin Korabelnikov
Soviet Trade Delegation, Berlin, 52, 61, 65
Soviet Union: The Incomplete SuperPower
    (Dibb), 16
Spanish Civil War, 58
Spanish intelligence service, *see* Centro
    Superior de Información de la Defensa
Special Branch, 137
Special Intelligence Service (FBI SIS), 157
Special Surveillance Group (SSG), 4, 43, 80
Spietz Laboratory, 143
Sporyshev, Igor, xi, 154
Sporyshev, Mikhail, 154–5
Spy Handler (Cherkashin), 168
Spy swap, *see* Andrey Bezrikov; Gerald
    Brooke; Anna Chapman; Lona
    Cohen; Morris Cohen; Willie Fisher;
    Lydia Guryev; Vladimir Guryev;
    Alexei Karetnikov; Mikhail Kutzik; Yuri
    Loginov; Konon Molody; Vicky Pelaez;
    Natalia Pereverzeva; Mikhail Semenko;
    Sergei Skripal; Igor Sutyagin; Mikhail
    Vasenikov; Gennadi Vasilenko; Elena
    Vavilova; Greville Wynne; Alexander
    Zaporozhsky
SSG, *see* Special Surveillance Group
Stahl, Lydia, 69
Stalin, Josef, 48, 50, 127
Staniford, Bill, 104

STANLEY, 75
Stasi, *see* Ministry of State Security
Steele, Christopher, 126
Stein, John, 8
Steinfeld, Ilse, 68
Stern, Moishe, 68
Stoebe, Else, 64
STONE GHOST, 136
Strategic Arms Limitation Treaty, 87
Strategic services Unit, 148
Strzok, Peter, 99
Stuchka, 53
Sturgess, Dawn, 143
Sugden, Steven, 104
Sulick, Mike, xi, 38, 47, 124, 169
SuperMax, Florence, Colorado, 168
Sureté, 48
Sutyagin, Oleg, vi, xi, 124, 157, 145, 169, 175
Svirin, Mikhail, 149
SVR, *see* Russian Foreign Intelligence Service
Swiss Labour (Communist) Party, 59
Switz, Marjorie, 70
Switz, Robert Gordon, 68, 70
Sypachev, Alexander, xi, 123, 175
Szady, David, 11, 27

Tacma, 99
Tailleur, Laurent, 103
TASS News Agency, 18
Tatarivnov, Vycheslav, 17
TAW, 10–11
TAYLOR, 59
TEDDY, 59
Tegorov, Nikolai, 165
Telmanshenko, Taras, 167
Tenet, George, 27, 38
Terentiev, Ivan (alias Ivan Lebedev), 144
Terlecki, Russell, 104
Theil, Wolfhard (GORT), 36
Thompson, Colin, 31
Thornburgh, Dick, 165
Tilley, Marjorie, 69
Tilton, Alfred, 70
Time, 69, 91
TINA, 135
Titov, Valeri, 108
Toledo, Alejandro, 127
Tolkachev, Adolf (AE/SPHERE), 10–11, 162
Toots, Alexander, 107
Travel All Russia travel agency, 97
TRELLIS, *see* Ethel Gee
Trepper, Leopold (alias Jean Gilbert),
    60, 62–6

Tretyakov, Helena, 84
Tretyakov, Ksenia, 84
Tretyakov, Sergei, xi, 83, 132, 157, 174, 176
Tretyakova, Revmira, 83
Trinity, HMCS, 156
    Trinka, Edmund (alias of Yuri
      Loginov), 2
Trofimoff, George, xi, 33, 75
Trump, Donald, 126, 156
Tsepov, Roman, 163
Tudeh Party, 76
Tupac Amaru Revolutionary Movement
    (MRTA), 81
Turner, Adm. Stansfield, 9
Tyashikun, Evgenni, 108

Ukrainian Security Service (SBU), 156
    Director of, *see* Vasili Gritak
Unit 29155, 142–3
Unschlicht, Max, 50
UNSUB, 31, 45
USA and Canada Studies Institute, 10
USA Today, 98
Ussotsev, Vladimir, 158

VAGIF, 77
VALENTIN, *see* Valeri Zentsov
Valtbach, Alexei, 108
Valtbach, Tatyana, 108
Varenik, Gennadi (GT/FITNESS), 8, 18
Vasenkov, Mikhal (alias Juan Lazaro), xi, 81
Vasilenko, Gennadi (MONOLIGHT), xii,
    5, 20, 24, 30, 37, 46, 122, 129, 152, 169,
    172, 175
Vasilenko, Ilya, 47
Vasilev, Fedor, 137
Vasilyev, Vladimir (GT/ACCORD), 19–21
Vauck, Dr Wilhelm, 63
Vavilova, Elena (alias Tracey Foley), xii, 99,
    169
Veitman, Vladimir, 107
VENONA, 75
Vernon, Wilfred, 70–1
Vertefeuille, Jeanne, xii, 24
VICTOR, 137
Vienna Convention, 71
Vietnam War, 2
    Vnesheconombank, 153
Vorontsov, Sergei (GT/COWL), 8, 18
Vyalkov, Igor, 108

Waldman, Louis, 69
Walker, John, 14

Walsh, Gerard P., 12, 15
WALTER, 59
Wang Ko–yi, 148
War Secrets in the Ether (Flicke), 61
Warrenton, Virginia, 8
Washington Field Office (WFO), 28–9, 31,
    42, 45, 74, 168
Washington Post, 128
Washington Times, 29, 39
Watergate scandal, 1, 9
Wauck, Mark, 43–4
Way, Bob, 35
Webb, Cindy, 47
Weiss, Ernest, 67–8, 70
Wenzel, Johann, 63–4
WERTHER, 58
WHISPER, 151
WHITE KNIGHT, 107
Wilson, Joe, 152
Wolff, Theodor, 64
Wood, Kimba M, 130
Woodman, Dorothy, 71
Woolcocks, Patrick (alias of Pavel Kapustin),
    120
Worthington, Eddie, 128
Wostwag (Eastern Trading Co.), 52
Wynne, Greville, 152

Yablochkov, Anatoli V, (alias Belashko), 164
Yakovlev, Sergei (alias Antonio de Jesus
    Amurett Graf), 105–106
Yakushkin, Dmitri, 5
Yandarbiev, Zelimkhan, 164
Yatsenko, Sergei, 153
Yefimov, Aleksei G., 23
Yermakov, Nikolai 107
Young Communist League, 69
Yurchenko, Vitali, xii, 11, 17, 28, 31, 169
    Yushchenko, Viktor, 163
    Yushenkov, Sergei, 163
Yuzhin, Boris (GT/TWINE), 18, 29, 169

Zaporozhsky, Aleksandr (AVENGER),
    xii, 24–5, 29–30, 43–7, 157, 169,
    173–5
Zaporozhsky, Galina, 46
Zaporozhsky, Maxim, 46
Zaporozhsky, Pavel, 46
Zemenek, Ludek, 73
ZENITH, 80
Zentsov, Valeri (VALENTIN), 106
ZEPHYRS, 11
Zharko, Vyecheslav, xii, 176

Zhomov, Aleksandr (GT/PROLOGUE), 9,
  22, 124, 130
Zimmermann, Agnes, 59
Zimyakin, Vladimir, xii, 4

Zloczower, 54
Zottoli, Michael (alias of Mikhail Kutzik), xii,
  89–93, 97, 169–71, 175